TO BE A CHINDIT

TO BE A CHINDIT

Phil Sharpe

The Book Guild Ltd
Sussex, England

The Book Guild Ltd.
25 High Street,
Lewes, Sussex

First published 1995
© Philip Sharpe 1995
Reprinted 1995
Set in Times
Typesetting by Southern Reproductions (Sussex)
Crowborough, Sussex
Printed in Great Britain by
Antony Rowe Ltd.
Chippenham, Wiltshire.

A catalogue record for this book is
available from the British Library

ISBN 0 86332 981 0

CONTENTS

MAPS

1

Wartime Cruise

Anchored in the Mersey, our troopship swinging lazily with the tide, we had begun to settle and accept this new chapter in our wartime service. For some, embarkation was no new experience, following soldiering in peacetime stations abroad, or more recently, in Europe, culminating in the Dunkirk evacuation.

Others no doubt saw it as a glorious temporary opportunity to escape from the boredom of drills and parades, and for a few it was a thankful escape from recent personal indiscretions, and an escape from certain retribution. For the majority, like myself, embarkation on this August day in 1942 was accepted as inevitable, but with some trepidation. So why were we in the Army?

In the mid 1930s, it had become increasingly evident to the British Government that Europe could well be on the brink of yet another major military confrontation. But the homeland population still held very vivid personal memories of the death and destruction in the comparatively recent 1914 World War. So at this time, any attempt to introduce conscription would have been rejected out of hand not only by the voting population, but by the Labour and Liberal opposition. Nevertheless, the armed forces needed a mass of well trained men as quickly as possible. So the Government, through the then War Minister, Hore Belisha, played a trump card. They would introduce conscription, but not under that name. Instead, a bill was laid before the House of Commons in April 1939 providing for all young men between the ages of twenty and twenty-one to register for just six months' training in the armed

7

forces. Surprisingly, this bill was passed without major opposition.

This regulation, which applied to me, appeared innocuous at the time. In fact, in my naivety, and as a keen athlete, I welcomed this service as a great opportunity to toughen my body with six months' hard training, not in those days so readily available. There were no sports centres, neither 'Outward Bound', or sponsored opportunities for budding athletes. So it would be ideal for me, a young wing threequarter in the Bath RFC and at twenty years of age already the holder of both the Somerset County Half Mile and One Mile Championships at senior level. So, passing A1 at my first army medical, I had no trouble at all in persuading my military interviewer that I should serve in the Infantry. In fact, this initial entry into the 'Militia', as it was then called, ensured that my service would not be for just six months, but in the event, well over six years.

The beginning of the war in 1940 ensured a radical upheaval in our lives. Plans we might have had for the future were brought to an abrupt halt. Future progress in education, careers, sport or family life, had to be put on ice, which in most cases melted away as the war dragged on. Our lives, and those of our families and loved ones, were caught up in the web of war. Even so, during our initial army life, we were able to maintain material links with our families. Periods of leave ensured that we still enjoyed some contact. Parents, wives or girlfriends, were in most cases just a bus or train journey away. Moreover, we were able to retain links with the civilian population and join in the social activities of wartime Britain. Added to this of course, there was the eternal optimism that the war would soon be over. So this embarkation was a watershed in our lives. We had said our farewells, the break was real. It was certainly goodbye for a very long time to come.

After initial training, my service during the first two years had been typical army routine, and relatively uneventful. In a newly formed battalion of the Somerset Light Infantry, we awaited the expected German invasion of the Kent coast, sheltered in hastily dug trenches, behind a few coiled strands of barbed wire, and precious little else besides optimism! We had watched helplessly as the German

Luftwaffe flew high overhead to bomb civilian, military and airfield targets, and in our capacity as signallers we laid and maintained telephone cables across the Romney Marshes. Now and again we were bombed, as the German planes jettisoned their bombs on the return journey to France.

On one occasion, they brought to an abrupt conclusion the ceremony of 'Beating the Retreat' with band and bugles on the Dymchurch seafront. The ceremony culminated with the lowering of the flag at Battalion HQ just before sunset. This tradition was to ensure that the sun never set on the Union Jack which represented the British Empire. However, the outcome was that the band and bugles beat a hasty retreat that evening for the last time.

We also had a visit from Mr Winston Churchill, accompanied by the divisional commander and other high-ranking officers, to inspect our sea defences. They were suitably impressed, probably because our total establishment of Bren and Vickers light machine guns, was rushed in advance to each Company due to be inspected.

Probably, the battalion's best effort was an attempt to bring down a slow low-flying aircraft, as it hugged the coast south-westwards. In the event only superficial damage resulted, which was most fortunate indeed, as the plane was taking Flight Lieutenant R.A.B. Learoyd V.C. to Lydd Airport, to accept the freedom of Littlestone-on-Sea, his home town! This Victoria Cross, one of the first awards of the war, was in recognition of his leadership in the determined low-level attack on the Dortmund Ems Canal, on 12th August, 1940. War Office orders at that time were that no plane should fly below 3,000 feet in the coastal area. No one had told the pilot!

Now I was no longer in the Somersets, but a corporal in the newly formed 45th Reconnaissance Corps. We had awaited overseas posting in Hereford, and begun our journey in the early hours of 23rd August marching in full kit, carrying kitbags and rifles the two miles to the railway station. 'Full Kit' meant just that. Travel detail was posted as follows: Best battledress, polished boots, khaki forage cap. Respirators slung over right shoulder, haversack over left shoulder. Full pack on back, greatcoat folded and secured bandolier fashion round pack. Rifles to be carried with bayonets fixed, scabbard firmly fixed to protect blade. Clasp-knife in right hand pocket with lanyard around waist. Luckily for all of us the left hand pocket was empty!

Security was strict and we had been confined to barracks for the two previous weeks, with no access to telephones, all letters had been censored and shoulder flashes and insignia removed. In truth, we could hardly have given any secrets away, as we had no knowledge at all of where we might sail from, let alone our eventual destination. By early afternoon we were in the railway sidings at Bootle, completing our journey to the docks in a convoy of requisitioned tramcars.

We then marched the short journey to Princess Dock, Liverpool, facing the troopship that was to be our abode for some considerable time. I vividly remember the boarding party of the Royal Military Police, who marshalled us to our gangplanks, making sure we had no chance to decamp. I was thinking how much I would like to change places with them, even though the 'redcaps' would not have won a forces popularity contest, and stay in England. Our forty-strong signals section was allotted Table 110 on Mess Deck B5. Since sergeants and warrant officers were allocated quarters on A deck, I was placed in charge of the signal operators, and my friend Corporal Ray Scully was in charge of the twenty despatch riders.

Arms, ammunition, all equipment, braces, belt and webbing pouches and respirators were immediately collected and taken to the hold together with our Tropical Head-dress, Universal Foreign Service, better known as 'Pith Helmets'. We retained our haversacks to keep our clothes and belongings together. For the duration of the voyage, canvas shoes would be worn, but we retained our army boots to use on inspection parades. We were issued with mattresses, Mae West-type life jackets, and emergency rations. Unlike the seaman's life jacket, ours did not have the battery operated red location light. Our emergency rations, packed in small, sealed tobacco-type flat tins, consisted of vitaminized chocolate. During the weeks ahead, these emergency rations had to be guarded like gold dust. They were easy to filch and the chocolate was excellent. Replacements changed hands at fabulous prices, but we soon learned and tied them to our life jackets, which we carried at all times.

Our quarters were outstandingly spacious, and with later experience we realised how fortunate we were. Very quickly we explored and located the adjoining quarters. The galley was near and so were the 'heads', lavatories to landlubbers like us. There were also plenty of showers and facilities for washing our underclothes. The only minor problem was that we were never able to obtain a lather in the salt water, although we were issued with special soap. Both our bodies and our clothes continuously seemed to be sticky.

Our troopship was the *Dominion Monarch,* 28,000 tons, a modern diesel cargo and passenger liner, pride of the Shaw Saville & Albion Line. Indeed, at this time she was the most up-to-date diesel liner in the world. She was built in Newcastle-on-Tyne by Swan Hunter & Wigham Richardson Ltd, launched on the 27th July, 1938 and completed in January 1939. Built especially for the Liverpool-Wellington run to return with New Zealand lamb, the liner had over one million cubic feet of refrigeration and cargo space. In addition, the *Dominion Monarch* had been fitted out to provide accommodation for over 500 first class peace-time passengers in absolute luxury.

War broke out during her maiden voyage, and after being hastily armed with lightweight guns in New Zealand, she came back unescorted to Liverpool. Because of the liner's limited accommodation, she was sidelined for a time until shipping losses became acute. We boarded the *Dominion Monarch* after the time of a partial refit to make her suitable for 1,500 troops. Later, her capacity was increased to carry 4,000. We were not the first, nor the last, of the 90,000 troops she safely carried during wartime, but were fortunate to voyage in her. It is sad to reflect that this magnificent liner had then less than twenty years' sailing time ahead of her. Post-war ascendancy of air travel caused her withdrawal from service. She was broken up in Japan in 1962. Later on in the voyage, we were able to inspect the immaculate engine room, with two banks of ten 20-cylinder diesel engines, operating four single screws, at a maximum of twenty knots.

During our first day on board, boat stations were

11

allocated, and in the first twelve hours we had three practice emergency musters. We learned this routine long before we left the Mersey. At the first muster, our two red and green fibre identity disks were checked. They were indented with army number, name and religion, and had to be worn at all times. They were threaded on a thin cord and worn round the neck. At that muster, not only were we warned that it was a punishable offence not to wear the disks, but that even on death, the green disk must be left on the body, and the red one handed in for records – a grim reminder indeed. One of our troop was Jewish and I remember his identity disk was stamped with a 'J'. So if he had fallen into German hands, they would have had no doubt as to his religion. The inconsistency was that, before embarkation, our religion had been blacked out in our pay books, precisely to avoid identification and possible discrimination.

The next morning, the majority of the troops on board were on deck, surveying the Mersey River and the Liverpool panorama. There was in fact much to see, as Liverpool in those days was a busy port, despite wartime restriction and reduction of shipping. Another troopship, smaller than ours, was already docked amidst a bustle of activity. There was a variety of vessels awaiting loading or convoy at the dockside. Behind the ships towards the city you could see the Dock Board offices, the Atlantic Tower Hotel, the Cunard Line HQ and of course, the Liver building. From our vantage point mid-river, we were surprised that we could see little sign of the extensive bombing of the docks and Mersey shoreline. Opposite, on the Birkenhead shore, there were row upon row of houses fading into the distance. Moving around deck, we met a Liverpudlian of the Lancashire Fusiliers who could actually see the roof of his house, a terrace off the Waterloo Road. Just half a mile away, his wife would have no idea where he was. As he said, he was 'So near and yet so far.'

Departures like ours were normal and frequent occurrences in the Mersey, with the all-embracing security, and matter of fact, unvarnished efficiency. There would be no cheering crowds, no regimental bands, no garlands, and certainly no ships' sirens. Just a few seagulls. As some compensation however, we did get frequent cheers and catcalls from the passengers on the Liverpool and Birkenhead ferry, which plied regularly across the Mersey. The girls were the main subject of attraction, but there were plenty of troops around the Liverpool area, and also on the ferries. So we exchanged pleasantries, and also less mentionable remarks. Separated by the water in between, and the knowledge that we were not likely to see each other again, removed all inhibitions. The troops would call out 'Get your knees brown,' and we would respond with 'Get some service in.'

We had some idea of our eventual destination, as back in Hereford we had been issued with full tropical kit, including pith helmets. So, could it be Gibraltar, we wondered? Not likely, not for a mechanised unit. The Middle East? Very probably, but this wasn't a popular subject of conversation. South Africa? Without doubt this was the most favoured destination. India? Burma? We were not yet to know. By the end of the second day of waiting in the Mersey, we were well established in our seaboard routine.

Compared to the average army rations, our meals were superb. Onboard stores were of course, obtained at overseas ports, where there was no rationing and no shortage. So meat, cheese, butter, vegetables, all the foods rarely seen at home or severely rationed, were available in abundance. It was peacetime catering for the ship's crew, augmented by the army cooks on board. In addition, the NAAFI canteen was well stocked: chocolate, sweets, tinned fruit, biscuits and in addition, plenty of cigarettes. Due to my interest in fitness at home, I had never made a habit of smoking, though my father smoked. In spite of their availability and low prices, I resisted the habit for the whole of my army service. Beer and spirits were not available in the canteen for obvious reasons, but an issue of beer was made available from time to time. The only restriction on our canteen purchases was lack of funds, but to be honest, we were never really hungry.

We already seemed to have been aboard for a long time and began to feel restless and looked forward to our forthcoming departure but we accepted the fact that we had no choice and that adventure lay ahead. There was not long to wait because, after breakfast on the Wednesday, there was

13

a great bustle as the crew moved to stations; the engines came alive and slowly the noise increased. With the pilot aboard, bells rang and the whole ship vibrated as she turned in the Mersey to face the sea. The last anchor cable was secured, and we were at last on our way past Wallasey and Bootle, through the narrow channel, with the minefield either side towards the open sea.

Two hours later, the pilot boat was on its way back to Liverpool, we were out in the bay and the land was receding. Hugging the coast northwards, we were joined by a convoy of six small coasters and a large escort, consisting of seven light cruisers and two destroyers. Soon, with the Isle of Man on our port side, darkness fell. We were tired out and slept well until 3.50 a.m., when we had a further muster, but this time out in the open sea. Although half asleep, we paraded in no time, all were adjudged to be present and correct, then we returned to our sleep.

When we went on deck next morning, we were anchored in the Clyde, just off Greenock, surrounded by hills in a vast natural harbour. Amongst many craft, we identified several warships, including the *Renown,* and off Greenock pier, the vast bulk of the *Queen Mary.* The 'Queens' used the Clyde as a base during the war years, as their previous berth at Southampton was dangerously close to the Luftwaffe airfields. Years later, on reading about the wartime service of these liners, I learned that when we saw the *Queen Mary* in the Clyde, she had come back from trips to South Africa and South America, and was being refitted to take additional troops. She was then to link up with the *Queen Elizabeth* on the North Atlantic run, bringing over most of the American troops who took part in the invasion of Europe in 1944.

That evening we had our last opportunity to write letters. I wrote home to my wife and parents, but the list of banned topics reduced the contents to personal empathy. This wasn't the time to write a newsy letter. Next afternoon we left our anchorage, joining the slowly proceeding line of merchantmen through the protecting minefield channel. Darkness surrounded us as we watched the Scottish coast slowly recede, on our way towards the open sea. Those of us on deck as the darkness thickened, heard distant firing ashore, and saw the tracery of vast anti-aircraft fire. In no time at all, this became the visible evidence of a major air raid, as parachute flares and bomb flashes lit up the sky. Soon a glowing red blanket of smoke spread over the eastern horizon. It was, we decided, yet another raid on the Glasgow Docks.

Next morning, we were really on our way, well out into the Atlantic, and according to my small button compass, sailing due west, with the convoy spread out around us. There were thirty-six vessels in total. We were the largest of the twenty-six troop and merchantmen in the convoy, and our escort consisted of two light cruisers and eight destroyers. The whole fleet zigzagged as one unit, changing pattern together. It was a most impressive sight. The *Dominion Monarch* was the commodore ship, and on board her, a senior naval officer assumed control of the troop and merchant navy ships, liaising with the senior commander of the navy escort vessels. The crew told us they now used a recently introduced very high frequency radio from the USA called TBS (Talk Between Ships), which made convoy control easier, and which to some extent superseded the use of flags and Aldis lamps. However, I noticed that as we progressed on our journey, the Aldis was still very much in evidence.

As we proceeded on this first day in the Atlantic, the weather worsened and we began to experience our first rough seas. Even on a vessel of 28,000 tons the movement was considerable, and the pitching and tossing began to take its toll. For the rest of the day, rations were in plentiful supply on the meal-time mess decks. Luckily, despite having a headache, I soon found my sea legs. Although the sea was rough, we were not confined to the areas below deck, and up on the fore deck it was a great experience as we met the waves head on.

The deck hands were noticeably busy, but of course they found plenty of time to talk. They also did not know where our destination might be, but they did not rule out the Mediterranean. Apparently, the Gibraltar-UK route was one of the most hazardous for allied shipping. In an effort to evade the German Air Command, and the U-boat bases in Western France, convoys went well out into the Atlantic, almost to the Azores, but although Britain and Portugal had long been allies and friends, American and allied planes and shipping did not use the Azores, due to Portuguese neutrality. It was not until the height of the battle of the Atlantic, that Portugal agreed to grant temporary facilities in the form of naval and air bases in the Azores and other Portuguese islands. So cover for convoys such as ours had to be based in Newfoundland, Iceland and the UK, thus leaving a vast expanse of water for the U-boats to operate in with comparative impunity.

We soon settled into a daily routine. Calls to muster at boat stations were frequent, even in the middle of the night. We were never quite sure if they were for practice or the real thing, but I must admit that they were essential at the beginning of the voyage, to ensure that the routine was well established. The ship's communication Tannoy system was first class, and could be heard clearly all over the vessel. It was used for all commands and communications.

Our day normally began at 6 a.m. with a roll call of the troop, which I took. My troop sergeant, Dennis Stringer, being nicely settled on the deck above, only appeared later in the mornings for our training sessions. Beds and bedding were stored away by 6.15 a.m. and at 6.30 a.m. breakfast was collected for the troop by a four man detail from the galley. This procedure was followed at the evening meal, when, as at breakfast, we ate from our mess tins. However, our main midday meal was issued to us in the galley in sectional trays with the meal and sweet all on one tray. We consumed this in the dining room. We were responsible for cleaning our own trays in a succession of large cauldrons. The first of these contained soapy water, the next disinfected water and the last one held hot salty water. It certainly was advantageous to be one of the first in the cleaning queue. Knives, forks and spoons, our 'eating irons' went through the same process.

In addition, we were able to collect cocoa and biscuits in the late evening should we still be hungry. Much later I learned how much wartime troopship feeding methods differed. On the *Queen Mary* and *Queen Elizabeth,* they only provided two meals a day in forty-five minute shifts. Of course, the situations were different as they carried upwards of 10,000 men each trip across the Atlantic, very closely packed, and with a stay on board of normally less than a week. After breakfast, unless the sea was very rough, we had P.T. on the boat deck for half an hour. Sometimes this was taken by the chief instructor, Don Welsh, who before the war had been a well-known professional soccer player. You may note that P.T., which stood for physical training, is now referred to as P.E., which stands for physical education.

At 9 a.m. GMT, the BBC overseas news bulletin was broadcast, usually confined to the headlines, followed by the mileage of the previous day, our speed and position, and any activities of interest for the day ahead. We listened avidly to the news, and were cheered by the successes of the Allied Forces, although I think we realised that much of this was propaganda.

Throughout our voyage, time on board was adjusted to correspond with Greenwich Mean Time, so at first, clocks went back as we journeyed west, and then forward as we began our eastern journey. Generally, our mornings were set apart for training and lectures; many afternoons and evenings being virtually free. A great deal of the training centred around our wireless, and wireless procedure, and stores would be collected each morning from the hold. We operated two army radio sets at this time, the no. 11 and no. 18. The no. 11 set was the universal set, in use during the first years of the war. It saw service in tanks and armoured cars, and in England we had used it in our Humber Snipe wireless cars, for communication between the Company and Battalion HQ and on to Brigade. To operate, it was basically two sets in one. The receiver worked independently from the transmitter and caused problems at times. With the microphone, speech was possible for up to around five miles in good conditions, but using the Morse code, it had a very long range. The no. 18 set was designed to be carried on the back like a pack, and operated by another signaller. In practice, it was much more successful when used in a static situation. On board of course, we could only theorise as the sets could not be operated, for obvious reasons! But we could practise our Morse reading with the keys and 'buzzer' sets, as this part of our training had been neglected. Many senior officers in my experience, looked at the wireless as a new-fangled toy. They were much happier with the field or GPO telephone.

Classes were organised for officers in the unit, but like most specialist subjects, they really did not have the time to become proficient. A lot of practice was needed, like learning to type or to play a musical instrument, and those sorts of facilities were not available. In retrospect, we certainly could all have had more widespread training in other capacities, such as in the use of mortars and anti-tank weapons. However, we were quite happy with what we were doing, and I am sure that the main objective of the military was to keep us from boredom, to make sure we kept fit and that we would be ready for action when we arrived at our destination.

My opposite number in the Signal Troop was Corporal Ray Scully, who in civilian life was a well-known racing motor-cycle rider. Although he was in charge of the despatch riders, he often joined me for training, and through him I became friendly with one of the ship's radio operators. He invited us to look over the ship's signal office near the bridge, which was normally out of bounds to all troops. The operation of the wireless room was smooth and ultra efficient, honed by wartime operation and experience. Indeed, it highlighted the difference between our signals, and even the difference between the troops on board and the ship's company. We had no real wartime battle experience, whereas they had been on active service on the high seas, and were always in danger when out of port. The *Dominion Monarch* wireless operators worked in eight-hour shifts. Outward communication was kept to a minimum to avoid radio detection, but I noticed that when they were transmitting their key work was in a different class from mine. From the signal room they also relayed all the internal information; broadcast relays, ship's announcements, in fact all internal communication.

The co-ordination of the convoy, as mentioned, was conducted from the bridge, and the Convoy Commodore and his staff had the use of short-wave radio and lamps for convoy control. Some of our afternoons were taken up by lectures, which did not necessarily pertain to our army responsibilities. The interesting ones that I remember were about MTBs, (Motor Torpedo Boats) in action, the British and Russian convoys, and German and Italian land mines.

In addition, there were the inevitable lectures on our responsibility in keeping fit and healthy in foreign countries, including as usual, the avoidance of sexual diseases. These talks were given by one of the padres or by medical officers. Without exception, the former offered moralistic considerations, extolling the benefits of living a chaste and monastic life. The latter, on the other hand, were much more practical and positive, offering more down-to-earth advice. They had the assistance of multi-coloured charts, which were very explicit indeed, leaving no doubt as to the organs involved and to their material condition. These lectures, I am sure, were designed to give a morbid fear of contagion, so for the benefit of all, the medical officers completed their talks by explaining the procedure involved in obtaining a free issue of contraceptives from the medical room.

The penalty for troops hospitalised through contacting VD was clearly laid down in army regulations: loss of pay of one shilling per day, and the likely stoppage of family allowance. There was more than a hint of blackmail in the latter regulations, for it meant that if wives or mothers enquired as to the pay stoppage, they would be informed that the soldier had contacted a sexual disease. The British Army was not interested in morals. During the war at various times and places, brothels were left open and organised for the troops. The High Command was in fact only concerned that the disease did not cause more casualties than the battlefield. It was certainly a new experience to listen to these lectures. Many of us in our young civilian life, had never been near a brothel, let alone visited one, due in most cases to our close family links and the shame of being found out. But now, we were off the lead as it were, so chance and temptation could well change the situation.

There were lots of other leisure activities aboard. Each troop had a suggestions committee, mainly to ensure that problems were brought into the open. The regimental adjutant was our chairman, with representatives from each other sections of the unit. Not only did I represent the Signal Troop, but I also had the onerous task of being secretary. Every Sunday, church services were held on all decks, and not being parades, were not compulsory. Nevertheless, a fair number used to attend. Some missed the service at home, some were bored, or as in many cases, they just enjoyed the singing. In fact, singsongs were often organised and were very well attended.

One of the most popular events was the request record programme, broadcast throughout the ship every evening at 7.30 p.m., which lasted one hour. The record library, assembled in peacetime for the first-class passengers of yesteryear, was most extensive. The presentations were chosen by units, or sections of the crew and transmitted very much like the BBC's pre-war 'Grand Hotel'. Selections varied of course, but usually fell into the same pattern of classical, popular orchestral, music from the shows, and Old time vocal favourites, all with a touch of nostalgia.

On the first of October, 1942, our selection was chosen for the broadcast:

Programme of records chosen by the
45th Reconnaissance Corps
on board *MS Dominion Monarch,* 1st October, 1942

1. *I'll Walk Beside You* sung by Webster Booth
2. *Selection* from Gilbert & Sullivan
3. *Boogie Woogie Bugler* sung by The Andrews Sisters
4. Mendelssohn's *Overture – Ruy Blas*
5. *Snow White Selection* from the film soundtrack
6. *If I Should Fall in Love Again* sung by Denny Dennis
7. *Bells Across the Meadow* by the Ketelbey Concert Orchestra
8. *Dear Old Southland* sung by Paul Robeson
9. Beethoven's *Moonlight Sonata*
10. *Vienna, City of my Dreams* sung by Webster Booth
11. *Joseph, Joseph* sung by The Andrews Sisters
12. *Serenade* from *The Student Prince*
13. *Along the Santa Fey Trail* sung by Bing Crosby
14. *On the Outside Always Looking In* sung by Flanagan & Allen
15. *Kashmir Indian Love Call* sung by Rose Marie
16. Selection from The Andrews Sisters
17. Liszt's *Leibestraume*

18. *The Warsaw Concerto* from the soundtrack of the film *Dangerous Moonlight*
19. *Intermezzo* from the soundtrack of the film *Escape to Happiness*

Without a doubt, these record programmes brought all those on board closer together; it was a bond with home. The nostalgia brought tears to the eyes of even the toughest individuals. I suppose it was the amalgam of all that was happening, the remembrance of times past with our loved ones, coupled with the thoughts of our prospects in the uncertain future ahead. Throughout the voyage, we also had free use of the extensive ship's library, augmented by paperbacks from the NAAFI, so we were never short of reading matter. The library was certainly the quietest part of the ship and ideal for letter writing. Another activity organised for our entertainment was a 'brains trust' based on the then popular current BBC Home Service radio programme. The competing panels were chosen from different units, sometimes according to rank. Apart from the morning physical training, we had a great deal of sports meetings, limited of course, by the confines of the deck. Tug-of-War was very popular, as were the obstacle races. I was too light for the former and not agile enough for the latter.

Meanwhile up on deck there was always plenty of interest, with the convoy all around us. Though I could not bother to participate, the most popular off-duty activity was called tombola. This is the only gambling game officially allowed in the navy, and no doubt the astute entrepreneurs who organised the schools were members of the crew. At home in civvy street at the time, it was known as lotto or housie-housie, and was the forerunner of the now ubiquitous bingo halls. Participants bought a card with three lines of numbers on, and the object was to complete a single line or, if possible, a whole card from the numbers announced by the caller. Those who have played will know that the numbers run from one to ninety. Those taking part covered the numbers as announced with bits of matchstick, so by the end of the day, the deck was carpeted with discarded slivers of wood.

Nearly every number had an alternative call which followed, such as number one Kelly's eye, number nine doctor's orders – because pill number nine was the medical officer's panacea for nearly all who reported sick, number eleven legs eleven, thirteen baker's dozen, sixteen sweet sixteen, seventy-six, seven and six was she worth it, and so on up to number ninety top of the house. No doubt these and all the other numbers have survived in present-day bingo halls. During the calling the silence would become more and more intense, until the call 'house' which was the signal for all participants to erupt into a babble of utter disbelief, and for the winner to dance forward to have his card checked and collect his winnings.

Below decks, the 'crown and anchor' boards, suitably tucked away, operated with warning scouts posted, and were ready to be covered up at a moment's notice. Participating in a crown and anchor school was a punishable offence in the services, and all the schools were aware of this. There were also the bridge fanatics. We also played pontoon or solo whist on our mess-deck some evenings.

We mingled with the crew, and got to know a number who related their experiences. Some of them had been sailing in the *Dominion Monarch* since she was commissioned. They were convinced she was a lucky ship. According to them, she was fitted with degaussing strips. These produced a dense magnetic field, which repelled magnetic mines. They also told us that the ship was fitted with paravanes. Basically, they were wires affixed to the front of the vessel, just below the waterline, attached to floats, which stretched the wire at a distance from each side of the ship, in theory for the purpose of pushing aside any floating mines. Ray and I spent a long time trying to discover these two devices but without success.

After a week at sea, the convoy veered southwards, and on 1st September, the nearest land was Cape Finisterre, the north western tip of Galicia in Spain, 700 miles away. Warrant officers' and sergeants' quarters on the deck above us, comfortably accommodated two to a cabin. However, the officers enjoyed luxury in single cabins. Segregated from us, on A deck was a party of nurses, all commissioned officers. It was rousing to get the occasional glimpse of them, even thought they were well out of our grasp!

Then just as we were really settled in and complacent, we had a rude awakening to our wartime dangers. At 2 a.m. on the morning of 3rd September, action stations were sounded and amid a great deal of activity, we threaded our way through the *mêlée* of activity to our muster stations. This time we knew it was for real because all the merchant seamen were on deck wearing their lifejackets. Depth charges were dropped around the convoy, which seemed to be proceeding at full speed. In the dark, we could only surmise what was happening, and rumours were rife. We had indeed been shadowed by a large plane the previous day, which according to hearsay was a Focke Wolfe Condor. We often got a glimpse of our own planes, the Catalina flying boats built in America, the odd Lockheed Hudson and once early on, one of our Spitfires. However, within the hour we were back in our sleeping quarters, and heard no more about the night's activities.

By a strange coincidence, the next day a special church service was held to commemorate the outbreak of war on 3rd September, exactly three years before. During a short service prayers were held, seeking a speedy end to hostilities. Few of us actually attended, the service was broadcast over the Tannoy system, but it had an impressive and forcible impact, especially after our experience the night before. By now, much further south, the weather began to warm up. The nearest land was now Africa, which was 900 miles away. Nights below deck became less comfortable and the following evening we were allowed to sleep on deck, which was most delightful as there was plenty of space, and from now on I took my straw mattress up on deck every evening. In different circumstances this experience could have been exceedingly romantic. The moonlit sea, the stars so much brighter than at home and the luminosity of the phosphorous, as the boat churned through the waves. This was an experience that became vividly imprinted on my memory. Around this time, and also much later in the Indian Ocean, we were accompanied by a school of dolphins, much larger than the porpoises and flying fish, both of which often accompanied us at this time. By the ninth of September we were only 200 miles from Africa. The weather was perfect.

During the morning, due to our impending visit to land, we were issued with tubes of mosquito repellent cream, and instructed that buttoned up shirts and long slacks must be worn on deck. The cream was not only greasy, but it also had a horribly pungent smell. Instructions were that it should be used every four hours in exposed areas, which meant face and hands. It would certainly have repelled most living things, let alone mosquitoes. The weather was certainly very hot now, so we were issued with a daily mineral water ration, as the water available below decks had to be boiled before drinking. However, just about this time, we discovered that a tap outside the galley on the port side of C deck dispensed almost icy water, direct from the refrigeration plant below decks. We tried to keep this find a secret, but before long there was a constantly moving queue during daylight hours.

The next day we had another experience of naval and air activity. Two Lockheed Hudson aircraft flew over the convoy, depth charges were dropped by the outer ring of destroyers' escorts, and we wore our lifejackets for an hour. Eventually, all quietened down, and the stand down was announced. At around 4 p.m. we passed close to a mass of floating debris and part of a lifeboat.

Years later, when censorship was lifted, and shipping losses allowed to be published, I read of the loss of the *Tuscan Star,* 11,500 tons of the Blue Funnel Line, sunk on the 6th September by U-109, with the loss of fifty-two lives, just off Freetown and I wondered if the same U-boat was the cause of our convoy's defensive measures. That submarine, incidentally, was eventually sunk in the Bay of Biscay by an RAF Sunderland on 7th May, the following year. The approach to Freetown was obviously a happy hunting ground for the German and Italian submarines at this time. There were numerous rich targets. Most of the convoys from the UK, Gibraltar, *en route* to South America, South Africa, the Red Sea ports and India needed to call at the port of Freetown for refuelling and for stores, before proceeding either to Cape Town or Durban on the Cape route, or across the South Atlantic. The Suez Canal and the Mediterranean were much too dangerous for the run of the mill convoys to pass through. Freetown was a major port, and one of the finest natural harbours in the world.

On the 9th September, land was sighted on the horizon, and the convoy formed into single file to enter the extraordinarily long approach, through the minefield channel protecting Freetown harbour, which certainly was a sight to be remembered. Seemingly miles wide, it contained what seemed to be a never ending assemblage of ships in a vast amphitheatre. The plains in the background looked lush and green, backed in the distance by the towering mountains. We were in Freetown harbour for three days, and we counted over a hundred large vessels, including an aircraft carrier which was too far away to identify. Although anchored almost a mile from shore, we were near enough to hear the traffic and bustle in the town and view the panoramic scene of storage tanks, derricks, cranes as well as the houses and buildings of the town.

The weather was damp during the monsoon period, which would run from May to October. Sierra Leone was known, like much of the tropical rain forest areas, as the 'White Man's Grave', because although the shore looked inviting, it was malaria-ridden. However, as we were so far off shore, we did not see or feel any mosquito bites. No doubt there were better targets inland.

The natives were soon around the ship in their heavily laden 'bum' boats, trading many exotic fruits, melons, coconuts, gourds and especially bananas, which we had not seen or tasted for years. We lowered our payment in envelopes on the end of pieces of string, and hauled up the fruit with change in return. We were not very pleased when we found that our change was in West African currency. All activities were of interest after so long on board, even the tankers that came alongside to refurbish the ship with diesel fuel and water.

We were given an interesting lecture about the colony of Sierra Leone, which would not become independent until 1961. It had been a British trading station in the 1600s and the capital, Freetown, was so named as it became a settlement for Africans rescued from the slave ships in the following century. In all, upwards of 50,000 West Africans were liberated by the British Navy, and thus Sierra Leone became a British Colony in 1808. When we were docked there in 1942, the population of the colony was 90,000, half of which made up the town of Freetown.

We eventually upanchored on the 13th September at 0645 hours, and were soon in the open sea watching the land disappear. It was a lovely sunny morning with a calm sea, and the church service held on the deck that Sunday was larger than usual. This was probably because of the start of another sea trip, or maybe it was just to relieve boredom. However, had there been a roof we would have lifted it while we sang *Guide me O thou Great Redeemer* to the tune of *Cwm Rondda*. We were soon 300 miles from land, the weather was wet and the sea was rough as we neared the Equator. Although it was warm, this was the comparatively cool time of the year, with quite a lot of rain. We crossed the Equator without ceremony on our deck, and time on board passed quickly, with the now usual routine. On the 17th September I noted in my diary that we had been on board for twenty-five days, nine in harbour and seventeen at sea. Now, as we steamed out of the tropics, our daily issue of mineral water ceased.

On 23rd September, we gathered on the main deck, to listen to our regimental second-in-command, Major Boileau. He revealed that our destination was in fact India, and that, when we arrived, our special duties would be to help retain law and order. There was a political problem at this time, as the Indian Congress Party which had always wanted independence from British rule, with the Japanese on their doorstep, had launched an all-out rebellion to embarrass the British Government. The rebellion consisted mainly of riots, and civil disobedience rallies, but transport had also been attacked and trains derailed. This insurgence had not been supported by the Indian Army who had remained loyal, and who were at all times an important component of the British Forces in India.

This news was well received by all. For those who wanted it, there was a chance of some sort of action. For a great number of us, it was a great moral boost. The War was nearly three years old, news on all fronts except Burma and the Far East was good. We were destined for India, for comparative safety and who knows, the war might soon be over and we could soon look forward to return and continue our civilian lives.

The regular soldiers, who had been returned to the UK from India to help form the basis of the regiment, were absolutely thrilled, and at once expounded their superior knowledge on our future environment. They regaled us with highly coloured tales of great danger. Lions, tigers, leopards, cheetahs and wolves prowled around all the camps ceaselessly. Snakes abounded under foot, in and out of barracks, especially the hooded cobra and the krait, from which, once bitten there was no serum antidote. Added to this they spoke of the unending columns of ants; large, small, red, black and white, and the ever-lurking scorpions and tarantulas. There were also the pestilences of cholera, yellow fever, typhoid, tetanus and malaria. We listened, but after nearly three years' service we took these tales with a pinch of salt.

In fact we enjoyed the companionship of these regulars. They cannily took their opportunities as for example when they first arrived back from India. Our medical officer had been a Territorial Army doctor from a civilian practice and he had never encountered a malarial patient, so a pulse raising cigarette, a small piece of soap under the tongue, a growth of beard and a pronounced shiver convinced him of the authenticity of the symptoms. The 'patient' was excused duties for three days, the equivalent nights out on the tiles and permitted a long lie-in the next morning!

Most regular soldiers in the regiment had been posted back to the UK from India soon after the commencement of war in 1940. This was to strengthen and stiffen the newly formed sister unit, the 6th Battalion, Somerset Light Infantry. There was one inherent and obvious weakness in this system, because as no commanding officer approves the release of his best men, so the resultant list would invariably include those men who were rebels, delinquents, misfits, or non-conformists in the view of the regiment. This was not to say they would not do well in the new environment; indeed many were glad to get away and make a fresh start.

We were now only 150 miles from Cape Town, which was our next port of call. The next day we had a lecture on South Africa and the Cape, and that evening the convoy formed up into its usual single line as it approached the protecting minefield channel.

On Friday 25th September, we were up early, and had our first sight of the mountains of the Cape. As we got nearer, the sun rose, lighting the scene in a most glorious fashion, now dominated by the unmistakable shape of Table Mountain and very soon Cape Town itself, in one of the world's most beautiful settings. Before midday we were in Table Bay, being turned slowly with the help of the harbour tugs, finally berthed in Duncan Dock, right against the quay. It was to prove a memorable stay.

First on the agenda was a pay parade. I drew four pounds, two weeks army pay, which at the time seemed very adequate. South Africa was then part of the British Commonwealth, so it used the pound sterling as currency. After over a month aboard ship, everyone was anxious to go ashore. The organisation for the issue of passes was badly thought out. I cannot now remember which higher command devised the system, but in the event it proved most unjust. A pack of cards was produced, and those drawing a seven or above were allowed ashore. Aces were low. The first day, I drew a king, and Ray Scully a five so I was lucky. On the first day, it was not known how long we would be in port, and the same system was employed on each day. In fact, we were to remain in Cape Town for over four days. Some troops on board were unlucky, and drew a low card every day. This nearly caused a riot. It was witless army organisation and the easy way out. On the fourth day, orders should have been given that those unlucky on the first three days should have been given priority. Those troops who had been unlucky went on to spend a further three weeks at sea, making a total of two months without setting foot on land.

Service personnel on convoys that docked in South African ports during wartime, will have experienced the magnificent and boundless generosity of the civilian population. As we looked out on that first morning, fleets of cars were waiting on the quayside, to take us to their houses, showing us the sights as they did and this was followed with entertainment and the provision of lavish meals.

I went ashore soon after midday with one of my signal

operators, Bill King. The sheer exhilaration of walking down the gangplank was wonderful, and equally, the feel of firm ground beneath our feet on the dockside. We were whisked away in a very large limousine, by a Cape Town lawyer whose name was Mr Hayes. First we toured the city, surrounded by the mountains. He showed us his office building in Adderley Street, and we had a beer opposite Government House. Then we had a trip along Main Road to see Green Point, and to the top of Signal Hill, which divides Camp Bay and Kloof Nek. Signal Hill offered an excellent view of the city at 1,200 feet above sea level. Mr Hayes was a keen cricket fan, and took us to see the Stadium at Newlands, famous as a test match venue for both cricket and rugby. We talked about the recent visit to South Africa by the MCC. We spent the late afternoon at our host's home in Collingwood Road Newlands, where we met his wife, who welcomed us like long-lost sons. We had an early tea in the garden, and later we had dinner of roast beef and all the trimmings, followed by peaches, ice cream, brandy and cigars. We did not talk about the war as such, but about life at home, in the army, and our families at home and how we missed them. Mrs Hayes wrote down our home addresses and promised to write to our families. My wife and my mother both had mail within a month of our leaving Cape Town. No wonder the hospitality of the South African people to the visiting wartime armed forces was legendary. Mr Hayes returned us to the quay, but the freedom still retained its magic, and we sat at a bar near the docks drinking beer, until our passes ran out at midnight. Subsequently, I wrote periodically to the Hayes family until 1959, when my letter was returned by a relative with a note saying that Mr Hayes, who survived his wife, had died.

Everything had impressed us, the hospitality, the magnificent friendly reception everywhere we went, the mountains, skyscrapers, buildings, the noise and bustle, but of course, the big impact was the freedom from the blackout we had left at home. There were bright lights everywhere. Even the *Dominion Monarch,* illuminated overall, looked like a cruise liner. I was off duty again the following day, but only just, because I drew an eight. Ray Scully drew a ten, so at midday we were away. The Hayes' had mentioned that the

29

YMCA in Victoria Street kept a list of telephone numbers given by locals who wished to meet and entertain visiting servicemen. We decided to go along and try our luck! The first number we selected drew an unanswered blank, but the second belonged to a Mrs Movsovic who lived in the seaside suburb of Muizenberg. Mrs Movsovic welcomed our call and gave us instructions on how to travel. We caught a train from Central Station, which linked Cape Town with the naval base at Simonstown, a distance of around sixteen miles. Muizenberg was about half way along on the same side of the peninsula facing False Bay.

The Movsovic family lived in Bridge End Street, almost on the seafront, and we were made very welcome. Mrs Movsovic's husband was away in the South African Navy, though he spent most of his time at the base in Simonstown. There were four children, Ella, Clare, Richard and Monty, who had arranged a picnic on the beach. I particularly remember the two teenage daughters who were most attractive. This was the cool time of the year in the Cape and the beach was almost deserted, but we could not resist taking a swim, although the sea temperature was around sixty degrees, and the breakers tremendous. We bathed in our underpants, having no costumes, and dried them in the sun afterwards. Later we went to a building called the Pavilion, on the beach for afternoon tea. We went back to the house for dinner and played table tennis, listened to classical music on the radiogram, and later a concert broadcast from Cape Town. We caught the last train back to Cape Town, having been invited back again the following day.

Sunday dawned wet and damp, with no sign of Table Mountain, but both Ray and I drew high cards, so we walked into town, had a meal in a cafe, and walked round the closed shopping centre. The skies cleared as we caught the train to Muizenberg. This time we had brought our P.T. shorts and a towel, so we had another dip in the sea, before going to visit the Movsovics again for an evening meal. We played pontoon, using matchsticks for money, and after dinner we played more games of table tennis. Mrs Movsovic had already written to Ray's mother and my wife Mollie, and for several years I kept in touch. Once again we just made it to the ship before midnight.

30

The following day we were free again, so Ray and I decided to go to the top of Table Mountain. First we had a meal of egg, sausage and chips at what we now regarded as our regular cafe. We then made our way to St George's Street and caught the bus to Koop Nek, the starting point for the cableway bus, which took us to the Table Mountain Aerial Cableway base station. The journey up in the cable-car was an unforgettable experience, and the view at the top was magnificent. The lower cable station is probably around 500 feet above sea level, and the cable a good half a mile long, rising to over 3,500 feet at the western end of Table Mountain. We had had no previous experience of cable-car travel, and this would have been obvious to the attendant. The first part of the traverse was swift and uneventful, but as the cable hung in a natural loop, progress to the top became progressively steeper and slower. The breathtaking experience must have shown on our faces. Of course, the affable attendant had witnessed the same situation many times before.

'Not nervous, are you lads?' 'Of course not,' we replied, probably with not much conviction. 'Very safe, tested every two weeks. Though cable-cars are prone to accident,' he added. We chuckled nervously. 'Unusual record has this one. Of course, we have a new main cable every five years just to be safe. As a matter of fact the new one is overdue, should have been fitted last week.' We managed another nervous laugh as we reached the summit.

The view from the top of Table Mountain was breathtaking. To the west, the azure carpet of the Atlantic Ocean faded into the hazy distance. Behind us to the east, the suburbs of Newlands, Claremont and Wynberg, and beyond them, towns and villages of the plain, the elevated grasslands of the veldt, merging into the far off mountains. To the south we could follow ,the peninsula all the way to Cape Point, or more correctly the Cape of Good Hope. We followed the line of the railway through Retreat to the line of beaches facing False Bay, St James, Fish Hoek, Glencairn to the terminus at Simonstown, everything spread out like a map. At this height we could even pick out the lighthouse on the end of the point, nearly twenty-five miles away. Finally to the north, seemingly right underneath our feet, we could see Cape Town and Table Bay, with a variety of shipping around the quay, including our troopship. Into the distance, as far as the eye could see was where the South Atlantic merged with the coastline.

The plateau of Table Mountain extended a long way eastwards. We walked quite a way along the rocky ground, almost bare of any vegetation, and as we stepped, we disturbed the small lizards which were sunning themselves on the warm boulders. We were extremely fortunate that the sky was cloudless. After this once in a lifetime experience, going back to the cable-car was almost an anticlimax.

Back in the centre of Cape Town, we realised that this might well be our last day of shore leave. The reprovisioning of the convoy had proceeded apace during the last few days, and there was a strong rumour that we would sail in the morning. So we decided to spend our last afternoon exploring the town and the modern shopping centre. As one would expect, there was an abundance of goods, with none of the signs of shortage and rationing we had experienced at home. We still had some money. Ray bought a wristwatch and other odds and ends, and I bought two rolls of film, black and white. My camera, a Kodak 6-20, which I still have to this day was packed away in my kitbag in the hold, as it was not allowed on voyage. I also bought two pairs of American nylon stockings, which were unheard of at home at this time, and the shop arranged to post them directly to Mollie, my wife in England.

On board ship there had been stories of the brothels in District Six, so after a couple of beers we decided to satisfy our curiosity, bolstered with a mixture of adventure and bravado, but only got as far as the military police, who made sure that this area was definitely out of bounds. We had expected to find the 'redcaps' patrolling the area, but surprisingly they were able to supply us with an alternative. For a fee they provided a list of brothels and cafes where prostitutes operated. These military policemen certainly had a nice little number in Cape Town. They must have had a steady stream of customers, as troopships docked in the harbour. It became a standard joke in the army to say that the quickest way to find a brothel was to look for a parked MP's jeep.

Sex was an inevitable and frequent topic of conversation in the services. Barrack room language, and instruction from our regular NCOs, had come as a violent shock to many of us young conscripts, who had previously enjoyed a rather sheltered home background. Maybe we had heard it all before, but not in normal conversation. For instance, I remember our early instruction in operating the Bren gun, and changing magazines in the firing position. Any hesitation in the drill would evoke the directive, 'You'd find it quick enough lad, if it had hair round it!' We got used to the coarseness as time went on. Likewise, we very quickly learned during map-reading instruction that the lines of latitude ran across the map, and those of longitude up and down, in that order. The instructor left us in no doubt by saying, 'You have to get across her before you can get up her.'

Our visit to Cape Town was now almost over, and as we walked slowly back absorbing the bright lights and the bustle all around us, we were very loathe to think of the morrow. Back at our 'regular' bar we had another beer and bought bananas and two pineapples at a stall outside, before wending our way back to the quay, handing in our passes as we left the gangway. South Africa at this time was part of the British Empire, and racial segregation did not appear to be a major issue, though, of course, we were only visitors, with no time to study the situation. All persons we had met in Cape Town, either black or white, had been outstandingly friendly and helpful.

Shore leave was cancelled the following morning and the last mail was collected. It was another fine day but Table Mountain was now covered with the 'Tablecloth', a layer of white cloud, just like the icing on a cake. The cloud seemed to form at one end, roll slowly along in the breeze and tumble off and fade away at the other end. Around midday, three tugs arrived alongside, the mooring cables were unhitched, the anchors raised and we were nosed into the centre of the harbour, to slowly turn to face the sea. We set out alone to go round Mouille Point, and then to turn due south along the coast of the peninsula. Soon after rounding the lighthouse at Cape Point, we were joined by a small convoy, five merchantmen and two cruisers, coming out from False Bay. They had probably been anchored in Simonstown. Slowly the mountain disappeared in the mist, and we said goodbye to Cape Town and South Africa.

The entry that day in my diary just about sums up my feelings. 'Ate last pineapple with Ray Scully, very browned off. Meeting the people of Cape Town was a joy, an unforgettable experience. They made us feel at home, and now we are homesick and rather depressed with the thought of the journey ahead. They were wonderful people.' In some ways the next stage of our journey seemed to go more quickly, probably because there was little change in the routine we had experienced on the first part of the voyage. Duties during the next eighteen days were very much the same. I was relieved of mess duties, but I was placed on the deck guard duty roster.

As we headed north east in the Indian Ocean, we ran back into the warmer weather, the mineral water issue was renewed, and we took the opportunity to sunbathe on deck. We were now travelling in convoy, having been joined by a cruiser and eight merchantmen. We duly recrossed the Equator on Sunday 11th October, and this time the ceremony of crossing the line was held on our deck. Officers and crew of the ship dressed up as King Neptune's Court, and King Neptune was the commanding officer of the South Lancashire Regiment, complete with golden trident, and draped in seaweed. Apart from the crew, very few on our deck had crossed the Equator before this voyage, so there were plenty of qualifiers for initiation. About thirty were accepted for investiture, lining up in front of the specially constructed 'swimming pool'. In turn they were copiously lathered, not too gently shaved with a large wooden cut-throat razor, and then toppled unceremoniously into the water. There was a great deal of harmless retaliatory horse play, all good-natured and enjoyed by all.

By now we were 750 nautical miles from the nearest land, which was still Africa. During the afternoon a battle cruiser joined the convoy, and a few hours later a large part of this convoy parted company with us. According to one of the crew, they were bound for the Red Sea and eventually Egypt.

On the morning of Friday 17th October, I was on guard

duties until 11 a.m., and just before that the cloud-like haze of the horizon revealed the line of distant land. As the ships formed up into line astern, we had our first glimpse of the skyscrapers of the Bombay skyline.

Small sailing craft, with multi-coloured sails sped around the bay, like a kaliedoscope of butterflies. It was probably the Bombay Sailing Club's Sunday morning competition. The white line along the horizon became a spread of white buildings, whilst throngs of large dragonflies surrounded the vessel. As we approached the dock we passed the Gateway of India, built specially in 1926 for the visit of King George V and Queen Mary as a hastily constructed white plaster arch. The arch we were looking at was actually more modern, built in 1927 as a more permanent structure.

There was a cruiser with three funnels in the dock. As we waited, it proceeded into the harbour with the assistance of the tugs that we were waiting for. We had already spent our last money in the canteen which was to close at 2 p.m., knowing there would be a pay parade before we left. Soon, the tugs turned their attention to us, so we turned slowly in the harbour churning up the muddy bottom as they shepherded us into the dock. At the pay parade, I drew fifty rupees, which was about four pounds at twelve and a half rupees to the pound. There are sixteen annas to the rupee and twelve pice to the anna. So for one rupee we received the equivalent of nearly two hundred coins. Our advance party left at 1900 hours and the rest of the unit was left to watch the passing scene.

We had all been issued with a new 31st divisional sign, and were ordered to make absolutely sure that this sign was also displayed in a prominent place on the baggage. When we sewed these on to our shirts the evening before, as always doing what we were told without question, most of us nevertheless expressed our views of the army in unprintable terms. Why could these not have been issued earlier? At the time we did not realise that this was for the benefit of the German and Japanese agents in Bombay.

During the evening, we bartered with the natives on the dock, where the fruit was very cheap. It was our first experience of the poverty in India. Destitute people were begging for small coins and huddled figures wrapped in rags were sleeping on the dock. We were soon enveloped with waves of sticky heat and a pungent stench. Above all this, there was the noise of car and taxi horns in an incessant cacophony, and we had not yet set foot on the Indian Subcontinent. Sleeping on deck that night was almost impossible, the noise in the background never ceased.

Soon after breakfast next morning we prepared to disembark. Already the derricks were in action, the booms were swinging the baggage across the deck to the bustling stevedores on the dock below. Our train was waiting on the dockside, and at 10 a.m. we marched to our coaches fully laden with all our trappings, kitbags and rifles. Most of us were sad to leave as we had made friends with the crew of the *Dominion Monarch* which had been our home for two whole months. It was the end of a great adventure, and we had memories we would never forget.

2

Training in Ranchi

We had been told before we disembarked, that our train was due to leave at midday, which would give us plenty of time to settle into our coaches. In the event, we found that the carriage doors were locked and the windows closed from the inside. This proved to be our first experience of Indian red tape and the trials of dealing with the country's officialdom. Apparently, certain formalities had not been correctly observed, and in the meantime, we waited not too patiently in the scorching heat which threatened to engulf us. Eventually, two wizened but smiling railway clerks arrived with a sheaf of papers and a very large brass turnkey. The omnipresent military police signed the requisite forms, the coach doors were ceremoniously unlocked, and we were able to get to work stowing our kit. As the coaches had been shunted into the sidings at first light, the interiors were like ovens and we sweated in the fierce heat.

Our train was composed of the standard compartment-alised military coaches, over seventy feet long. Each compartment consisted of six wooden slatted bunks, three each side, supported by thin metal stanchions which ran from floor to ceiling. Both top and middle bunks each side folded down to allow daytime occupation, although we soon found out that the top bunks each side were good places to be. If you could ignore the heat and the noise you could sleep undisturbed all day.

Eventually, just after midday our steam locomotive arrived, the coaches were coupled and we clanked slowly over the uneven track in the sidings through the straggling tenements of Bombay city, gathering speed as we threaded

37

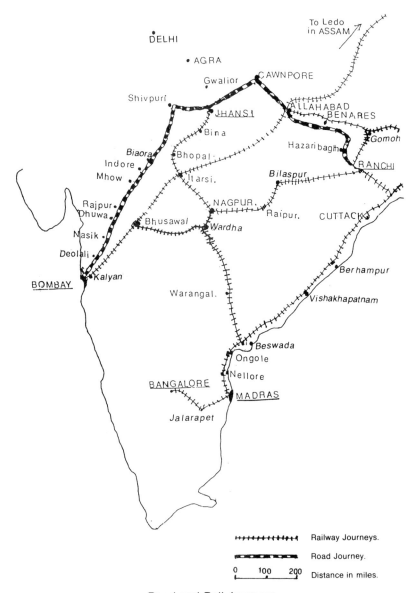

DELHI

AGRA

Gwalior

Shivpuri

JHANSI

Bina

CAWNPORE

To Ledo
in ASSAM

ALLAHABAD
BENARES

Biaora

Bhopal

Hazaribagh

Gomoh

Indore

Mhow

Itarsi.

Bilaspur

RANCHI

Rajpur

Dhuwa

NAGPUR.

Raipur.

CUTTACK

Nasik

Bhusawal

Wardha

Deolali

Berhampur

BOMBAY

Kalyan

Warangal.

Vishakhapatnam

Beswada

Ongole

Nellore

BANGALORE

MADRAS

Jalarapet

Railway Journeys.

Road Journey.

0   100   200   Distance in miles.

Road and Rail Journeys.

through the better class suburbs, and finally out across mile upon mile of the flat open paddy fields towards the distant hills. Yesterday was our first experience of the Indian sub-continent. Today produced a plethora of new encounters, and an insight into the future. All these new experiences were difficult to assimilate in such a short time.

We had not gone far before we came to a halt, and learned that troop trains in India were bottom of the list of priorities. The mail trains had absolute precedence over all other traffic, and these express trains were almost always on time, mainly because the line was made clear up to an hour before the time of passing. This caused great delay to other train movements, especially as many of the secondary routes consisted of single tracks. After about an hour's travel we were diverted into the sidings at Kalyan. Here we found confirmation indeed of the poverty of the Indian masses and the need to fight for survival. There were many beggars pleading for 'baksheesh', a call for alms, and a multitude of traders offering tea, fruit, knives and trinkets, in a struggle for subsistence. We were, of course, more than grateful for the tea, and from now on the tea-boys known as *charwallahs* became part of our lives. We also bought a lot of fruit, especially bananas, dates and mangoes. Here our steam engine disappeared and we awaited the electric locomotive which would take us over on the modernised lines up the steep climb to the plateau.

At this stop, the Railway Transport Police were on duty. They collected all the fake divisional flashes we had so carefully sewn on our khaki shirts. I never again heard or read of a 31st British Division, though certainly the Japanese 31st were to make a great name for themselves in the operation around Imphal and Kohima much later. Considering that the collection of flashes was eagerly watched by all and sundry around the station precinct, there was certainly no security and I wondered if this ploy fooled anyone at all.

On this journey we were provided with two meals a day, dished up from temporary cookhouses organised by the Indian Army in the railway sidings, and we missed the luxury of our troopship meals. But luckily we were always able to supplement these meals with fruit and tea, which we got used to calling 'char' from the vendors. The water on the train was supplied from tanks in the roof, so it was always tepid or hot from the daytime sun. However, we soon discovered the Indian *chagul*. This was a canvas water bottle with a narrow neck and tying tapes, holding around a gallon of water. As the canvas was porous, the slowly leaking water evaporated and considerably cooled the residue in the waterbottles. We hung them from the carriage windows and doors, so the heat of the sun and the movement of the train made the water almost icy cold, and in the prevailing circumstances, most delicious. Later, these were to be a standard addition to all our transport, and at a cost of eight annas, equivalent to about nine old pence, from the railside vendors, they were a good buy and a real life saver.

Talking of water, there was the question of ablutions, and the 'squat' toilets at the end of each compartment in the carriage. To say that they were very basic would be a compliment. Toilets obviously did not appear on the railway cleaner's list of duties. Those who could hold their breath while performing the essential functions were at a distinct advantage. Habits may well have changed, but we observed very early on, that the majority of inhabitants did not consider toilets a necessity, as squatting in the street or the fields was normal. If confirmation were needed, this was provided as we passed through the Indian countryside early mornings at first light.

There was little to do during our journey in the way of duties. A train guard was mounted at night, and I did one duty. When we were not viewing the scenery, we played cards, mostly pontoon, to while away the time. On the third day we arrived at Nagpur, which was a magnificent station, and there we witnessed the arrival and departure of the Calcutta Mail, which was scheduled to stop for one hour. This was to enable the first-class passengers to consume a five-course meal in the station restaurant. We had arrived half an hour before the mail train, and would not move until it was well on the way to Calcutta, so we had plenty of time to explore the station and get a good view of the diners. The whole meal looked luxurious, and the service was impeccable, the waiters in the white livery, bright red turbans and broad cummerbunds of the Indian railway restaurants, the whole company cooled by the breeze created by the *punkah* high in the ceiling. The *punkah* was a heavy strip of cloth, fixed to a long beam. This beam was swung back and forth by means of a rope unhurriedly pulled by an Indian servant, hidden away in the background. We were told that all first-class passengers on the mail train were served in this way. Meals could be ordered in advance at the previous stop. All other passengers had to obtain food from the vendors on the platform unless, like many, they had brought their own.

We noticed how wide the railway track was, five feet six inches as compared with those at home which were four foot eight and a half inches, which was why the carriages were built so much wider. At Nagpur we were roughly half-way through our journey, having passed through many stations, including Bhusawal, Akola and Wardha. From Nagpur, our route lay through Bhandara, Raipur, Bilaspur and Raigarh. We certainly saw and learned a great deal during this first troop-train journey. The initial panorama of the Indian scene included elephants, camels and monkeys, before the fifth day on Wednesday, 21st October when we eventually arrived at the railhead sidings at Bakakana Junction. We had a long wait and managed to get a shower under the railway water tower on the platform.

Eventually, a procession of Indian three-ton lorries arrived. They were to take us to our camp, twenty-six miles away. As we climbed aboard, we learned that our destination was Ranchi, four miles along the road leading to Ramgarth. It was a long and dusty journey up the winding foothills to the Ranchi plateau, and we arrived at the camp just in time to collect our kit from the baggage dump before the sudden dusk turned to darkness. The encampment had been recently established and we were completely housed under canvas, eight men to a bell tent. We were issued with a mosquito net each and a hurricane lamp hung from the centre pole. But we did not need any light as we were completely exhausted by our journey and took no time at all to fix our nets and slump on to our groundsheets fully clothed. In spite of the uneven ground we slept well.

The next morning we found the open earth latrine, a deep trench under two long parallel poles which became standard from then on. An overhead tank and buckets which sufficed for our ablutions, were filled by an Indian Army Service Corps tanker daily. The rest of the day was spent finding our way around, unloading stores and handing in our rifles for the armourers to check and inspect. During the next few days we were quickly brought down to earth, and we returned to a soldiering routine.

My section had to be properly dressed and fallen in for inspection outside the tents, thirty minutes after being woken up by bugle calls. We had to march to breakfast and all other meals and other parades. If we passed an officer we had to 'march to attention' and 'eyes left' or 'eyes right'. All routines were tightened. We had been spoiled on our voyage from home. Our easy life had ended. Added to this, our vehicles were still on the high seas, so we did not have the luxury of transport, except for some three-ton lorries of the Royal Indian Army Service Corps. Using these, a rota was quickly established for evening leave trips to Ranchi. They were known as 'passion wagons'.

At the cookhouse for our first meal, we encountered the skill and nerve of the Indian black kite which we knew as kite hawks; these perched like vultures on the nearby eucalyptus trees. Carrying our breakfast plates of fried bread, sausage and beans across to the open-air trestle tables, the kites swooped at breakneck speed and with split second timing, delicately removing the piece of bread or sausage. Naturally, we soon learned to cover our plates, but we immediately changed the name of this bird. In future references the letters 'sh' were substituted for the letter 'k'.

The following morning we were all washed, shaved and breakfasted by 7 a.m. when our Signal Troop fell in, prior to joining the HQ parade half an hour later. Those who have done service will know the routine. Following this inspection, we formed up with A, B and C Squadrons, to endure a further regimental inspection by the orderly officer and the adjutant in preparation for the arrival of Colonel Trotter, our commanding officer, who arrived to take the salute and address the regiment at 9 a.m.

Climbing on to a jeep, with amplifying equipment provided, he informed us of our new role, and the present situation. We had now become part of the British 70th

Division, commanded by Major General W.G. Symes. Originally formed in the UK, they had served in France, fought in the Mediterranean, including the siege of Tobruk, and were a first-class battle-hardened unit. We were suitably impressed and proud to be accepted into this Division. Overall, we were part of India Eastern Command, commanded by General Sir Archibald Wavell.

No doubt this was a 'breather' for the 70th Division. They were considered to be in the army reserve but for the last six months they had been engaged on extensive duties in Eastern Bengal in an effort to quell the India Congress Party riots. India had for some time, under the leadership of Mahatma Gandhi, been wanting independence. Although Gandhi and the Congress chiefs were now imprisoned, their subordinates had organised a 'Quit India' campaign. The subsequent rioting was centred in Bihar and Eastern India. In Calcutta, vehicles were set on fire and telephone cables cut. In the provinces, action took more serious patterns. Attempts were made to decapitate motor despatch riders by stretching wires across their paths and the railways were attacked. Stations were looted and set on fire, signals destroyed, lines torn up, and in isolated cases passengers were dragged from trains and murdered. At one time, large areas of the Eastern Provinces were isolated, including the large towns and cities, and the supply of arms and provisions to the Burma front cut off. In fact, throughout the middle of 1942, GHQ Delhi considered that the Congress Party campaign was more dangerous than a possible Japanese invasion attempt. But we had to come in at the tail end, and now towards the end of October, civil power was slowly being established.

As so often happened in army service, the parade that day was quite over the top. The information conveyed was most interesting, and put us in the picture. It began at 7 a.m. and lasted until 11 a.m. when I dismissed my section, the speech lasting for fifteen minutes, but we were not yet used to the heat, so several men collapsed that day. Admittedly we wore the cooler khaki drill uniforms of open-necked shirts, shorts, ankle socks and boots with *topees* as headgear, but I wondered if it was really necessary to wear our respirators at chest height in the ready position.

This would be an opportune moment to compare the differences of our soldiering in India with peacetime service. There were many analogies of course, but the picture painted by the regulars amongst us did not materialise. Regular battalions in India were steeped in tradition, segregated in brick-built quarters away from the Indian town or city. Barracks were known as cantonments, which on the whole were similar to self-contained towns. They were centred on large parade grounds surrounded by the offices, guard room, armoury, separate living quarters for men, NCOs and officers, cookhouses and messes. There would be separate bungalows for married quarters, a small hospital with medical staff, a church and a separate shopping bazaar. When the troops went on leave, it was usually to the hill stations, to live in similar conditions. The only time that barracks were vacated was to go on manoeuvres. Of course, there were brick-built army camps in the Ranchi area, which was the HQ of Eastern Command, but as the build up of troops continued, more and more camps under canvas were established.

The pattern of soldiering and training closely followed that of peacetime. Inspections and parades tended to be organised to take place in the early morning or late afternoon. During the heat of the day, we had free time or less active tasks. The hot and humid monsoon season which was from May to October in the Bihar area, was now over. The days were now dry, hot and cloudless. As winter approached, the evenings and early mornings cooled. Later, the nights became very cold, so that we experienced very great extremes of temperature. Like the regular troops in previous peacetime India, we had the opportunity of being waited on, depending on how much we wished to spend. In the eyes of the Indian tribesmen and camp followers, the British soldier was a very rich man. Establishing connections with soldiers in army camps could be a lucrative experience. Thus we had a host of would-be servants, who would perform tasks for trifling sums of money.

Communication was comparatively easy as Urdu was the camp language. However, due to the British occupation of India, English was the second language and it was well understood. If not, it was very quickly learned by the natives. So from the first day we had calls from the *charwallah* the *dobhiwallah*(washing and ironing) the *nappiwallah* (shaving and haircutting) *durziwallah* (tailor). All these callers were most efficient and trustworthy. The *dobhi* would take our shorts and shirts in the early morning, and they would be returned, washed and ironed by the evening. We also had other callers, including one cheeky and persistent young rascal who enquired, 'You want *bibi* (woman) *sahib,* my sister (always his sister), very good jigajig, very cheap, very good!' The universal response was 'What's your mother like?' He always grinned back but I wonder if he really understood our humour.

Tea is the universal beverage in India and our *charwallah* adopted us from the day we arrived. He was a hardworking, cheerful character who became part of the Signal Troop establishment. Outside our tents before reveille, he was still around even late in the evenings. He must have lived in one of the small local villages, because he was never far away. He wore a long white shirt, called a *dhoti*, a yellow waistcoat and a red fez hat. His tea urn had a charcoal fire, and the tea was always hot, strong and sweet, with goat or buffalo milk. We were never sure which of the two. He also carried a large tin box, which contained cakes, sweetmeats and chapatis on which he would spread a concoction resembling marmalade. We were good customers. Moving from tent to tent, he used to shoulder a wooden yoke, the tea urn hanging from one end and the tin box on the other. It must have been a hard life, but without doubt he was better off than millions of his fellow countrymen.

Ali, which was the name we gave him, lived in a dream world. He imagined that we all lived in tents in similar conditions back home, and that permanency of employment in England, as our charwallah, would be only a matter of time. He said to me, 'I know Birmingham cantonment *Sahib,* very good barracks. I be very good charwallah in England.' My camera had already been rescued from the bottom of my kitbag and Ali featured in one of the first snaps, complete with his wares.

After a few days, more tents arrived and we were able to make ourselves more comfortable. Four to a tent was normal, and I shared a tent with Ray Scully. We were then able to have *charpoys* which were roughly constructed beds. They were fashioned from thin tree trunks, from which the bark had been removed. The frame measured roughly six by three feet, it was supported by legs at each corner, and the central area was interlaced with lengths of rough sisal rope. Compared with our previous sleeping areas on the ground, they were a great luxury, and soon they were standard sleeping accommodation in the camp. They were snapped up at two rupees each. Even so, we were probably overcharged.

After a couple of weeks, we had settled to a regular pattern of soldiering, although we still awaited news of our transport. Reveille was at 6.30 a.m., breakfast at 8, midday meal known as tiffin at 1 p.m. and the evening meal at 6. We now had early morning P.T. before breakfast. Our rifles were returned from the armourer, and we had kit inspections, lectures, cookhouse and other fatigues, guard duties but very little training on signals. However, a great deal of time was allocated to sport in competitions between our own companies and other nearby units. The most popular of these was football, but gradually other games were organised, such as hockey, cricket, baseball and even rugby. Plans were made to construct a rough running track and eventually it was to be my responsibility.

We looked forward to our pay parades, and the weekly visit of the mobile bath unit. Actually, this was nothing more than a glorified shower. On the other hand, the most hated days were Tuesdays between 9 and 10 a.m. when army respirators had to be worn without exception. The drill was most uncomfortable and suffocating, especially considering the heat. This really was an unnecessary chore, no doubt thought up by some higher authority in GHQ. The danger of gas was less than minimal, and we had all been in the army long enough to know the drill if indeed a raid did occur. We had also had plenty of practice wearing respirators.

By now we had received our first batch of letters. I had letters from my wife, parents, brothers and sister, as well and the Hayes and Movsovic families, so there was plenty of letter writing to do. The quickest communication was by airgraph. This form, about quarto size, could be purchased in camp from the orderly room post corporal and it cost three annas. There was a box at the top to insert the address and the rest of the space was for writing the message. Once censored, these forms were micro-filmed at Delhi GHQ, thousands of letters on one roll of film were flown to England and developed. The resultant printout, about a quarter the size of the original, was then delivered via the normal post Those I sent to South Africa arrived very quickly, so the facilities must have been available for all the Commonwealth countries, and certainly for the USA. These forms were similarly available in the home country, and delivered to us by the reverse process. Specially decorated forms were available for all occasions such as birthdays, Christmas and Easter.

There was no mains electricity in the camp, so our Signals Troop had the duty of providing electric lighting. derived from twelve-volt bulbs run from our heavy duty batteries, for the Officers Mess. Whether this was the practice in other units, or a mad scheme of Signals Officer Tony Musselwhite to impress the CO, remains unanswered, but it was most expensive to install and operate. Adequate Tilley lamps were available in abundance and used in all other offices and mess tents. It was sheer extravagance as we used yards of line cable, masses of bulbs, bulb holders and switches and all our accumulators to provide the lavish set up. The accumulators only lasted one night, so our two 350 watt petrol generators were in constant use, and it took two men to lug each accumulator back and forth to the officers' mess. To add insult to injury, the lights were so successful that the CO and adjutant decided they would also indulge in the luxury, so we had to go to the divisional Royal Army Service Corps for more wire and accumulators.

After less than a month in India, I was detailed to attend a week long 'watermanship course' for NCOs, to begin on the 15th November. This instruction was operated by the Royal Engineers of the 70th Division at Ratu, about forty miles away. The camp was situated on the edge of a large 'tank'. In India, all man-made artificial lakes and storage ponds were known by this name. The course proved to be a most constructive and beneficial experience, and it was put to use in future manoeuvres. Certainly it was also a chance to get away from the now re-established formal parades and training.

Here we learned how to cross a wide and deep expanse of water, while keeping our arms, ammunition and clothing completely dry. The initial procedure was to spread out our army waterproof six by three foot groundsheet flat on the ground. Then a thin strong cord was threaded through the eyelets round the border, ready to be pulled taut. We laid down our rifle as a keel, end on in the middle of the groundsheet, together with heavy items such as ammunition, boots and steel helmet. A layer of brushwood was then spread over the whole, to a depth of about twelve inches. Finally we stripped down to our underpants, laying our clothes and equipment on top of the brushwood. The edges of the groundsheet were then carefully drawn together around the whole package and the cord was pulled tightly and tied securely. In doing this we had to make sure that the corners were correctly folded to ensure a watertight boat. We then launched our craft on the water, and were amazed by its excellent buoyancy. By holding on and pushing the whole craft ahead, even a non-swimmer could make reasonable progress across the water. If it was done correctly, all the contents remained completely dry. Even a radio set or a heavy accumulator, which we tried later, could be successfully transported in the same way. We also learned sailors' knots, which we were to use on future exercises. A simple reef knot, the bowline, a bowline on a bight, how to shorten a cord or rope with a sheepshank, the figure of eight, the round turn and two half-hitches, the clove hitch, half hitch and seized back and several others. All of which I have now forgotten except the granny knot.

We then progressed to major projects, like transporting jeeps and other vehicles over a river. From the bamboo thicket nearby we cut canes of suitable lengths, and making use of our freshly gained knowledge, we lashed them together into a correctly sized raft. The hollow compartments of the bamboo added an extra buoyancy and we had success with our very first attempt at launching a jeep. Even more fascinating were the methods used to waterproof vehicle engines, so they could be operated and driven under water for short distances, at a depth dependent on the driver's height in the chassis. The secret was to waterproof all exposed electrical points, leads, spark plugs and distributor with a type of plasticine, and in addition, to extend the exhaust pipe upwards with a flexible tube, so the extremity was above the waterline. Amazingly it really worked. We also learned to handle rowboats, skiffs and punts and how to attach and fix outboard motors to assault craft and inflatable dinghies. Our one night manoeuvre, which was a test of our recently acquired watermanship knowledge was not so successful. Our section sank with a jeep and all hands, when our raft overturned. But the week was not all work. In the afternoons we played the REs at football, hockey and handball and in the evenings we played whist or pontoon. In addition we had a 'race meeting', when a selection of films of horse racing in the USA was shown. Each film showed eight runners and we bet on the result. On the last working day a regatta was organised between us and the REs. The highlight for us was winning an assault boat race against the resident experts. Four of us, Sergeant Cameron, Corporals Poole and Blackburn and myself paddled Red Indian fashion over a 200 yard course, and won by inches.

On the other side of the tank, opposite to our normal working area, there were two very old temples, joined by a long concrete and stone platform, with rows of steps leading down to the water's edge. The two temples were identical, very small and they were not regularly used. Basically they were four round pillars holding up a flat stone roof, with a small area inside which had probably once been used for prayer and sacrifice. We were quite surprised one Saturday, when we noticed a crowd of villagers bringing a variety of items and setting up stalls, tables and platforms. Then we heard the noise of music, drums and the odd firework. Evidently a celebration was planned.

During the early afternoon, the throng increased, many firecrackers exploded while music was being played. Many of the Indians seemed to be in special costumes, the women in brightly coloured saris and the men in white shirts and striped bathing trunks. Then we noticed that they were stepping in and out of the water and realised that this was a Hindu ceremony. Our camp servants told us that this was a holy lake and a ritual bathe. Later, towards sunset, we were urged by our *dhobi* and *charwallahs* to join in the festivities. They both insisted, '*Sahib,* bring all *hath-butti,*' so around ten of us lit our hurricane lamps from the tents and made our way round the lake. We noticed that many Indians had brought Tilley lamps. We joined the throng and received a cheerful welcome.

We now realised that the lamps were needed because this was the Hindu Festival of Lights, and everyone carried lamps, torches and lanterns, some of which were scooped out of gourds. It was like a mixture of Guy Fawkes Night, Halloween and local carnivals at home. We later learned that the Hindus called the festival *Diwali,* which was celebrated all over India. Above the commotion we could just about hear the 'band' which was made up of long guitar-like instruments, with gourds attached to increase the sound. Some with seven strings which we discovered were called *sitars* and *vinas,* were almost silenced by the cacophony of sound produced by the numerous gongs, conch shells and drums. Later, I was to listen to other music in India, in more peaceful surroundings. The scale is so different to ours, having twenty-two divisions to the octave, as opposed to the thirteen in European music.

There was plenty of food available, and it was pressed upon us as though we were special guests. They called us *Bura Sahibs,* meaning 'important men', (because they had benefited financially by our presence) which I suppose we were at that time. Lots of cooking had been organised, the main attraction being a whole lamb roasted barbecue fashion over a charcoal fire, along with several chickens and a whole variety of vegetables, rice and spices. Most of us decided on the lamb, together with a mixture of rice, beans and lentils, which were all very heavily spiced. Large plantain leaves served as plates, and we mopped it all up with pieces of chapati. We sat down amongst the throng on the bare earth, using our fingers to eat. At this time we had not learned the Indian conventional code of only using the right hand and fingers to handle food, but as we were mostly all right-handed, no one seemed to notice. I finished my meal with a mango and some bananas, but there were melons, pomegranates, figs and coconuts available. By now it was getting late, but by no means the end of the jollity of the festive occasion. This was enhanced by the liquor. Bowls of Indian 'firewater' gin appeared and we were invited to partake. It was certainly my first experience of the local distillation, and it tasted like methylated spirits which, maybe it was! However, in this environment and with the passage of time it became most palatable and acceptable.

We eventually decided to outsmart the drums by beginning a sing-song. We rendered our version of 'She'll be coming round the mountain' and several other ditties with even ruder words. Our hosts did not understand the lyrics but seemingly enjoyed our contribution, applauded and proffered more firewater. Then, just after midnight they produced several hundred little boats, constructed of leaves, cardboard or very thin earthenware, all about five inches in diameter and quite shallow. These little vessels had been filled with oil on which floated a small wick. The wick was ignited, and the containers gently launched into the water. I shall never forget this most beautiful sight. They drifted slowly out on the gentle breeze, bobbing and twinkling like so many stars. It was an enchanting array which eventually faded into the night. My camera was not with me, but a black and white picture would not have done justice to this colourful occasion. Sometime during the early hours we found our way back round the lake, and collapsed on our charpoys.

Not surprisingly, I was not the only one to wake up with a shocking headache but luckily there was no parade on this our last morning at Ratu, as we were due to leave after midday tiffin. Being young and fit, most of us quickly recovered and we went for a last dip in the water.

Lieutenant General Sir Philip Christison had succeeded Lieutenant General William Slim as Corps Commander in October, and now as part of the 70th Division under Major General Symes, we were under his command. He told us during a talk on 23rd November that civil disobedience in Bengal, Bihar and Eastern India had been 'cracked' and now we could look forward to the business of thrashing the Japanese. We must step up our jungle training with more ambitious plans, including the use of tanks and armoured vehicles. He said we must be keen, tough and ensure that we were ready for the final push, which would ensure victory.

Marching back to Dipitali, breathing in the thick red dust thrown up by the passing military lorries, we wished that someone somewhere would speed up the arrival of our own transport that was on the high seas.

During the afternoon, our *charwallah* created some excitement when he killed a small snake on the edge of the scrub near our lines. In the event, it was not a krait, but a harmless species. This was the first time that we had been reminded of the vivid and exaggerated picture of the perils we would face, as had been described by the regulars on the *Dominion Monarch*. The fictional situation created by books and films, showing snakes chasing people did not exist. The main danger would be in surprising a snake sunning itself on a rock, or seeking warmth or moisture in buildings. Most snakes could feel the vibrations of footsteps long before the person approached. Of course, like any creature they will attack in self defence. However, several small snakes, including the dreaded krait were often killed by the natives around the camp. In one isolated instance, a dead snake was placed in a comrade's bed by a stupid halfwit. The culprit was placed on a charge for creating a disturbance, fined two week's pay and given cookhouse fatigues for the same period.

The only wild animals we heard but rarely saw, were wolves which prowled around at night howling. There were lots of wild dogs, called 'pi dogs', who were always on the scrounge. We saw many tame animals, especially on the road to Ranchi. There were laden camel trains, occasional elephants and performing bears and monkeys. There were also sacred cattle everywhere, which roamed through the camp, often decorated with garlands or coloured with dyes. They were extensively used as beasts of burden, double-yoked to wooden carts, and they were terribly thin and scraggy. Here, on the Bihar plateau, we were far from the real jungle areas. Even if there had been larger wild animals around, they would not have approached, due to the movement and noise created by the troops and inhabitants around Ranchi.

We did not get rats, mice, cockroaches or bed bugs at this

time, as they only frequented permanent buildings in the towns and cities, but we did get insects. Flies were far and away the main misery. They disappeared at dusk for a good sleep and arrived on parade in their hordes at sunrise, all ready for breakfast! At mealtimes one hand had to be kept on the move, to keep them away from our food. They followed instinctively, and were a prevalent upset wherever we went. Great efforts were made to contain or eliminate them, but we were fighting a losing battle. Waste food was collected, binned and buried, latrines regularly fumigated and lime spread in liberal quantities. Nevertheless, they were always present during our necessary visits.

During this time I frequently recalled the schoolboy joke of the 1930s, when privies were more commonplace. It began with a little girl who visited her grandparents in the country, and who around midday, needed to visit the garden privy. 'I don't like your privy, Grandma,' she said, 'it's full of flies.' Well,' replied Grandma, 'don't you worry. If you can wait a minute Grandad will be carving the joint, and they will all go up to the kitchen.' The little girl had my sympathy, but it wasn't so funny here. Unfortunately, these were the days in India before the arrival of Dichlorodephenyl-Trichloroethane (DDT). We were unable to reap the benefit of this chemical until after our adventures in Burma.

Other flying insects abounded, and were a nuisance, especially at night. If the tent flap was opened, in they came. Our hurricane lamp became a funeral pyre, and needed to be cleaned almost every day. On the credit side were the little grey and green lizards called gekkos which pursued the insects around the tent sides with limpet skill, and were always very welcome. The other problem was created by the termites, also known as 'white ants'. They channelled along or just below the surface, and built huge nests as hillocks several feet high. These mounds were riddled with tunnels and galleries, and the whole structure was brick-hard and bound together with their excrement. We encountered them everywhere when camping in India. The big nuisance was that they could consume and destroy virtually everything except metal, and as our tents were pitched on the bare earth, even they were unsafe.

Overnight they could gouge out a sizeable pattern from

the soles and heels of army boots, and even our charpoys were not immune We soon countered by putting a brick under the bed at each corner and hanging our clothes and equipment on the tent pole or mosquito net supports. In addition, most of us purchased tin boxes to preserve books, papers and other valuables. Many losses of kit and equipment were attributed to the destructiveness of these termites. They were the salvation of every soldier, especially the regimental quartermasters' staff. Both we and the regimental stores used white ants as an excuse for the loss of kit and equipment. 'Eaten or damaged by termites' appeared on countless inventories at audit time. I once heard that the loss of a Bren gun carrier was attributed to action by these insects, but cannot substantiate the story.

Another problem, of course, was mosquitoes, but it was the dry season on the Ranchi plain, we were some distance from the nearest water, and we wore long-sleeved shirts and slacks an hour before sunset. Nevertheless, there were mosquitoes around and they did bite, so we were glad of our nets as without them, we would have had sleepless and uncomfortable nights.

So far we had not been issued with more anti-mosquito cream or given any of the new mepacrine tablets. At this time it was probably a matter of balance between cost and the risk of casualties. Few of the unit went sick with malaria, and probably due to the fact that we had a regular medical officer who had served in India before, the time we spent serving as soldiers was unaffected by malaria.

At Diptali Camp, we were only four miles down the road from the large town of Ranchi, which had contained a permanent peacetime garrison, but had now been much extended due to the wartime situation. If we were off duty in the late afternoon or evening, we did not need to obtain a pass to leave camp, as long as we took our army service book, part one, with us for identification, and as long as we were back in the lines by midnight. We had to rely on the divisional transport, and travel passes were restricted. However, alternate conveyance was available in the form of rickshaws. These were known as *garris*, the Hindu word for cart, which had two long shafts joined to a two-wheeled vehicle. The garriwallah, who was usually a skinny little man, would get between the shafts and pull two big soldiers the four miles to Ranchi for the sum of eight annas. Admittedly, the road was tarmacadamed in the centre, and the four miles were almost flat across the plain, but it was slavery, and made some of us embarrassed. Nevertheless, *garris* were always available, their owners waiting for custom in the equivalent of a present day taxi rank. Ray and I went to Ranchi during our first week at the camp, but found the town much too large to become familiar with in one visit. We subsequently got to know it well.

The town was very crowded, full of servicemen from many units, British, Indian, Gurkhas and Chinese packed the streets and cafes. Although the military police were always in evidence, we were able to explore without reservation. First impressions were similar to the initial ones in Bombay when we had first arrived. Overall there was an incredible noise of Indian music from the various establishments mingling with that of the slow moving traffic and the sound of many tongues. Vehicles and persons were held up by the roaming sacred cattle and beggars, but above all there was the striking sensation of many pungent smells, a heady mixture of fragrance and foulness.

On the credit side, there were many modern shops, offices, a variety of market stalls and places to eat and drink at some risk of getting stomach upsets. For a while early on, we were mystified by the speckled red stains on pavements and roadways everywhere, but we soon noticed the constant expectorations of the Indians. The redness was caused by betel-nuts which they constantly chewed. The nut was freely available and on sale at stalls and from street vendors. It was grown chiefly in Southern India, cut into slices and wrapped in a betel-nut leaf, with added lime and flavouring. When chewed, it reddened the mouth and saliva, and blackened the teeth, but as an antiseptic it was supposedly beneficial.

Ranchi did not have many buildings of major historical interest, but it did contain one little gem as far as I was concerned. This was the cathedral called St Paul's, which was built by the Christian community in Ranchi near the cantonment area, surrounded by elegant buildings, with lovely lawns and gardens. I cannot remember how old the cathedral was, but it had many plaques and memorials dedicated to those who had come to serve, work and die in the Ranchi area. It was quite a small building, more like a parish church in England, and very similar in shape and space to St Luke's church in Bath, where I was a chorister and also deputy organist for a short time. Later, I was able to practise in Ranchi and play for some of the divisional church parades.

3

To Bombay for Vehicles

At last, after six weeks in India, word came through from GHQ Delhi that our unit transport had arrived in Bombay. Our vehicles had been delayed, due to a mechanical breakdown of the steamship *Bangkok,* which had left Liverpool in another convoy. She was in fact being repaired in Cape Town while we had been docked there.

I was delighted when after this time it was decided that Signal Sergeant Dennis Stringer, our NCO, would monitor our progress across India with a wireless detachment. We now had an opportunity to travel and see much more of the continent, and exercise our specialist ability, even if due to the distances involved, we would not be back before Christmas. So we left camp on Wednesday, 9th December, travelling down from the plain in the usual Indian fifteen-hundredweight transport, to Bakakana Junction. Special coaches had been reserved on the Calcutta-Bombay Express. The word 'express' was a misnomer. It meant that it would have a much lower priority than the mail train, that it would stop at a lot more stations and almost certainly arrive late at Bombay. However, supposedly it was speedier than the scheduled troop trains.

Our compartments were identical to those we had travelled in previously, but this time we had plenty of room. My companions for the journey were Ray Scully, Bill Key, Eric Nightingale, Harry Cresswell and George Bell; all excellent company. We had brought our rifles and a quantity of ammunition, which we stacked in a compartment under guard. My rifle had been issued to me at the beginning of the war, a Lee-Enfield · 303, and as an issued firearm was a very personal responsibility. It was a crime not to remember the number without hesitation. For that reason alone, I will never forget the number J 9989. Similarly, one's army number stayed with the individual for the duration of the war, irrespective of the number of postings to other units.

I was the official post corporal for the train journey, which meant that I was busy for one hour each morning, selling stamps and airgraph forms, and unofficially accepting mail for posting in Bombay. The regimental orderly room had lent me a small tin trunk with a lock which was my 'post office'. At night I used to deposit it in the guardroom. I also had a long list of 'wants' such as stationery and pens for regimental HQ, and a similar list of needs for our signal stores. Altogether I had over 400 rupees, which was about thirty-five pounds, so I was glad of my security trunk. As expected, we made slow progress, but the food, supplied by the Indian Army Service Corps, was reasonable.

We travelled the identical route of our initial journey, in the reverse direction, but it all looked new, and in any case there were areas we had previously passed during night-time. Some of the larger towns and cities we passed on our way to Bombay were Raigarh, Bilaspur, Raipur, Nagpur, Wardha Junction, Bhusawal, Manmad, Kalyan and Thana. This rail journey was much more direct than our impending road journey. The latter was no doubt geared to take advantage of possibly better roads, and the army cantonments and depots *en route*.

We arrived at Victoria Station, Bombay in the early hours of Saturday, 12th December, and were lifted to the Bombay transit camp in the now familiar Indian Army fifteen-hundredweights. The drivers all looked the same and drove just as madly.

The vehicles were in the lines, but work was not to start until the next day – Sunday.

At first we strolled around, bought bits and pieces and picture cards, and had milk shakes in the Hornby Cafe. Then across the road we saw that *Beyond the Blue Horizon* with Dorothy Lamour, was the evening film at the New Empire. Another serviceman told us that we had to book to see the film, which we did, despite the fact that there were plenty of seats to spare. We again went to the cafe and found out about Breach Candy, while having egg and chips. Breach Candy Swimming Club, in Bhulabhai Desai Road, was just over a mile away, and at the time mebership was only available to white Europeans, but troops if they were white, were allowed free admission. So we caught a bus out, and had a most enjoyable afternoon sunning ourselves and swimming in the pool. The time soon went and as the sun set we made our way back to the city centre.

Sunday was a working day and we had lots to do. Our transport had received no attention, so far as we could tell, since leaving England. We gave our eight Humber Snipe wireless trucks a full engine maintenance, and then began fitting our number eleven sets, erecting the aerials and charging the accumulators. The top speed of the Humber Snipe was fifty-five miles per hour, but they had been fitted with a governor which brought the maximum down to forty-five. They only did twelve and a half miles to the gallon, had no synchromesh gearbox, so we had to double de-clutch to change gears. In battle, they afforded little protection as they were not armoured. The rear canvas waterproof hood was spread over a metal frame, so that the whole unit could be removed and used as a tent. In practice this was rarely done, as the whole operation was too time-consuming.

As the wireless set was mounted sideways in the back, no forward facing seats were fitted, so operating the set on the move was a nightmare. It invariably gave operators headaches and in some cases violent sickness. To make matters worse, even the tarmacadam of India had wide dust verges, so that on the move, a vacuum was created behind the vehicle, sucking up the dust and sand and depositing a thick haze. This turned breathing, let alone operating, into an ordeal.

On the dashboard there was a sliding arm which operated the accelerator so when the vehicle was stationery and out of gear, the accumulators could be charged. Previously in the UK, when on straight main roads, we had often set this device to a fixed speed, to avoid the use of the foot operated accelerator. This was unauthorised and at best a lazy and dangerous practice. We also had some reconnaissance cars called ARCs, which were 'armoured' with very thin steel plates and which we equipped with mounted Bren guns and wireless sets. We fitted these out with the radio sets, but thankfully these were not to be part of communications on the way back.

Having bolted down the no. 11 sets in the Humbers, we erected the aerials and connected up the accumulators. It was time to test and try out the radio network. Tony Musselwhite, our signal officer was to be in sole command of personnel and radio, but it was my duty to organise the communications.

Each Humber Snipe was to have a team of four, all driver operators, two in the front and two in the rear. Duties would be on a rota, so all would have a change of responsibility, taking turns in the rear. Each squadron would have one wireless van, with A Squadron leading, followed by B and C Squadrons and regimental HQ taking up the rear. The number eleven sets would be reasonably near to each other during the 1,400 mile journey, so we would communicate with relatively primitive plastic hand-held microphones, with moulded rubber mouthpiece. A button on the stem was depressed for transmission and released for reception, which we picked up on headphones.

When on the move, the convoys were to operate in battle order as a training exercise, and were only to keep listening-watch. There would be halts of ten minutes on the hour and at this juncture, messages were to be handed in and transmitted. There would be times when the regiment might be split during the overnight laager, so if units were at separate locations, communication could be established between 1900 and 2000 hours. However, in the event this provision was rarely needed

We did not expect transmission problems during the daytime, as the no. 11 set was capable of sending and receiving well over ten miles, and the convoy should never stray that far apart.

Using the correct jargon appeared much more important at this time than getting the message across. The only reason for alphabetical identity was to ensure that the words of messages could be identified through atmospheric or other radio interference, or weak signals due to distance.

The word 'Repeat' or the phrase 'Repeat your message'

was not allowed over the air. Instead, the correct request was 'Say again' which was an inordinate precaution dating from the First World War, when only telephonic communication was available. Then, the word 'Repeat' might be heard by the support field artillery, who would have understood it as meaning 'Fire again'.

However, much could go wrong and it often did, even under the most ideal conditions, and the simplest of radio communication systems. Causes of possible malfunction were distance, atmospherics, equipment, power failure or human error either in not being on listening-watch at the correct time, or not using the final word 'Over' at the end of a message, thereby preventing transmission from other stations.

All official communications were pre-written before despatch on army form C.2130 (an example of which appears in Appendix I), which was designed to accommodate all categories of message sent by radio, telephone, despatch rider, runner or carrier pigeon. Conversely, messages received by telephone or radio were recorded on this form, and were filed to form the equivalent of a log book. Any error in despatch, receipt or action could be readily traced back to the culprit.

On the passage back to Ranchi, we would be very dependant on our batteries for powering the no. 11 sets. These accumulators were very heavy, nearing eighteen by nine inches, housed in well-constructed teak boxes with solid metal lifting handles at each end, so that they could be easily moved to the charging unit. Six storage cells of approximately two volts each, connected in series, gave a total of twelve volts for forty-eight ampere hours. It was essential to keep the accumulators well maintained at all times by topping up the storage cells to cover the lead plates with distilled water, and checking constantly that the electrolyte was of the correct specific gravity. We used a hydrometer for this, and a voltmeter to test the voltage. Lead plates left uncovered could soon lead to permanent damage due to the heat and consequent evaporation.

In addition to the routine communication programmed for the return journey, we were to conduct an interesting experiment, by contacting our base in Ranchi during the evening hours between 1900 and 2000 hours, an initial distance of over 1,000 miles as the kite flies. Both we and base would be operating no. 11 sets using a long-wave frequency, with morse key transmissions. This was well over the radio specified practical operating limits, but we would be able to log our efforts and the response from Ranchi. They would be on listening-watch at the agreed times, starting on Wednesday, 15th December.

Communication over long distances depended on a number of complicated factors. The chief of these was that radio waves needed to be reflected back to Earth by ionised layers in the atmosphere. These layers varied in height and thickness due to climatic changes, caused by reflected heat from the Earth. Consequently, the quality of signals varied considerably, especially between day and night-time, and in addition there were the obstacles of 'sun spots' and magnetic storms to contend with.

To boost our transmission distance, we decided to experiment with an end-fed aerial, which was a directional aerial of bare copper wire, cut to match the frequency length, and set up to point towards the receiving station. We used an exact compass bearing on Ranchi. To operate it we joined a weighted rope to one end of the wire, threw it on the compass bearing into the highest tree branch we could manage, and then we joined the other end of the aerial to the set terminal. The communication would have looked like this in diagrammatical form.

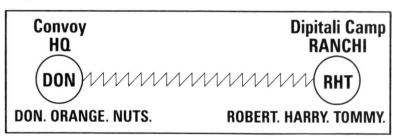

When we planned this experiment, we did not realise that later in Burma, this method of communication would become a crucial link between success or failure of the entire operation.

By Sunday evening all our sets were operational, the frequencies to be used had been allocated, our vehicles loaded, and we were ready for 'the off'. It had been decided that we would leave at first light on the Tuesday so this order would enable us to have a whole day off on Monday in Bombay. Some of the troop went in to the city that evening, but I spent the night catching up on correspondence, writing to my wife Mollie, my parents, brothers and sister. I posted these letters in the General Post Office the next day, and they arrived without censorship. Anyway, they would know that I was in Bombay by the postmark.

The next morning I had purchases to make for the regiment, so I went off on my own, straight after breakfast, arranging to meet my friends back at transit camp for midday meal. We already needed to economise, but I booked six seats for the evening film at the New Empire, called *Defeat of the Germans around Moscow*. On the way back to transit camp I realised how hot the weather was, over ninety degrees Fahrenheit at midday. However, I enjoyed the hot weather, and of course we had not yet experienced the humidity of the monsoon period. Evenings seemed cool at this time of year, even if here in Bombay the temperature did not drop below the mid-sixties.

Straight after the midday meal, the six of us who had travelled down together in the train, left camp for Breach Candy. As we were waiting for a bus, we were lucky enough to be offered a lift by two off-duty military policemen. This saved us both time and money, as they were also going to the club for a swim. We had a very good time, and made the most of every minute. After swimming in the pool, we had soft drinks and then sat on the rocks of the nearby shore. Breach Candy Swimming Club was right on the coast, on the Arabian Sea. The water was rough and we let the breakers roll over us.

The afternoon passed much too quickly and it was soon time to head back to the city centre. So we took photographs, had more drinks, and then boarded a crowded single decker bus along Marine Drive towards the city. We descended at Churchgate Bus Depot and threaded our way through the side streets, towards Victoria Station. On this visit we could enjoy but a fleeting glance of this dynamic historical city, of which there was so much to see and so little time to explore. Many nations, cultures and religions merged here. On the streets there were Europeans, Hindus, Muslims, Sikhs, Arabs, Parsis, Christians and Jews, including traders and exiles from many lands. There was an exciting hustle of humanity cramming the streets, a good illustration of the mixture of extreme poverty and untold wealth to be found here. We still had much to see: the fine parks, Malaba Hill, the Parsis Towers of Silence, the Hanging Gardens, the magnificent Victorian buildings, the docks and much more of the Bombay scene, so that evening I made up my mind, that if or when, leave was granted, Bombay would be my choice to spend it in. Back in Hornby Road, we ate at a cafe of that name: pork with chips, salad, chapatis and a chilli sauce, followed by mango and melon, and vast amounts of tea; a 'special' for the forces. We then crossed the road to the New Empire, for the film, *Defeat of the Germans around Moscow* which we did not rate highly, sensing that it was propaganda.

We had enjoyed an exhaustive and colourful day, but even so, we had caramel custard and milk shakes before seeking out the bus that would take us past the transit camp. The next morning we had to be up at 6 a.m. to prepare for our journey. We had already breakfasted, collected our arms and ammunition from the guardroom and made sure that all was ready and loaded, when A Squadron, leading the 45th Reconnaissance Corps transport, pulled away, joined by the Humber Snipe wireless van and the operators assigned to them. It was 0930 hours on Tuesday, 15th December. They were followed out of the Bombay Transit Camp by B and C Squadrons, and it was more than an hour later when we got the order to move. Traffic was congested through the suburbs of Parel, Dadar and Dhavari, and progress was sporadic as we crept along the main road towards Sion Causeway and the interior.

Centuries ago Bombay had been a natural island, separated from the mainland by the Mahim River to the west, and the Sion River to the east. Over the years a great deal of land had been drained and reclaimed, so Bombay now appeared to be an isthmus. Neverless, there were only two road routes out of the city. To the north the Mahim River

Bridge fed road traffic along the coastal plain towards Ahmadabad, whilst the Sion Causeway provided an egress past the salt flats for the road and rail link to the east and south. No doubt since 1942, these roads have been improved and widened, but as we trailed along the narrow tarmacadam strip, it seemed as if we would never clear the suburbs. However, once we had crossed the causeway, traffic thinned out and we began to make progress on a flat road with miles of paddy on either side, lines of cacti hedges, short, stunted trees and the occasional grove of tufted palms. We passed through the towns of Thana and Kalyan, between which a large diameter pipe line was being laid.

On the granting of independence to India in 1947, changes were made in the names of many cities, towns and streets, especially if the names were connected to British rule. The towns mentioned above appear in my diary as Kasala and Kurld. Almost all the street names in Bombay were altered, making identification and reminiscence most difficult. Even the infamous Grant Road became Mautana Shaukali Road. On the first day we travelled a mere fifty-five miles. Overnight stays had obviously been planned in advance, as we were to spend several stops in cantonments on the way. This initial laager, pleasant and peaceful after the noise and heat of the journey, was by the side of a river, surrounded by mango trees and adjacent to a small Hindu temple. Most of us took the opportunity of a bathe in the river before our meal. It was a tremendous relief to wash away the red dust which penetrated and covered us from head to foot. During the rest of the trek, dust was to prove an absolute bugbear and irritation. This first day was just an initiation.

A fifteen-hundredweight truck converted into a field kitchen was attached to each squadron and the regimental HQ, and from it they produced a substantial evening meal of the usual 'bully' stew. During the trip, they also provided breakfast when we were not in barracks, which was usually sausage, beans and fried bread, sometimes with an egg for good measure. Most of our vehicles had rations aboard, consisting of army biscuits, corned beef, butter and marmalade, all out of tins. Our *charwallah* also did good business, although we had plenty of our own tea, tinned milk and unrefined sugar.

On the first evening I was on the air and transmitting the call sign at the agreed time, but the only reply was a jumble of noise and atmospheric static, so after a while I joined the majority of the company round a camp fire with the inevitable sing-song, before making up our beds round the vehicles and erecting our mosquito nets with pieces of bamboo, or in my case, with sections of spare aerial rod. There was very little sound after 10 p.m. The next morning, although we were not due to move off until 0900 hours, we operators rose early to check the network because our B Squadron set had had problems the day before.

In many respects our second day on the road was typical of the days ahead. We were now well away from Bombay and the city traffic, there were to be no more towns or cities with suburbs, just small hamlets and villages alongside the road. Traffic was sparse and from now on, even the main highways would be constructed of gravel and packed earth. When we did approach larger settlements there would often be a strip of tarmacadam in the centre of the road, which was just about wide enough for one vehicle.

No one drove on the left. Everyone hugged the centre of the road. Bullock carts and pack animals comprised the bulk of the traffic, so we had to continually pull over on to the earth-packed edge. This evasive action created a cloud of penetrating dust; a continual hardship for the whole of the journey.

Virtually all motor traffic consisted either of Indian Army or long distance buses. The latter heralded their approach with a fanfare of prolonged hooting and as they passed in ever thicker dust cloud a shrill applause rose from the passengers who were either clinging to the sides or squatting amongst the rooftop baggage. Later we witnessed accidents, but life seemed to be considered cheap. Almost every day we had a long midday halt, and concocted meals from the rations we carried on the vehicles. One of the days included a twisting ascent up the ghats, a climb of over 3,000 feet to the central plateau. Mr Musselwhite, our signal officer, had commandeered a despatch rider's Royal Enfield motorcycle so he could career up and down the convoy. That conveniently left his place vacant in the Humber, so I was able to share duties with his driver Trooper Tom Moffat. Tom had been a member of the peacetime Territorial Army, and we considered him, at thirty-eight years of age, to be a very old man!

Just before we arrived at our evening halt, we passed through the town of Deolali, spotting the large cantonment in the distance. Deolali cantonment was and had been for many years, the main transit camp for reinforcement troops arriving in India. It also housed a mental asylum, which was the assembly point for deranged army patients on the way back to Netley Mental Army Hospital in England. 'Gone Deolali' or 'Deolali Tap' pronounced by the forces as Doolali accordingly came to mean 'a bit round the bend', and the expression became universal both in India and home as early as the nineteenth century. The word 'Tap' originated from the ancient Sanskrit word *Tapa,* meaning heat, pain, torment or fever. No doubt a great deal of mental illness in the early army in India was related to the after effects of malaria and other fevers. In 1946, long after the war in the Far East had ended, one of my friends was encamped in Deolali, with many others awaiting repatriation, as there was an acute shortage of troop transports. He confided that for a long time the symptoms of 'Gone Deolali' were just around the corner, as far as he was concerned.

We arrived early in Nasik, where we were allowed to park our vehicles in the cantonment area. We slept out either in the open or in our trucks, but could use the barrack washing and toilet facilities. In addition, we had orders to hand in our firearms to their guardroom for the night. On those evenings when we made our own camp, a guard was detailed and arms and ammunition stacked with them. Before that, a fatigue party was assigned to dig latrines.

Vehicles were refuelled every evening from a supply lorry in the convoy, petrol being stored and distributed in two-gallon petrol cans. Oil levels and tyre pressures were checked and in our case, accumulators recharged. Recharging our accumulators by using our 'chorhorse' petrol operated charging unit, was a noisy business. Wherever it was sited, we evoked moans from the would-be sleepers. In addition to our ablutions, we had the additional task of removing the dust and grime from the wireless sets and auxiliary equipment. Early on, we found out that a three-inch paint brush was by far the best dust remover.

From the barracks we looked down on the temples and shrines of the Godavari River, which at this point was wide even though it was near its source. This river rises very near the west coast of India, north of Bombay, but flows in the opposite direction, right across the peninsula, to join the waters of the Bay of Bengal at Rajahmundry. After our evening meal and my second unsuccessful attempt to contact Ranchi, a few of us decided to take a look at Nasik centre. However, as we neared the town outskirts, we heard the noise of rifle fire. Congress party supporters had been throwing bricks and stones at the resident Indian army troops, and they had reciprocated by firing into the air. Although at this time there were no restrictions on our visits to towns on the way, we were ordered not to get involved or provoke trouble on this journey, so we made a hasty retreat back to our lines.

After an early start the following day, we made rapid progress across the Nasik Plain. We drove across undulating country at a height of around 2,000 feet. We passed through the towns of Chandor and Malegaon, eventually making camp on the banks of the River Panjhra, near the town of Dhulia. After the usual meal and bivouac routines and another blank reply from my signals to Ranchi, I spent some time by the camp fire, and then had an early night. Although the days were very hot, on the plains at this time of year the temperatures were extreme, and the nights were cold. I took my groundsheet and blanket, and slept in the back of the Humber wireless car.

Early on Friday, December 18th, I travelled in the back of the regimental HQ wireless car, and did a session of operating. Concentrating on controlling the network, while travelling sideways, rolling from side to side and surrounded by a constant haze of dust was a really disagreeable experience. The one shift of two hours was more than enough. We then descended from the plain to the fertile valley of the River Tapti. Here we enjoyed a long three-hour midday halt. It was a wonderful relief to swim naked in the waters and wash our clothes in the fast flowing stream, which was narrow at this time of year.

After 3 p.m. we climbed from the river valley back up to the Plain. By the time we had halted for the night near the small town of Rajpur, we were once again enveloped in dust. That evening, during the agreed radio operating time, I definitely heard my call sign DON (_D. / _Q _/N.) but my reply evoked no response. My directional aerial was amongst trees, whilst the set at Ranchi was no doubt sited well out in the open. I recorded strength QSA 2, and readability QRK 2 in my log book. For our Morse Code recordings, we used the International Signal Scale.

We were scheduled to spend the weekend in the cantonment at Mhow, which was only fifty miles on. Soon after our start we crossed the Narmada River, which flows into the Gulf of Cambay in the Arabian Sea. Although the bridge was half a mile long, only a small stream wound through the central arch. The monsoon, on its way north in June, would bring torrential rain, and then the whole waterway from bank to bank would be a raging torrent.

Soon after midday we were in Mhow, and we were allotted space in a barrack block, which was the first time we had been able to enjoy proper sleeping facilities since starting our journey 400 miles away. Mhow was completely different from other military stations we had so far encountered. It was very clean, extensive and absolutely British. A considerable number of the troops had permanent postings with wives and families present. It was also the main Royal Corps of Signals depot in India, and it housed a wartime Officer Cadet training unit, OCTU. It is still operated to this day by the Indian Government as a major military training establishment.

The central area of Mhow was refreshingly different with high-class goods in a well-lit shopping complex. We noticed that a great deal of the merchandise originated in America. At such a large base, there would be many permanent peacetime troops and their families. We noticed two cinemas, and I was able to purchase some two-pin plugs and telephone cable for the signal store back in Ranchi.

For the second time running, I heard my call sign from Ranchi, but they did not hear my reply. One of the reasons they did not hear me could have been that the no. 11 set was not a transceiver. In other words, one half of the set transmitted and the other half received, so the dial which rotated to pick up the incoming signal, was not linked to the transmitter dial. At this considerable distance, a small error could mean failure to link the two signals.

The next day was a rest day, but we had to fall in and parade for meals and march to the barracks' cookhouse. The food was appreciated after the makeshift provisions on the journey. At 11 a.m. I strolled over to the garrison church and attended the morning service. There was a great number of the residents, and most of the troops were in civilian dress. It could easily have been a Sunday service back in England. This revelation certainly emphasised the difference in living between these peacetime base troops, and we wartime troops fresh out from England.

After leaving Mhow, we journeyed a further 130 dusty miles passing through many villages and towns including the large town of Indore. In the centre of the Plain, vegetation was mainly scrub with the odd clump of trees. Communication betwen the squadron sets was excellent. At one time A Squadron were eighteen miles ahead and speech reception was strength 5.

Up to this point, the weather had been constantly cold at night, becoming very warm in the day with cloudless skies. But today, we had a few clouds and several bursts of rain. Apparently at this time of year, sporadic rain was experienced for a few days on the Central Plain, and was well-known as the 'Christmas Rains'. To us, it was quite unexpected but a welcome relief, as it certainly helped to minimise the dust clouds.

That evening we followed our now routine camping practice, pulling off the road just past the small town of Biaora. We had more rain and most of us slept in the vehicles, though space was limited and we could not stretch out our legs. Then at around 2 a.m. we were woken by a gang of *Gandhiwallahs*, that is Congress Supporters, who threw a few stones and boulders at the vehicles. Those who were on guard or awake were soon after them, and no damage or real resistance was encountered.

We ran into very heavy rain the following day, but it cleared before the midday halt. Here, we shared the halt with a camel train, about thirty in number, and we took photographs. By evening, the skies had cleared, and on the edge of jungle country we made our camp near Shivpuri. Here the road divided, one fork continuing north to Gwalior, the other east to Jhansi, which was our next destination. During the evening, several operators toook turns on the spare radio, in an endeavour to contact Dipitali Camp, but there was no response. We were, of course, still 500 direct miles away. We had more than the usual numbers of helpers to replenish the logs on our comforting camp fire that night as we listened to the wolves and jackals.

At our main halt the day after, near a large palm tree plantation, we watched natives climbing the trunks, cutting slits in the bark and hanging small tins to collect the sap. We thought that they were collecting rubber, but our *charwallah*, in a very rough translation from a language that was not Hindu, assured us that the collected liquid was fermented and used to make 'firewater'. Later in the day we took a photograph of an Indian with a performing monkey. They both enjoyed corned beef and army biscuits.

Just before Jhansi, we drove past a massive reservoir near Dinana, arriving to spend the night at Alexandra Barracks. Once again we slept by our trucks in the cantonment area. We had now spent nine days on the road, travelled over 700 miles, and in spite of the many diversions, we were tired. We slept early for a dawn start. We of the regimental HQ were to lead the convoy this Christmas Eve, so that the adjutant could be the first in the Lancashire Fusiliers officers' mess, or so it was rumoured.

The ground quickly fell away as we approached the vast fertile valley of the River Ganges basin. To our right was the huge Betwa River, and on the left, the canal of the same name. We followed the railway line through Moth, Orai, to Kalpi, where we crossed another great river, the Jumna, by pontoon bridge. This river had already flowed through Delhi and Agra. These rivers, the Betwa and Jumna, would merge at Hamipur, before they in turn flowed into the Ganges at Allahabad. There was so much water, even in the dry season.

All day we passed irrigation canals and sugar beet in abundance. Livestock, mainly cattle, sheep, pigs and goats, also abounded. At midday near Bhognipur, we encountered a family of monkeys. They were wild but not really shy, and approached us warily to be fed. We tried to catch them and Harry Cresswell chased two up a tree, but they were too wily for him and came back down another. We arrived at Cawnpore, now known as Kanpur, at 1500 hours and we camped outside the barracks. The afternoon was spent doing a major clean up of vehicles, inside and out, and we had to act like soldiers again. We were allowed to use the washing facilities of the Lancashire Fusiliers, but were required to parade and march in threes, complete with washing kit and towels.

The next day was Christmas Day, so we removed the frames from the Humber Snipe chassis, and made them into semi-permanent shelters on the ground. There was still no reply from Ranchi and we spent a rather miserable evening as we were not allowed into Cawnpore, neither could we light fires.

On this trip, sets were not to be used other than on the frequencies pertaining to the exercise, and that was an order, but it was possible to pick up All India Radio. But with headphones available we did break the rules; we listened avidly to the news. Before the trip I had written: Nov 5th – good news about Libya. Nov 8th – Americans land in North Africa, and Nov 12th – thousands of German prisoners taken by the Russians at Stalingrad. But during this journey, in December 1942, news could not have been striking because I made no reference to the war news until Christmas Day. Here is the exact extract from my diary on 25th December, 1942.

Cawnpore Christmas Day 1942

'Woken at 0600 hours by the bugle calls of the Lancashire Fusiliers. Dozed until 0830 hours, Washed, shaved, ready for breakfast parade at 0900 hours. Whole troop to fall in, but no inspection!!! Marched in threes to cookhouse in cantonment, and after the meal back again. Listened to the news. Darlan assassinated. Morning off-duty, wrote letters home. Troop on parade again at 1230 hours. Marched them to the soldiers' club, (built by Lord Roberts) for special Christmas dinner. This arranged at short notice by the local WVS. Greatly appreciated. Roast beef, all the trimmings and Christmas pudding. A great surprise not expected in the circumstances. Off-duty for the rest of day!!! Took photographs of each other around the armoured wireless car (ARC). Then with Ray Scully to have a look at Cawnpore. Not very impressed with what we saw, mostly squalid and depressing. Bought tea and cakes in the cantonment canteen, and then went to the Garrison Theatre to see a good film, *How Green was my Valley*. Then back to the lines, under truck shelter to play pontoon, by the aid of an inspection lamp. Opened tin of bully beef, mango jam and spread separately on army biscuits. Lots of char. So ended Christmas Day. Could have been much worse.'

We left Cawnpore early on Boxing Day, after reveille at 0700 hours, following the Ganges valley, through one of the many towns in India with the name of Fatepur. This was not the Fatepur Sikri, near Agra, which is now a major tourist attraction. Nevertheless, this town had many old and attractive buildings, including several mosques and temples.

We followed the railway line all the way to Allahabad, and as we neared the city, we bordered the Ganges to our left. This was our first glimpse of this great river, which is fed by streams from the Southern Himalayan mountains and joined by many other large rivers, before joining the main stream of the Brahmaputra. Allahabad is situated on the left bank of the Jumna, which flows south of the city, whilst the Ganges loops around the northern conurbation, so Allahabad is almost surrounded by these two great waterways. Just to the east of the city they become one. Every year, vast numbers of pilgrims come to this confluence for a fair of great antiquity.

At Allahbad, we were due for a pleasant surprise. When we arrived in the early afternoon, it was to enter the

McPherson Barracks, where for the second time we were provided with beds for the night. Later in the afternoon, a precautionary innoculation was given to the whole detachment. Apparently smallpox, a highly contagious virus infection, had broken out in the Benares area, with a very high mortality recorded, and we would soon be passing through this territory.

A few minutes after 1900 hours, we made our first positive two-way radio contact with Dipitali our base camp in Ranchi, which was still 250 miles away. It had not been easy to erect the end-fed aerial in an ideal position at previous halts. Here, on the edge of the cantonment there was a large climbable banyan tree in the right line near our wireless truck. Harry Cresswell, not a signaller but a despatch rider, was our tree climbing specialist, and he shinned to the top with the wire. Though interference and static were heavy, the Morse signal came over at strength three in both directions, and we passed several messages.

This project had been set up unofficially, so there were no authorised messages, but to us, transmitting a distance of around 250 miles was a novel and exciting experience. Mr Musselwhite was especially enthusiastic, and he suggested we try to link up, using speech transmission. Not surprisingly, our efforts were fruitless, and after the agreed five minute trial period, both stations reverted to key.

Was this distance of communication ever exceeded between two no. 11 wireless sets? I have been unable to trace records, but it would be interesting to know if any documentation exists. Of course, the operation of a more powerful set at base, such as the 12 HP 33 or the WS 53, would have greatly increased the range of the no. 11 set.

Meanwhile, most of our company had found the soldiers' canteen, a large building in the residential area. It offered substantial meals, and astonishingly, unlimited quantities of tinned beer. Inevitably, quite a few of them had more than a good time, and it was 2 a.m. before we were able to get the last of the drunks to bed. So much for the anticipation of a good night's sleep in luxury, which eventually lasted for just four hours. But it was a real joy to stretch out in comfort and enjoy civilised hygienic facilities.

On the way out of Allahabad barracks our leading scout

car took the wrong turning and approached the imposing ancient archway of the city entrance. This was an out of bounds area, but I was able to take a photograph before we turned back. We soon found the correct route, and left the city over the Ganges just before its confluence with the Jumna, crossing by the Curzon Bridge. This magnificently built box girder bridge, supported by several piers, was over half a mile long, and built in one single span of two levels. The railway used the top section, with the road running directly underneath. Lord Curzon was Viceroy and Governor General of India from 1898 to 1905. He carried out many reforms and was responsible for the restoration of the Taj Mahal. Unfortunately, his confrontations with the Commander in Chief of forces in India, Lord Kitchener, led to his resignation.

Our road to Benares ran alongside the railway, north of the Ganges. We had now dropped almost to river height at around 250 feet above sea level. A vast waterlogged expanse greeted our eyes, with endless rice fields stretching into the distance. Without incident, we arrived at the military barracks of Benares early in the afternoon.

The cantonment was just north of the main station, but today there was to be no excursion into the town, because in addition to the smallpox epidemic, there were riots taking place in the region. However, there was an excellent canteen and because we were now much nearer to Ranchi, we again had a successful radio communication. I had an early night and caught up on my sleep.

Leaving Benares on 28th December, we again crossed the Ganges, this time by the Dufferin Bridge, which then accommodated all traffic both road and rail, as it was the main road between Delhi and Calcutta. We had to wait half an hour for the mail train to pass, as the rails ran in the centre of the narrow span.

Benares, or Varanasi as it is now called, is a most holy place. Hindus arrange travel to the city to die or have their bodies transported from the town of death, to be cremated beside the river. As we crossed the Ganges, the *ghats* and temples glistened in the early morning sun. Distance lent enchantment. The river was absolutely filthy, and no doubt still is to this day, where white plastic bags have replaced the shrouds, which were used to cover the dead. We could also see human remains from the funeral pyres on the *ghats,* and numerous dead animals. Our view was brief, lasting for just the time it took for the train to come. As we crossed the Dufferin Bridge on 28th December on the way to Sasaram, I took a photograph through the box girders. It shows the pontoon bridge, half a mile downstream. Even more interesting is the view at the end of the bridge, as our rear vehicles crossed. In the foreground are the curious Indian civilians and vendors, and in the corner of the print you can see an old fashioned stone milepost: Calcutta 418; Delhi 487; Karamnasa 25; Sasaram 69.

We made camp just short of the town of Sasaram and during the late afternoon we were approached by an Indian, speaking good English. It transpired that he was a local schoolteacher, and curator of the nearby mausoleum. Those of us who accepted his invitation to view were not disappointed. This was a gem, an excellent example of Pathan architecture. The mausoleum stood in the middle of the lake and could only be approached by a narrow causeway. Built in red sandstone, it contained the remains of the Emperor Sher Shah of Sur, a great Muslim ruler from the sixteenth century. It also contained the tomb of Sher Shah's father and the unfinished tomb of his son. That afternoon, the slanting rays of the setting sun glowed on the red sandstone, and the still waters below formed a perfect reflection.

Swami, our guide, was absolutely thrilled to have so many interested visitors. He was a most enthusiastic curator in this voluntary commission, and his knowledge of the Mogul Empire was extensive. A graduate of Patna University, where his parents still lived, he had moved to Sasaram with his wife and infant son, to teach at the local school. We fifteen soldiers may well have been the largest group of overseas visitors he had encountered. Few peacetime troops would have been likely to come this way, so ours was a chance encounter. Even to this day, the modern guide books and popular tourist literature do not mention Sasaram, or include the town in their itinerary, which is strange, because it is only seventy miles from Benares.

When we were back in the camp, I passed several

76

messages to Ranchi before joining our gang round the camp fire. One message that evening surprisingly revealed that we were to spend the night of 31st December at the barracks in Hazaribagh. That was surprising, because as today was the 28th, it left us three whole days to travel the 100 miles, which we could easily have accomplished in one go. The simple answer was that the officers had been invited to celebrate New Year's Eve in the officers' club. These were my memories of Sasaram and after our meal we once again sat round a camp fire, listening to the howls of the prowling wolves and jackals.

In spite of the fact that we had so much time to spare, the next morning we again departed at dawn. After a short journey, we came upon a vast expanse of water which at first sight appeared to be a lake. This was the River Son, which flows north to swell the Ganges just before Patna. We crossed the river by a narrow bridge, which was well over two miles long. This was on the main road and rail route between Delhi and Calcutta. If the Japanese had gained a foothold in India, this span would have become a prime target.

We were allocated one hour, between 0900 and 1000 hours for the convoy and other road traffic to cross. The Calcutta–Delhi mail train was due from the opposite direction at 1030 hours! Once across we began to climb, leaving the vast irrigated flat lands of the Ganges Basin behind, the scrubland gradually thickening into semi-jungle. At midday we left the main road and eventually halted, well away from habitation. Although we were amongst bamboo thickets, wild banana palms and large banyan trees, this was not like the rain forests we were to encounter later in North Burma. Here, there was plenty of room between the trees to park our transport for the next two nights and would enable us to complete the remaining few miles to Hazaribagh on Thursday, 31st December.

The next day was officially declared a rest day so we had no parades. I inspected the radio sets of the A, B and C Squadron detachments in the morning. The feeling amongst most of the troops was that we should have kept on going to Ranchi. We had all had a long journey and now wanted to get back to camp, in spite of the regimentation there. My knowledge of the real reason for the delay was not, of course, divulged.

In the afternoon Ray Scully, George Bell, Gordon Shales, Bill Key and myself took a compass and went out to explore our surroundings. We climbed the steep slopes of a nearby hilltop, a good 500 feet above the camp. From the top we were able to see the way we had come, right back to the valley of the River Son. We encountered several monkeys and flying foxes, and clumps of very solid bamboo. We also traced a thick pall of smoke which turned out to be nothing more than a charcoal burner's crude furnace.

Coming back around the base of the hill, we discovered a completely abandoned village. There was a central stone shrine with red marks and drawings on the walls. We recognised a tiger's head, but the rest to us was grafitti, and we could not comprehend the meaning. All around the temple, at various levels, was row upon row of clay pigs, of mixed sizes. On closer inspection, we decided that they could well be meant to represent boars, but they must have been offered on feast days over a long period of time. A few of the village huts were still intact with their walls and bamboo thatch. In front of two of the huts, there were moulded steps and seats made of mud. The seats were smoothed into beautiful curved comfortable shapes, and had set hard as concrete. Inside one of the huts they had built a fireplace oven and niches for storage in the same manner.

Outside, around the central banyan tree there were perfectly moulded troughs for cattle yet all around was quiet and completely deserted; evidently no person had lived in the village for a long time. Apparently, the use of mud to mould furniture and buildings was an art practised by the Santals, one of the largest aboriginal tribes of India, residing mainly in West Bengal and Bihar and to a lesser degree, in the State of Orissa. It seemed sad and mysterious that this once beautiful village had been deserted for no apparent reason.

On our return we realised that our exploration had taken its toll. We were covered with insect bites, and had collected ticks which had made a bee-line for our private parts. We removed the ticks with lighted cigarettes, and then went to see our column medical orderly.

I was to get no sleep that night, not because of the bites, but because I was again guard commander. Once again this was not a full twelve-hour guard, but a night shift. However, we were miles from other troops and civilisation, so we had to be particularly vigilant. Our accompanying tanker vehicles had almost run out of water, so during the night we filled our chaguls from the nearby stream and constantly brewed char over the dying embers of the fire.

Orders were given the next morning to fill water bottles from the watercourse and to add purification tablets. The night had passed quickly, without untoward incident.

As guard commander, my first early morning duty was to wake the cooks, then the officers' batmen, and finally the section leaders. Then at stand down, I paraded the guard by the guardroom (the ammunition lorry) and collected the six live rounds from each man, obtaining a signature from the armourer. Then I gave the order 'Present arms', followed by 'Unload,' even though the rifles were empty. When the bolt was withdrawn and the thumb of the right hand inserted in the breach, with the thumb nail pointing upwards, if I could see each man's thumb by looking down each barrel, I could ensure that all rifles were unloaded. On this particular morning no officer was present, so it was less formal than usual and I dismissed the guard myself. Guard mounting back in Ranchi, for squadron or regimental twenty-four hour sessions, was comparatively a much more exacting and disciplined parade.

The final leg of our New Year's Eve journey to Hazarabagh was relatively uneventful. On the midday halt, one of our troop saw two scorpions sunning themselves and succeeded in encapsulating them in an empty matchbox. After he had gingerly displayed his captives to all who were interested, we persuaded him to return them to their natural habitat. They were not fully grown, and probably harmless, and besides they were not really suitable for pets.

We had a miserable evening parked in the cantonment in Hazarabagh, especially as the soldiers' club were having an exclusive New Year's Party restricted to resident troops. We were unexpected and unwanted, in fact they were not at all pleased to see us. On the other hand, we could hear our own officers' jollification well into the early morning at the nearby officers' club. The only advantage was the use of the barrack toilet facilities, and what little sleep we had, was by the sides of our vehicles.

New Year's Day, 1943, marked the final stage of our journey back to Ranchi. Forty miles out, we were met by a party from the camp, headed by the RSM, and they escorted us back to Dipitali, where we arrived at 1300 hours. We had been away exactly three weeks, but it was a great experience and seemed much longer. There were stacks of mail awaiting, including a cable from my mother telling me my grandfather had died. It made me sad and very homesick, so I spent the evening writing letters and getting ready for the next morning's parade.

4

Standing By

During our absence from Dipitali Camp, day-to-day
routine had been reorganised to present a tougher regime.
In addition, the encampment presented a much more
solitary aspect. The whole regiment was still under canvas
but old tents had been realigned and new ones struck, so
that we all had more space. One especially joyful addition
was a large marquee by the cookhouse, where we could eat
in comfort, away from most of the flies and shielded from
the forages of the marauding kites. Discipline had to be
maintained at a high level in military units, but its intensity
and application could vary like the seasons. Over a period of
time, slackness and inertia were apt to creep in, but on an
impending visit from the 'top brass', transference to a new
command, or just the adjutant's troubled conscience,
drastic upgrading would suddenly be reintroduced.

A new day-to-day regimen awaited us. We now had earlier
reveille, longer P.T. and drill sessions and the enforcement
of falling-in, and marching to all meals and duties. In
addition, whatever our duties were on Thursdays, we had to
wear our respirators between the hours of nine and ten in
the morning. Part Two Orders outside Squadron HQ Office
read as follows:

	Monday to Saturday
0630	Reveille.
0715-0745	Physical Training.
0800	Breakfast.
0830	Sick Parade.

0900-1000	**Monday, Wednesday, Friday** Rifle Inspection, Weapon Drill, Musketry. **Tuesday** Tent and Kit Inspection. **Thursday** Fatigues as detailed. Respirators to be worn. Pay Parade. **Saturday** Vehicle maintenance.
1000-1030	Morning Break.
1030-1230	Specialist Training.
1300	Midday Meal.
1400	Organised Sport.
1800	Evening Meal.

At first glance, details like this looked much more exacting than they really were. We had all experienced tougher conditions, especially in our initial basic training. Besides that, afternoons were virtually free, and if we were not taking part in the many sporting activities and if we were willing to miss the evening meal, we were permitted to leave the camp. Visits to Ranchi for most of us were purely regulated by lack of finances. This routine was continually superseded by other events. During the coming months we were often out of camp on exercises, some of these lasting a full week. Getting prepared for these 'schemes', as we called them, disrupted other duties. Special duties also disrupted the daily routine: such as regimental guard (NCO and twelve men), and squadron guard (NCO and six men).

One of my duties, such as marching men to meals, a distance of only seventy-five yards, was a complete waste of time, it took longer to get the men on parade than it did to march them to the cookhouse. As sergeants had their own mess tent, they were not involved. One boon at this time was that except for once a month, church parade was voluntary. When in camp, I attended and played for the service on the padre's folding squeeze-box harmonium. There was a divisional parade once a month, with all the spit and polish, though I usually evaded this by travelling ahead in the padre's transport. Otherwise, Sunday was a free day with meal times the same, but reveille an hour later.

By now, a great number of evening activities had been organised. Budding actors could volunteer to practise for the 'regimental showtime' which was to be presented at the garrison theatre in Ranchi. Naturally, musicians were needed and a surprising variety of instruments was conjured up. Also, card schools abounded, with unofficial games played in individual tents, but crib, whist, bridge and chess could be played in the mess tent and for those not wishing to exert themselves mentally, there were bingo sessions twice a week.

In the Signal Troop, we had an additional advantage, which was the signal store and training marquee. In the evenings we often listened to radio programmes from far afield on our radio sets with the special outdoor aerials. We kept up to date with the new popular songs and listened to a great deal of classical music. We had also smuggled in a very old wind-up gramophone from England with about a dozen records listed as stores. On one of the records, we knew the tunes so well that we could put the needle down in precisely the correct grooves for our favourites. In our circumstances we became exceedingly nostalgic and this homesickness was crystallised for many of us when listening to the music.

My earliest recollections had been of listening to the first 'talkie' I had experienced in 1930 entitled *Show Boat*. The tune *Old Man River* brought memories of those times flooding back. The sound was not well synchronised with the film track, the music following the actions fractions of a second later. Another melody of this era was *Sonny Boy,* but memories of this soulful song was somewhat tarnished by the army version of the lyrics: 'I know what you're after, feeling up my garter, I'll tell your ma Sonny Boy.' There was also *Smoke Gets in Your Eyes* of 1934, and the lovely *The Way You Look Tonight* of two years later. These had been my teenage school days. For a different reason I will never forget the last dance *Goodnight my Love,* that I had with Mollie, my wife, just before embarkation.

We now listened to the new tunes of the 1940s like *White Christmas, In the Mood, Room 504* and *The Last Time I Saw Paris.* Also popular, and only a few years old at that time were *Begin the Beguine, Wish me Luck, I'll Walk Beside You* and *A Nightingale Sang in Berkeley Square.* These and many more, were the songs that we had listened to and shared with our loved ones before embarkation.

Coupled with these were the songs of the First World War which we had sung on our route marches in England. *Tipperary, Keep The Home Fire Burning, Pack Up Your Troubles* and *Mademoiselle from Armentiers.* At this time, we reckoned that route marches were a thing of the past, but it would not be long before we had a rude awakening.

These evenings, listening to the music from the radio or on our gramophone records, made us feel homesick and rather depressed. We had nothing to complain about in our actual service duties, or in the day-to-day routine. In fact we had been lucky so far, having had the excitement of sea travel, the new sights and the experiences in India, the busy army routine, plenty of opportunities for sport and plenty of free time in the evenings. Nevertheless, this life was not of our choosing. We were away from home and out of our natural environment. The Army held us in a time capsule, and at this juncture we were free wheeling, wanting the war to end. There was the ever-present and dreadful realisation that we would most probably have to fight. There was no way ahead until Japan was defeated. In this situation we were neither cowards nor heroes, we could only look to the future with hope.

Meanwhile, army life followed the described pattern, though we became more and more a part of the 70th Division. It was now early January, and there were none of the usual clues through the 'grape vine' as to how long we would remain in the Ranchi area. Certainly, all the indications were that we would be staying on the plain for quite a while. Divisional exercises had been planned for some time ahead, there had even been rumours of a possible leave roster. However, it was more likely we were being held here in reserve for the future. The Japanese were now well entrenched in Burma, with established sea-supply lines, so troops and shipping were required for the second front. Our supply lines in the eastern area were fully extended.

Back in camp, those of us who had been on the road during the Christmas period were given a special Yuletide dinner on 7th January and excused all parades for the day. This came as a most welcome and pleasant surprise.

At the end of January we took part in a big jungle training exercise involving the whole of the 70th Division. The scheme lasted fourteen days, we were based about ninety miles west of our camp at Dipitali and we had very mixed weather. On the way out, we became bogged down in a river bed, and getting the vehicles out had not of course been planned as part of the exercise. Otherwise it was not very energetic, our radio network worked reasonably well, and those involved seemed noticeably satisfied with the Signal Troop. The only benefit was a relief from routine parades, and the chance to improve our wireless communication standards.

During the first day at the camp we engaged three natives to build us a shelter, which turned out to be almost a proper hut. The three of them cleared an area, leaving a few trees standing as uprights, and then constructed a framework for the roof and sides with cross-pieces, thatching the roof to make a completely waterproof shelter. We took a photograph of the workmen during the construction, for which they charged a total of one rupee. It really was a marvellous job.

The only real excitement occurred towards the end of our stay, when a certain Lieutenant Benson and seven men became lost in the jungle. We formed a search party, but they were eventually located by others. The jungle we encountered in this area was comparatively sparse, when contrasted with the tropical variety, nevertheless it did command respect.

Towards the end of the exercise, we assembled for the first of many lectures on the Burmese jungle and Japanese military tactics. This particular talk was given by an ardent young captain from GHQ Delhi, who presumed that we were champing on the bit to see some action. His opening words were: 'Every man here this afternoon is waiting to get his chance to fight the Japanese, and´ throw them out of Burma. That chance will come.' He would have been given full marks for content for his lecture, which contained a brief description of the country, some history, information about industries, Burmese village life and how to keep healthy. He concluded, 'We must return determined to be victorious, hitting the Jap good and hard, and we shall get all the co-operation from the Burmese, provided we behave as soldiers and gentlemen.' Inspired though it might have been, his talk in general fell upon very stony ground indeed. Had we been poised to attack Rangoon harbour from assault craft moored in the bay, or paratroopers about to drop on Mandalay, this would have been an excellent call to arms. As it was however, we had just completed an exercise, and were looking forward to the return to camp in Ranchi and comparative comfort.

Soon after we returned to camp, orders were issued that sun helmets had to be worn between the hours of 1000 and 1600 hours. This rule had to be rigidly observed, even if we moved five yards to the next tent, and even on the few rainy days The army still seemed to cling to this rather old fashioned rule, emanating from the days when the *topee* was the all-year traditional Indian Army headgear, like the bowler hat was in the City of London, all part of the scene. Going even further back in the history of sunstroke precautions soldiers used to wear a strip of canvas with insertions of thin cork strips, down the back of the neck inside the shirt which must have been very uncomfortable. The astonishing absurdity of this order to wear helmets, was that we frequently played games between these hours without headgear of any sort. Later in the year, with the sun directly overhead, these encumbrances were superseded by berets.

In the army, the announcement that one of the 'top brass' was due to make a visit inevitably triggered off a frenzy of activity. So when it was known that the Divisional Commander, General W.G. Symes, intended to visit us on 21st February, this tradition was well maintained. One hundred and fifty men were detailed to form a special guard of honour, and were rigorously drilled by the RSM for three days before the event. The rest of the regiment were employed on general fatigues, making sure that no rubbish or paper was in sight, and that all tents were correctly pitched, with guy ropes taut. Tables and chairs in the mess tents were scrubbed and the pots and pans in the cookhouse were scoured. On the morning of his visit, our beds were made up and inspected, everything being left out on display. Each troop was issued with a detailed list of training activities, so everyone would know what to do if the general made a tour of the lines. Everything was geared to make an outstanding impression. In the event, he arrived on time and drove past the troops lined up for inspection, straight to the officers' mess. After a hasty lunch, he was away again even before one hour had passed. I only hope he had noticed the guard of honour.

Periodically, our troop was given the duty of fumigating the latrines. We used one of the Humber Snipe wireless trucks, attaching one end of a flexible pipe to the exhaust, and dropping the other end into the pit which was temporarily covered with a tarpaulin. Presumably, we were given this task because the armoured vehicles were heavy and less manoeuvrable. After running the engine for around twenty minutes, toxic fumes were produced, most of them seeming to escape from under the edges of the tarpaulin. It was never explained what benefit, if any, this fumigation had, and how it affected the contents of the latrines. However, I do know that I had several violent headaches, as a direct result of this operation. No doubt modern day ecologists would have been flabbergasted at this preposterous hazard to health, and detailed reports would have been made.

Mail from England arrived in batches, and often awaited our return to camp. My wife, Mollie, wrote at least once a week, and my parents, younger brothers Cyril and Ralph, as well as schoolgirl sister Audrey, also wrote quite regularly. I also heard from friends including my new-found ones in South Africa, the Movsovics and the Hayes. It was a great morale booster to receive mail, and I certainly found no difficulty in replying to the one-off letters. But as the weeks turned to months, love letters to Mollie became more stereotyped, and obviously rather repetitive.

The long separation had become a permanent stress factor. Back at home, the weeks apart had been sustained by the promised excitement of our next meeting, whereas here the break seemed endless, with no light at the end of the tunnel. Like so many young wives, Mollie was now working in a munitions factory, constantly subject to the temptation of wartime liaisons. Time was to prove that I would be one of the lucky ones whose wife waited faithfully for nearly four years.

Letters brought both good and bad news, for example, towards the end of March, I was shocked and saddened to learn that R.A. Gerrard, a captain in the Royal Engineers had lost his life in the Middle East. I knew 'Gerry' well, due to playing both rugby football and athletics together. He had won no less than thirteen international caps against South Africa, New Zealand, Ireland, Scotland and Wales between 1932 and 1936. Being rather older than myself, we had only played together twice in the Bath second team, he as a centre and myself on the wing. Gerry was coming back after injury at the time, at the end of a long career, and I was just a budding junior. But we knew each other better due to athletics. He held the Territorial Army shot put championship, and in the two summers before the war, had put the sixteen pound weight for us at the Bath and County Athletic Club. None of our competitors, including those from Bristol University could match him.

We now used to go into Ranchi quite often, maybe three or four evenings a week. When we were in the money, the *garriwallahs* were engaged, otherwise we added our names to the leave list to go on the 'passion wagon'. Often I would be placed in charge of the evening detail. It entailed collecting the list from the orderly room, accounting for the numbers and detailing a guard for the vehicle when it was parked in Ranchi. The guard was usually drawn from troopers on 'defaulters'. Once I had forgotten about the guard and had to do the shift myself!

Another problem could arise when the driver himself had had too much to drink. Unless he was troublesome I took no action, allowing his mates to look after him in the rear, then driving back myself. This was not an onerous task, the Studebaker three-ton lorries were a joy to drive. They had an enclosed cab with synchromesh gears between third and top and no speed governor was fitted.

Ray Scully and I made our main eating place in Ranchi the Central Cafe. Like the Chinese restaurants, they cooked in oil instead of the *ghee* that the Indians used. But the main attraction was that we soon came to an understanding with

88

Ali the waiter. He would lose the bill in exchange for a large tip. I have to admit that we made full use of his services, even on Sundays when we had come straight from worship at Ranchi Cathedral.

In February, a new edict came from GHQ Delhi, that all cameras must be registered with units. Some had brought cameras from home, others had purchased them in Ranchi where modern cameras and films were available. We were never given a logical reason for this check. Cameras were certainly never deregistered! At the time we took a great number of films and got them developed reasonably cheaply. Prints were sent home but like our correspondence, they had to be censored. They were stamped on the back with the unit rubber stamp, which was a one inch circle with 'Unit Censor India' round the outer rim and in the centre, D45, which must have been the number allocated to the Reconnaissance Corps.

Those who could afford to, sent home presents, such as neckerchiefs, scarves and ties, and sometimes lengths of dress material. Articles would be carefully packed, stitched in a canvas outer by the resident tailor or *durzi* before the green declaration form for customs export was attached. Transportation was slow, taking up to three months but goods usually arrived safely.

The local aboriginal tribes of the nearby village were employed to help build and maintain the tracks and roads. They excavated the red earth with primitive tools, putting it into tins or flat reed baskets. Whole families worked and it was left to the women to transport the earth in the baskets and metal boxes, gracefully balancing the containers on their heads. They were engaged by the Royal Engineers and needed little supervision, Working from 9 a.m. to 4 p.m. they each earned five annas per day, and they were amazingly cheerful and friendly, although I must admit they did well with the occasional gifts of food. As the midday sun got hotter in the summer months they all worked stripped to the waist, even the women.

To most of us, wholly sex starved for months, these dusky Indian women became younger and more attractive by the hour. This engendered temptation both to the troops and the villagers. A poorly paid family with a consenting wife, could earn more in a few minutes than by labouring for a full week. Liaisons took place quite unofficially on a large scale, mostly with the same few troops participating. The majority, in spite of the temptation, had more respect, morals or fear of contagion, not necessarily in that order. Only once did real trouble materialise. Shots rang out from the direction of the village, a native was injured in the leg and the military and local police were involved. Eventually, no charges were made and nothing officially recorded. Both road work and nocturnal activities continued.

However, as usual in the army, a story slowly emerged. The wounds had been caused by a Smith and Wesson revolver, which used $0 \cdot 38$ calibre ammunition. As these weapons at this time were only issued to officers and warrant officers down to sergeants, the field was narrowed. But we were on active service, so that checking ammunition around several units and inspecting all Smith and Wesson revolvers would have been time consuming and probably futile. Had the injuries been to British soldiers, then enquiries might have continued. We heard through the *dobiwallah* that the shots had been fired by a sergeant who had refused to pay the woman's husband who confronted him.

Thanks to the efforts of Captain Adams and Lieutenant Potter, we had been able to construct a fairly flat sports pitch. Initially, we had the use of a bulldozer for a week, in addition to the help of the natives. The area had been a paddy field and was not perfect, but we were able to use it for soccer, hockey, cricket, athletics and later when the rains came, for rugby.

My main sporting interest was athletics and I was a representative on the Regimental Sports Committee. We had already visited the 290 Battery, Royal Artillery, and won a contest against them. Relay races at this time were different from now. For example the mile was not 4 x 440 yards, but 880, 440, 220, 220, in that order. I ran the 880 yards in the winning relay and also won the individual 880 and 440 yards. We lost both the sprints to the Royal Artillery, but scraped enough points to win the contest. We also beat them in a hastily arranged cricket match by 88 runs to 76. On the very rough pitch, it was a wonder that runs were scored at all and no bones broken. In our regiment, sporting 'stars' got no favours at all. The RSM was our problem and he would not agree at all to the reallocation of duties.

The regular units in the division were much more sport conscious and were able to field their best teams. This was highlighted later in the year when a divisional cross country race was arranged. This was a big sporting occasion, scheduled to take place near Ranchi Aerodrome on 5th April, when the divisional commander, Major General W.G. Symes was to start the race. We were one of the twenty teams due to take part, fifteen men to a team, the first twelve of the squad home to count for points. Some of the units had selected their men in February and allowed them to train free of their duties, until the day of the race. After a great deal of lobbying by Captain Adams and other officers, we were excused duties for one week before the event by our commanding officer, Colonel Trotter.

Winning a major sporting contest was a great fillip and engendered pride in a unit. With three hundred men in the contest, we wanted to have a nucleus of men in the first fifty. In the event, seven of our team managed that and we came in fifth, but two things had beaten us. Firstly, we were ill-prepared, and secondly we were not acclimatised to the conditions. Although the race was started at 6 p.m., it was still very hot. The winners were the 2nd Battalion Leicestershires, regular troops who had been in the Middle East or India for the last three years.

We often spent a whole day at the firing ranges, especially now that wireless communication was used to control the operation. When we went for actual firing practise it was to fire our rifles and on a couple of occasions, the Bren gun, with live ammunition of course. The whole procedure was very strictly controlled, with rounds issued and double checked to avoid the possibility of accident. Much more frequently, our visits were as a fatigue party, primarily to operate the radio sets but also to act as 'pasters'. There were two locations, one at the firing point and the other at the targets. The former position was a snip, all that had to be done was to relay the orders from the officer in charge. At the target area there was much more work to do. The view from the firing position duggout and target area was as illustrated:

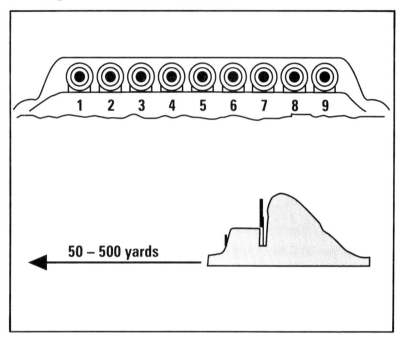

The firing point could be anything from fifty to 500 yards away. The actual targets were like huge dartboards, with a centre bull and outer rings, hoisted aloft on wooden frames for the actual firing. We used our no. 38 short range man pack wireless sets, one at the firing point, the other in the trench at the target area. They were considered superior to the old army DS telephones which needed miles of cable to operate. Today our sets would be considered even more ancient compared with the modern crowd control 'walkie-talkies'. The officer in charge of the firing would order the targets to be displayed, he would order targets to be lowered and individual hits, if these were recorded e.g. number one: one bull, one inner, one outer; number two: two inners and so on. This done, we would 'paste up', covering the holes with paste and paper, ready for the next session.

5

Leave in Bombay

At the end of March, much to our amazement, it was announced that a fourteen-day leave roster was to commence at once. This confirmed the general feeling that our division was being held in reserve at present, though we knew from experience that army plans could be changed overnight.

We were also pleasantly surprised by the wide choice of leave centres. These included Simla, Darjeerling, Agra, the Kashmir Valley, as well as Madras and Bombay. However, the choice was tempered by the fact that except for the last two locations, leave centres were organised very much like army camps, and apart from the beauty and coolness of the hill stations, it did not afford a great change. In any case, I very much wanted to have another look at Bombay with plenty of free time, so I had no hesitation over making a decision.

Strange to say, quite a number of our comrades did not apply to go on the leave. Unlike being at home, where most serving men had a family to go to with free accommodation, here in India we had to pay for our board and keep. Maybe for this reason, I found myself included in the first draft, along with Ray Scully and several of the Signal Troop, leaving for Bombay on the twelfth of April. It is difficult to compare money values in 1943 with those of today. Even so, the 150 rupees drawn on the pay parade the day before we left was not a fortune. This sum, equivalent to ten pounds, included ration and other allowances. My pay as a corporal was six rupees a day, or nine shillings – forty-five pence in today's currency.

Luckily I had saved another twenty rupees, so this was a bonus. Armed with a free army rail warrant, we left Ranchi station at midday on the narrow gauge line to Muri, changing to the broad gauge for Tatanaga. Here we were due to board the Calcutta–Bombay mail train at 2130 hours, second class accommodation having been reserved through the Railway Transport Office, the RTO. When the train arrived, our carriage was completely crammed with travellers of all ages, complete with bedrolls and goats. They had boarded without tickets at Calcutta in the hope of an undisturbed journey. This was quite normal all over the Indian railway network. When we turfed them out on to the platform, they seemed to enjoy the experience and bore us no grudge. As the rest of the train was crowded, they would join the throng on the platform, and patiently await the next train. Time was of no importance, and camping on the station was free.

Our carriage was very much like the troop train format, both the middle and top bunks could be pulled down for sleeping. We travelled along the same route as before via Nagpur, but much more quickly, an overall total of thirty-seven hours for the journey of something like 1,200 miles. This was by no means a fast trip, at around an average of thirty miles per hour, but even this top class mail train made numerous stops, for water, engine changes and meals for the first-class passengers at station restaurants. These meals were bookable in advance at the previous stops, but to us they were expensive. There was also a restaurant car on the train.

We arrived at Bombay Victoria Station eventually, then we clambered into *garis* to take us to the Salvation Army hostel. It is very likely that the Red Shield hostel in Shahid Bhagat, run by the Salvation Army today is the same building. Accommodation had been reserved for us by the station staff officer, the local army commander, for bed and breakfast for our fourteen days leave.

We booked in, paying in advance, at a cost of seventeen rupees each for the whole period. Four of us shared a room, which fronted onto a wide verandah, overlooking some gardens. Everything was bright, fresh and airy. Our beds had clean white sheets, with real mattresses, mosquito nets and a large overhead fan high up in the ceiling. An even greater luxury was the showers and European-style toilets. We had not experienced the latter since leaving the *Dominion Monarch* over six months before. At this time western-style toilets were almost non existent in India. Squat toilets were the norm in all houses and public buildings. In fact, at this time the ordinary Indians in the street were not too particular about using toilets at all.

Our first priority was to visit the station staff officer in the Railway Transport Office to register our leave passes in Bombay. We were given an authorisation certificate covering the duration of our stay, to present to the military police if challenged. Many British and other troops had deserted in India, and Bombay was one of the easiest places to go underground. Given the right contacts, shelter and material help was available from the Congress Party.

The city was a great attraction for troops on leave, and crews from the Royal and Merchant Navies swelled the throng on the streets. Several of us were interested in playing tennis, and we visited the Hospitality Committee at the YWCA to find out details. The tennis courts were just across the road and free to service personnel. Consequently, every weekday we played tennis, usually before breakfast or late in the afternoon because of the hot weather. Raquets and balls were available for use without charge, and there was an Indian tennis coach and smartly dressed ball boys, *Chokras,* in attendance. We did not have a lesson from the instructor, but gave the ball boys plenty of tips. This interlude playing tennis was most enjoyable and my game improved, but it was to be three years before I had the chance to play again.

It was absolute luxury to be able to sleep in our beds at the hostel, and some mornings I must confess even the prospect of playing tennis only just got me out of bed. Breakfast-time was fairly flexible, and we were usually out for the rest of the day. When we did stay there for a meal at midday or evening, it was good value but no cheaper than in the city.

The first afternoon we made a bee-line to Breach Candy and enjoyed the swimming. However, we now found that the drinks were expensive, as they were geared to the higher paid officer class. We heard that the Back Bay swimming baths were on our doorstep and free to service personnel, so that was our only visit to Breach Candy. We finished our first evening in Bombay at the Empire Cinema to watch the film *Song of the Islands.* Bombay was very much hotter than it had been in December, but we were relaxed, on holiday without the army routine, so life was most agreeable.

We visited the baths at Back Bay nearly every day. They were crowded and noisy, bringing us into direct contact with the Indian youngsters who seemed to live in the baths. One day for a change, we had a bathe with some of them in the sea in Back Bay itself. Although it was not out of bounds to troops, bathing in the sea was frowned upon by the authorities as being most unhygienic. It probably was, but we had a fine time in the company of the urchins who swam with us and continually demanded *baksheesh.* All the boys swam naked and one of them took a photograph of all of us using my camera.

Even in the 1940s, Bombay was the film capital of India, producing a multitude of movies in the many local studios, mostly in Hindustani, Marathai or other Indian dialects. We were fascinated by the colourful lurid advertising hoardings outside the cinemas, but we did not watch any of the Indian productions, preferring English and American films which we mostly saw at the Eros cinema. This picture theatre was housed in part of a vast corner building, with a high tower over the central structure. The area was called Reclamation, as together with the Marine Drive, it had been built on land reclaimed from marshland in the 1920s. I noted three of the films we watched: *Just off Broadway, Kings Row* and *Life Begins at 8.30.* Also in Bombay at this time was a well known dance orchestra called Ken Mac's Band with Beryl Templeman. We watched the performance at Greens, a city dance hall and afterwards we wished we had been able to join in the dancing. However, with female partners in the ratio of something like 1 to 200, and being without an army commission, the overall odds were very much against us finding partners.

On the first Sunday of leave, I attended a service at St Thomas's Cathedral. Afterwards I walked round the interior, reading the names on the profusion of plaques and the stone and marble memorials. These persons had served

India well over the years, and a great number had died in battle. The chairs used by King George V and Queen Mary during their visit to Bombay in 1911, were exhibited.

The following Sunday, 25th April was Easter Sunday. I went to all the services, not because of any religious fervour, but because I enjoyed the hymns, the singing and the complete change from army life. This was a different world, and in a way it created a bond with home and family. The war seemed very distant at times like these. We loved the colourful panorama of life in Bombay, but the continual and persistent demand for *baksheesh* was an irritant.

It seemed to us that Bombay must be the mecca for the begging fraternity, we were constantly accosted wherever we went. They represented a cross-section of the populace, being both young and old. Some were really poor or had life-crippling diseases and they were wholly dependent on charity. However, a greater number of them made begging into a worthwhile profession and we witnessed many instances of this. Babies in arms were at best often pinched by their mothers to make them cry, or at worst, maimed at birth to evoke permanent sympathy, but all had the same objective. Multiple amputees would team up on display for sympathy. As we slowly approached Victoria terminus, station in Bombay at the beginning of our leave, I took a photograph of three turbanned Indians, all with only a stump on the right shoulder. In good spirits with a holiday ahead, these were the first beggars we encountered, and many pice and annas were thrown beside them on the track as the carriages went past. But later, there were so many of them pleading that we just had to turn a blind eye.

In contrast, the Bombay traffic police presented a smart and colourful display in their dark blue uniforms. They had plus four breeches just over the knee, bare legs and black sandals called *chaplis*. They wore wide black leather sashes and holsters and belts with heavy brass clasps. Around their necks they wore white lanyards and whistles and from wrist to elbow they wore white detachable ármbands. On their heads they wore a blue pill-box hat, trimmed in red, kept in place with chin straps. The showpiece however, was the large white umbrella firmly planted in a holster attached to the belt, and held in place higher up the shaft by an attachment to the sash. Thus equipped, they were able to keep the traffic moving, with protection from the midday sun. Bombay was well inside the Tropic of Cancer, so for several months in the summer, the sun was directly overhead.

Night-time revealed the most colourful aspect of the Bombay scene. The evenings were comparatively cool, and it seemed that everyone found their way out on to the streets, including the sacred cows which wandered unhindered everywhere. Although there was much splendour to see, there was also much poverty in this prosperous city. We had to step carefully over and around the many sleeping forms on the pavements, avoiding the filth. There were hovels built against the commercial buildings of the rich companies and on the edge of the parks, yet the majority of the moving throng looked so clean.

We wandered around the streets and looked into the brilliantly lit shops but spent very little. At Crawford Market we admired the displays which seemed to reach the roof. Here at various times we bought apples, bananas, pineapples, melons and tangerines. Even on our army pay, fruit was very cheap. In the daylight hours we looked at some of the most famous buildings, though visiting architectural buildings was not high on our list of priorities. Buildings at the other extreme were blocks of flats over the offices and stores. Some looked like blank crossword puzzle squares, five cubes high by six cubes wide, each the home of large families with a twelve by twelve foot frontage, with a six foot high iron railing facade. Through this barrier the occupants looked out onto the street, like so many animals in a zoo.

The most worthwhile experience we had was not planned. One of our party, Sergeant McQuade, expressed an interest in looking at the Hanging Gardens near Malabar Hill. I think he had in mind the Hanging Gardens of Babylon. What we had heard was only hearsay as we had no guide book. We caught a bus routed to Malabar Point and had no difficulty in getting off at the correct stop. All the travellers in the bus spoke English in a lilting voice very much like the Welsh. But the Hanging Gardens were most disappointing, as we had expected something more spectacular. There was plenty of greenery, the terraces were bordered with small trees, with larger ones round the extremities and there were many exotic flowers, shrubs and hedges. At home these would have been called Botanical Gardens.

We then walked slowly to the top of the terraces and entered a road leading back to the coast. This was obviously a wealthy area and we passed many elegant residences. As we walked, we passed a long high wall on our left, and further down we came upon an elaborate wrought iron gateway, flanked by two large pillars. Inside there was a room that looked like a guardroom. We stopped to look through the gate and two uniformed men approached us. This certainly looked like a military establishment. Both men were Sikhs with elegant uniforms of dark blue fabric, red turbans, wide black leather belts and holsters, with large brass buckles. They carried staves, but otherwise they were unarmed. In fact this dress very much resembled that of the traffic police. We exchanged words of greeting and they explained that this was the Parsee cemetery. Now I realised where we were, especially as they talked enthusiastically about their duties. They were in charge of the workmen who trimmed the lawns and hedges and bore the bodies aloft. These were the Parsee Towers of Silence.

One of them invited us to enter through a side gate, for which we needed little encouragement. He led us up an inclined path, winding across a lawn flanked with many tall trees, mainly cypresses and palms. Suddenly, the landscape opened up in front. There, high up on the slope, were several very tall circular stone towers with metal cages on top. The guard explained in gruesome detail exactly what was happening. Because of the rise in the ground we could see nothing of the grim remains, but his description left little to the imagination. The vultures were certainly in attendance, circling high above the towers or perched on the metal grills above the columns. We did not stay long, and back at the entrance gates we gave each of the Sikhs a five anna tip, which they received graciously but with a hint of expectancy.

There is no doubt in my mind that this dereliction of duty was a usual way of supplementing their wages. The whole area was very quiet, and the gardens and trees screened the view for possible onlookers. Years later in England I was to read about the Parsees, largely because of this lucky visit. Today the towers are zealously guarded at all times and visitors and tourists are not admitted to the cemetery.

The Parsees arrived as immigrants in Bombay towards the end of the seventeenth century from Persia, rather than face the Arab occupation. Their Zoroastrian religious belief is that earth, fire and water are too important to defile. For this reason, the bodies of their dead are laid high up on the towers on grills, by burial squads who are not Parsees. In theory, the grills are constructed in such a way that the vultures can consume the flesh but not carry away the bones which then drop into wells at the base of the towers. Rumour has it that this does not always happen in practice, and pieces of limbs have been found in the area. It is a fact that Rudyard Kipling's mother was distressed when she found a child's hand in her garden.

There must be some truth in these rumours and stories, because in 1881 for most certainly hygienic reasons, the three large reservoirs which supply the water to Bombay city were covered over. These are now safely under the terraces of the Hanging Gardens which were designed, constructed and largely financed by the Parsee community.

The Parsees live mostly in Bombay, and they have wielded a major influence in Bombay and India far out of proportion to their numbers. Best known are the Tata family, who built the Taj Mahal Hotel in Bombay, and who over the years have launched innumerable successful business ventures, including the iron and steel works at Tatanaga, the massive textile works at Wardha, electricity generating stations, ship building and the airline which eventually became Air India. But above all, the Parsees have always been philanthropic, with a benevolent civic responsibility, and over the years they have donated great sums of money to hospitals, schools and the needful causes that are endemic to India.

Our fortnight away from the unit flew by, and in no time at all we had just a few days left. In that time we attended the combined Festival of Music and Dance on the esplanade, and found the rhythms and medley of fractional tones difficult to understand. However, listening to the music and watching the dance forms was a great experience. The music of the sitars, vinas and reed trumpets produced a timeless spiritual and ethereal quality. Almost next door was the War Exhibition. This was purely propaganda and featured mainly the Indian Army and the war in the Middle East. In less than a month's time, the North African Campaign would end in victory, all due to the troops of the Raj! No mention was made of the Japanese Army which at present held all the cards in the Far Eastern conflict.

Only two days of our leave now remained. So far, none of my companions had strayed into the brothel areas, which were very numerous in Bombay. They ranged from the sordid notorious 'cages' in Grant Road to the 'high class' establishments, the escort agencies and the call girls, in the Taj Mahal Hotel.

There was also a brothel officially supervised by the army, one of the many operated in India by the military, and situated near the transit camp. At this brothel, overseen by the military police and the Royal Army Medical Corps, troops paid five rupees and were given a condom and the number of the room to visit. The girls were examined regularly by the RAMC doctors and paid a wage. Two of our leave party had gone along the evening before, but they were turned away by the MPs because the brothel was due to close at 10 p.m. and the queue was already considered to be too long.

Later in the year, subsequent leave parties found that all these official brothels had been closed. This was due to protests from various religious communities, coupled with the appointment of a very high ranking officer to India Command in Delhi. According to reports from the RAMC, soon after the Delhi brothels were closed down, the previously almost empty VD ward in the military hospital was filled, and another ward opened up.

I cannot recall how it came about that three of us decided on our last evening, to go and look at the 'establishment' at 20, Lamington Road. We had certainly heard about the 'hostesses', and the fact that the girls enjoyed a chat and a drink, with no obligation to indulge. You could blame our action on a misplaced sense of adventure or bravado, or something to do, but circumstances alter intentions and we had naively set the scene. We ensured we had brought enough money as we climbed into two *garis* and asked for Lamington Road.

We duly arrived at our destination; the whole area looked very respectable and number twenty looked much the same as the other dwellings in the row. We had got so far and there was no escape. We were now committed and one of us pressed the doorbell. After a short delay, it was opened by a tall, bearded, well-dressed Indian gentleman in a grey lightweight suit, topped by a large Rajput turban. I well remember his words: 'Good evening, gentlemen, welcome to our household, do please come in and have a drink.' We were then led into a very large comfortably furnished room, where over a dozen young and beautiful girls were standing in groups and talking. All of them were tall and slim, wearing flimsy evening gowns. They welcomed us and introductions were exchanged all round. It was a long time since we had enjoyed such friendly female companionship.

We were like moths around a candle flame. As we chatted 'madam' came around to each of us in turn very unobtrusively, to let us know that if we required a friendly liaison, the girls' 'pocket money' would be ten rupees. The girls were well trained because they left each of us in turn with madam.

I must have shown an interest in one of the girls, maybe due to a nervous smile, because in no time at all she had invited me to have a drink. The 'bar' was through an alcove in the main room and she led me by the hand, poured me a glass of beer and had a lemonade for herself. There was no mention of payment. We sat and talked, and exchanged names. Her name was Julie. Meanwhile, my two companions had been prompted to join us at the bar with their escorts and indeed several other girls, and it still seemed to be just a pleasant party. Then, all at once, I became most conscious of the warmth of Julie's body next to mine, and her hand on my thigh. We drew even closer and looking round, the room was empty, my companions and the girls had suddenly vanished.

Now, all clear thinking and caution had evaporated. The excitement of being so close to this girl was uncontrollable, my judgement was upended, and fierce raw passion had taken over. After months of sexual deprivation no further incitement was needed, I was totally aroused and fully committed. We ascended the stairs to her room, our arms entwined. She mentioned the money and I had it ready before we entered a very small cubicle with a bright unshaded light hanging from the ceiling. In spite of my ardent desire, I noticed a small wardrobe, a dressing table with chair, a large bed, the mattress covered with a white sheet and in a corner, a small table with washbasin, water jug and towels.

I believe she gave a choice of options and how she could fulfil my desires, but now with my nakedness revealed, it was obvious that no time remained for deliberation. There was no lovemaking, no precautions, and in no time at all it was all over, culminating in her practised moans of artistic expression.

I took advantage of the washbasin, cleansing myself with the purple manganese peroxide, and dressing very quickly. Then she showed me down a back staircase to the hall, where I joined my waiting companions. Outside, the air seemed very clean and fresh, and we were all very quiet with little conversation. The *gariwallahs* were still waiting. They were well accustomed to the night-time habits of service personnel.

Back at the hostel in a blue funk, my first concern was to have a long, soapy shower whilst amid apprehension and contrition, I considered my foolhardy escapade. We had been lectured and warned about brothels time and time again and I was a victim of my own stupidity. But later, with my companions enjoying a beer, normality began to return.

Thursday, 29th April was our last day of leave in Bombay. My first waking thoughts were my previous night's stupidity and my witless action in joining this brainless escapade. During the next few days, this reckless exploit would continue to haunt me like a bad dream. However, my first act was more practical. I took another thorough shower before joining my companions for our last game of tennis. Earlier in the week we had taken a photograph of the marker and his four ball boys, and as we left, we presented each of them with a print. They were absolutely delighted.

After breakfast we went to the Back Bay baths for a swim, a last look at the seafront and I went for a haircut, which was most essential after fifteen days neglect, before returning to the hostel for a late lunch.

Most of the afternoon was taken up with packing, then we said our farewells to the staff of the Salvation Army and headed for Victoria Railway Terminus. We were in plenty of time to catch the Nagpur Express, which was just as well because when we made enquiries, it transpired that the RTO had failed to book a reservation. After a much heated debate, telephone calls and efforts to gloss over their error, the RTO managed to provide an alternative. A special coach would be attached to the next Calcutta Mail. This change created two previously unforseen problems. The Calcutta Mail was routed via Allahabad, which was much further than going via Nagpur, and there were no official rail connections on this scheduled train to get us to Ranchi. Our first concern was that we should be late back from leave and marked absent without leave AWOL. Our second worry was that assuming the journey could take an extra two days, our finances, which were already strained, would run out. Luckily, Sergeant McQuade, the senior NCO in our party of thirty-six, managed to persuade the Bombay SSO to send a message to our unit, via the 70th Divisional HQ in Ranchi.

However, we had no success at all in our efforts to obtain a supplementary payment from the field cashier's office at the SSO. We had our paybooks with us and under the circumstances a small advance would have been justified, but unfortunately our request was made too late in the day. Although we were at war, the field cashier's office kept normal office hours and the authorising officers would not be back until the next morning. Luckily we were not all without funds and Sergeant McQuade had unspent money from the President of the Regimental Institute, the PRI, allocated for purchasing unit provisions in Bombay, some of which had been unavailable. So we were able to pool our resources, while writing out numerous IOUs.

The mail train left on time and the hastily provided extra coach was comfortable with enough room for twice our number. We slept all night and awoke the next morning as we were leaving Bhusawal. Travelling north-east all day, we arrived at Allahabad just after midnight, after twice crossing the Ganges on very long railway bridges. Saturday, 1st May dawned, and at around midday our coach was detached from the express and we were shunted into a siding which appeared to be miles from anywhere. This was the rail junction of Gomoh where a branch line ran south to join the other Bombay–Calcutta route at Jamshedpur. There was only one passenger train each day and the next connection was not due until 0527 hours the next morning.

We were very hungry, short of funds and completely isolated, but half a mile away was the very small town of Gomoh. We made our way down the hill to explore the locality, and there we were in for a most welcome surprise. The inhabitants were mainly Eurasian or Anglo-Indians as most called them, the descendants of those white men who came out to work on the construction of the railways and married Indian girls.

The British who came to work in India, many of whom were young and with technical skills, had been made redundant due to the closure of the Cornish tin mines, and the completion of most of the local railway network at home. They met and subsequently married the attractive Indian women here, and eventually made permanent homes on the Indian continent. Social scales the world over, have always been tipped heavily against Eurasians. In India, their descendants could not escape the disabilities of being in an intermediate position. They were shunned by the British Raj and the Indians alike, and called 'chee chees' because of their lilting speech. They lived in limbo between the two races, forced to remain aloof in virtual isolation. Unlike the Parsees in Bombay, they lacked education and wealth. So these families became an embattled group, living around the railway centres they had helped establish, working on the railways and with postal and clerical employment. In a way they were more British than the British, remembering the past and trying to live the lives their great grandparents had enjoyed in the home country.

Gomoh was a typical example of these communities. Several of our party were invited to meals, and in the evening we were all guests at a social at the Railway Institute, a regular Saturday evening event. Obviously, they rarely met British troops in this corner of India, and they gave us a wonderful evening. Trooper Snell and his partner won the lucky waltz, which was actually the only dance of the night, then the ladies of the institute prepared us a special supper in the railway canteen. As all was free it could not have been available at a more opportune moment and we were very grateful.

We were on the move the next morning, attached to another train, and we soon arrived at Ranchi Road station and transferred our kit to the local bus that passed our camp. It was a long climb up the ghats to camp and the engine overheated twice, but we arrived eventually, in time for a very welcome meal. There was a quantity of mail which had accumulated during my absence, so having read that and answered the letter from my wife Mollie, I prepared myself for the return to camp routine in the morning.

6

Courts Martial

It was with some trepidation that I attended the first muster of the day for all those who had returned from leave. Normally, I would have considered this a waste of time, but this sick parade had rather more significance due to our 'socialising' in Bombay. We stood with our nether garments removed while the medical officer made his routine inspection. Eventually, he singled out one of the party, sending him to the 119 Field Hospital for treatment. I went back to my duties with a great sense of relief, and the clouds lifted somewhat.

I was away the next day on a divisional exercise, mainly involving our senior officers. Wireless communication was required but no troops were involved. This was a tactical exercise without troops, better known as TEWT. At my level I had no idea what it was all about; all the messages were put into cypher and it was good operator training. We were away for five days, fifty miles from Ranchi, and certainly it made a change from normal parades and duties. On the other hand it was very boring. The officers had tents and Tilley lamps and batmen to prepare them an evening meal. We slept on the ground around the wireless vehicle, heated our emergency rations and played pontoon in the evenings. It poured with rain one evening so we all huddled together in the vehicle, but there were too many of us to get a proper sleep.

Amidst all our other duties, we were pleased to hear the good news from the Middle East, and we heard on the radio on 13th May that the North African campaign had ended with the capture of 150,000 prisoners. Following this, the 21st

May was declared Tunisia Day, and we were given the day off. We went to Ranchi in the evening, the streets were decorated, mainly with leaves threaded on string and held aloft on bamboo poles very much like a clothes line, augmented by lots of bunting, flags and coloured lights.

On the fourth of June, I was obliged to march Harry Cresswell to the regimental guardroom to be placed under close-arrest. I stress the word obliged. Putting men on a charge was nothing new to me, but most NCOs would avoid making out a charge sheet unless it was absolutely necessary. Charging a man and writing out the evidence was exacting and it involved much time. Also, after over three years' service, most troopers accepted the tough discipline of army life and realised that orders were orders. King's Regulations were not unfair when properly administered, although once put on a charge, a soldier could rarely expect to be given a 'not guilty' verdict. Minor offences invariably resulted in either a loss of pay or fatigues. In camp here, being confined to barracks was not the punishment it would have been in home surroundings. Nevertheless, men were often sentenced to forty-eight days hard labour for an offence which in civilian life, even in those days, would have collected nothing more than the penalty of being bound over.

Harry Cresswell had always been an enigma, almost a masochist. He was a hard worker and a man you would choose to share a crisis with, who would stand by you in a rough house, and he would have been the first to find his feet on a desert island. Fit and strong, he would support his mates, come what may. All this was proved later, during action, but he was a rough diamond and he hated authority, especially from officers. Like Don Quixote, he tilted at windmills, without fear of the possible consequences, always treading a dangerous path. Sergeant Stringer and us NCOs understood his foibles and sometimes turned a blind eye to his initial reactions.

On this particular day, I was called to the HQ troop office, where the adjutant ordered me to find him a replacement driver to take him to Ranchi. His duty driver had been commandeered by Colonel Trotter, our CO, to go to Divisional Headquarters. Unfortunately for all concerned.

Harry Cresswell was outside the office. I had to find someone quickly and I thought he would do, so my words to him were, 'Trooper Cresswell, report to the adjutant straight away with your vehicle and take him to Ranchi.' He replied, 'Oh, not that xxxxxxx bastard.' Outside the flimsy walls of the marquee, there was no escape for either of us. His reply had been heard loud and clear. The adjutant stormed out. 'That man is a mutineer, put him in the guardroom.' Actually, it was hardly a mutiny, more a confirmation of general opinion but I did not hesitate. In the words of the army, his feet did not touch the ground, and we were on the way to the guardroom. I left Cresswell with the regimental guard commander, and went to the HQ office to make out the charge sheet with the help of the orderly room sergeant.

The War Office Manual of Military Law sounds and is most complicated. I was glad to have Hedley Chapman, the orderly room sergeant to help me. Part I classifies, under a variety of headings, the military offences for which persons subject to military law are punishable by company, regimental or court martial procedure. The charge was found in Section 9 (I): Disobeying in such a manner as to show a wilful defiance of authority, a lawful command given personally by his superior officer in the execution of his office. This disobedience may be of a trivial nature, right up to the most serious description pertaining to mutiny. Not fully understanding an order is not necessarily wilful disobedience. For instance, a soldier not understanding an order to fall in on parade is not disobedient. But there was no doubt that Cresswell's reply was deliberate and obstinate, so there could be no way out. The charge sheet read as follows:

'The accused, no. 5673908 Trooper Cresswell H., 45th Reconnaissance Regiment, a soldier of the regular forces when on active service, is charged with disobedience in a manner showing wilful defiance of authority, a lawful command given personally by his superior officer, in that he at 1630 hours on 4.6.43, when personally ordered by Corporal Sharpe P.G., Signal Troop Reconnaissance Corps, to report for duty as a driver to

Captain Booth, Adjutant, 45th Reconnaissance Corps, did say "not that xxxxxxx bastard".'

The next morning we went to the Squadron Office. Cresswell pleaded guilty, so our CO, Captain Hennings had no alternative other than to formally remand Cresswell to appear on commanding officer's orders on Monday, 7th June, at 1230 hours. The only person who seemed to enjoy the proceedings was Harry Cresswell himself, deriving delight in being the centre of attraction. In a way he was the only person who did not have to worry. All in attendance had to wear their best uniform and ensure that no mistakes were made in procedure. In fact, it was very much like being on stage in a production.

At 12.15 p.m. Cresswell had been marched to the CO's office from the guardroom. We had all lined up outside, Cresswell, one of the escorts and myself. Dead on time, the RSM appeared and brought us to attention.

'Accused, cap off,' (handed to escort). 'Accused, escort and evidence left turn. Quick march left right left right left right march to attention left right left right halt.' (All in one breath). 'Right turn, evidence and escort stand at ease.'

Captain Booth and the CO, Colonel Trotter, faced us. The charge sheet was read out by the regimental orderly sergeant. Cresswell pleaded 'not guilty' now, and refused to accept the CO's punishment, requesting a General Court Martial.

This plea caused a certain amount of consternation. Army law is complicated at the best of times, and I have no idea in fact whether the CO could have given punishment in this case. After much deliberation and debate, this request was granted and Cresswell was released on open arrest, pending court martial. This meant that he was back on duty but confined to camp, reporting to the regimental guard room twice a day, morning and evening. Back in the troop, Harry Cresswell was as cheerful as ever, with not the slightest hint of trouble, with no resentment towards myself at all. To some, he was the man of the hour, a bit of a hero.

The GCM was eventually convened on the 18th June, starting at 0930 hours and lasting one and a half hours.

Cresswell was given forty-eight days field punishment. During this time, he was mainly employed on fatigues around the camp area, including digging latrines and of course he spent his nights in the regimental guard room. Pay is not deducted in these circumstances. His meals were brought to him from the cookhouse, and overall he seemed to enjoy the whole experience. During the GCM Cresswell, standing to attention, had continually been chided by the RSM, who prodded him with his baton, telling him continually to 'stand still,' 'speak up' or 'keep quiet.'

During my early service, I had been on a charge several times and had come upon this bullying myself. In England before Dunkirk, I had had the same experience when charged for something that was not my fault, for trying to defend myself. But I got my own back at a later date, when I was definitely guilty. Marching to attention past the regimental guard room in the centre of Wakefield, a private and myself were talking. The RSM rushed across from a side street, putting the NCO in charge on open arrest for allowing us to talk! Private Sainsbury and myself were placed on close-arrest. While peeling potatoes in the cookhouse awaiting charge we were visited by the lance corporal and we hatched a plot.

My name of Sharpe was the solution. We said we had been marching to attention when Lance Corporal Maidment called out 'sharpen your pace up.' I looked towards Sainsbury who said 'Not you.' A likely story! Nevertheless, the CO gave us the benefit of the doubt and the charge was dismissed. The RSM was furious. But in the army you can never win. This time the RSM saw to that. During the next week, Lance Corporal Maidment was charged with having a dirty rifle on guard mounting and lost two week's pay as a result. Private Sainsbury was charged for not having his forage cap on at the correct angle and lost one week's pay and I was on a draft to join the newly formed Reconnaissance Corps. I think I came off best because at least I left the infantry and learned to drive!

When stationed in Ranchi, we were only about one hundred miles from the town of Jamshedpur and the railway junction of Tatanaga. Jamshedpur was at this time the largest industrial iron and steel works in the British

Commonwealth, and produced a million tons of steel a year. We had seen something of the area when we had changed trains to go on our Bombay leave.

These days we would describe the layout as a 'new town'. It had originally been established by Yamsetji Tata in the late nineteenth century, created from out of nothing in the Bihar jungle, close to the deposits of ferric oxide ore and the Jharia coalfields, and expanded by his Parsee family over the succeeding years. Now, the offshoot industries produced railway engines, lorries, armoured cars and light vehicles as well as railway lines, tin plate, cables and nails. One of the vehicles they were assembling in Tatanaga for the army, was the Tata armoured car, and these operated in the 70th Division area. Three of these vehicles had to be collected by the regiment in June and I was one of those chosen to make the journey.

In the sergeant's mess, there was talk that they had found pice coins used as washers, in some of the vehicles constructed in Tatanaga. There was of course no proof of these stories, but these coins had been used for the odd repair, when a washer was required during maintenance to any of our own vehicles.

This particular coin with a hole in the middle was only minted from 1943 until 1947, which was the year that India obtained independence. It seems the only possible reason for the hole was to save metal. During the five years the coins differed slightly, but the first pice coin minted had a diameter of ⅞ of an inch, and the hole was ⅜ of an inch across. It was struck in bronze, with the British crown, date and value on the face, written, in English, Persian and Devanagari, with a floral scroll on the reverse. It must have been very costly to produce and the first mint was one of 165,000,000 in Bombay, identified with a diamond under the date. Subsequently many millions of these coins were cast, not only in Bombay, but also in Pretoria, South Africa, where there was a round dot below the date, and in Calcutta, where it was clear below the date. Metal washers were expensive at the time, but the purchase of the pice coin required a much lower monetary outlay. Two thousand eight hundred and eighty for one pound in English currency!

112

When we had completed our training as Driver Operators in the newly formed Reconnaissance Corps, back in April 1941, we had received the addition of tradesman's pay, and this had been entered in our soldier's service book, part one, on the 10th April.

Since that early training, no effort had been made to upgrade us as operators, or even to test us to see if we still merited the extra three pence per week. Some of us had no doubt improved our Morse Code sending and receiving, but it was quite possible that many had fallen behind, especially as much of our communication had been radio telegraphy, i.e. speech, on the many exercises. Higher authority must have noticed this so it was announced in May that a three-week upgrading course would take place in addition to our other routine duties. A very large marquee was erected and classes were organised. Incorporated into this training was instruction on the newly-arrived no. 48 set, an improvement on the older no. 38 set, used for short wave radio telegraphy communication.

Regimental duties took preference during the time we were on this signal course, so nearly everyone had to miss part of the training. There is no doubt that at this time, playing at soldiers, cleaning rifles, wearing respirators, mounting guard and marching to meals were regarded as much more important than the special technical skills involved in radio communication.

The final examination took place on Monday 14th June, and was conducted by the Royal Corps of Signals personnel from the divisional HQ, so that no favouritism from internal sources could be expected. We had to complete a written paper in the morning, and in the afternoon we had to transmit and receive a number of messages. When transmitting, the key work had to be perfect and messages received written clearly and correctly on the message pads provided. My previous interest in the Morse Code, especially the long distance operating during our trip to fetch the vehicles, had given me extra useful experience in practical work, and when the results were announced on the 18th June, my grade had gone up three notches from C.III to B.III, so I was awarded a pay rise of three pence per week.

Lieutenant Tony Musselwhite had been a great source of encouragement to us during the classes, being an excellent operator and instructor. We were therefore most disconcerted when he was replaced by another officer, Lieutenant Riley, just as the sessions ended. I do not say surprised, because some of us had received background information from the grapevine. There is no doubt that Tony Musselwhite suffered because he had been 'one of the boys'.

A distinction between men and officers was seen by the army as absolutely fundamental to the maintainance of discipline. To maintain discipline in the forces, any undue familiarity between troops and officers was rigorously discouraged, and sometimes carried to excessive extremes. The fact that many officers remained aloof from the other ranks was not because they wished to do so, but because this was the rigid norm laid down by the army. Tony Musselwhite's friendly attitude did not mean that we had not respected his authority. In fact we were much more likely to follow him as a leader. But it did not concur with the rigid army rules, in that he had often met us in Ranchi for a meal at the Chinese restaurant, and he had been warned by the CO about his conduct. Matters came to a head when he was reported by the military police for repeating this 'serious offence'. There may well have been another official reason given for his transfer, but we were well aware of the real facts of the case. So we lost a popular officer who had been considered too much of a friend, and he was transferred to one of the fighting squadrons. The following year he was killed leading his men into battle, two weeks before we were flown out of Burma.

Another officer who was most popular and did everything possible for the troops was Captain Adams. As regimental sports officer, which involved extensive additional duties, he also organised classical gramophone recitals and trips to Ranchi Cathedral, when musical recitals were organised after the Sunday service. On such occasions, we NCOs and troopers went our separate ways for a meal before meeting again for the return trip. Sadly, like Tony Musselwhite, Captain Adams died in Burma. Seriously wounded in the thigh, we had to leave him behind as we had too many casualties to cope with. He wrote a note for his wife, and after a shot of morphia, he requested a loaded revolver and grenades, ready to fight to the death.

A further illustration of this unbelievable rigid army regulation on fraternising with men of different ranks occurred in September 1945. My brother Cyril was at the OCTU in Bangalore, and I managed to get a three day pass to meet him, the first time for four years. The War was over and I was a sergeant awaiting repatriation. In the High Street of Bangalore, he was reported by the military police to the commandant of the Officer Cadet Training Unit for 'fraternising with a non-commissioned officer.' He was summoned by the OCTU adjutant and in spite of explaining the special circumstances, he was instructed not to go against protocol. When he refused to comply, various threats relating to 'indiscipline' and 'un-officer-like behaviour' were made, and when these threats fell on stony ground, the bright suggestion was put forward that civilian clothes would be acceptable, and that these could be provided for him to wear when the two of us were together in public. Being by nature a bit of a 'Harry Cresswell', my brother refused this compromise on principle, so he was hauled before the OCTU commandant. After maintaining his stance and being formally threatened, that if he wanted to be commissioned, he had better step back into line, he was eventually told that 'discreet' meetings during my visit could continue.

The question as to whether this was a victory for common sense over a nonsensical army regulation, is answered by my earlier comments about not being able to beat the system. Not long after this episode, my brother was indeed commissioned, but instead of being posted to the unit of his choice, or returning to one of the Special Services units operating in the Far East, which as an ex-commando he was qualified for, he was submitted to the indignity of being commissioned into the Indian Army Ordnance Corps. He spent the remainder of his service in various store depots in India. So the system finally got its pound of flesh, but the Sharpe family honour remained untarnished. In the army then it was very much in order to have a brother officer, but not a brother who was an officer! One suspects that such attitudes have not changed much over the years.

By the middle of June, the monsoon period in Ranchi was approaching and we had several electric storms, with brilliant white multiple flashes and enormous cataracts of torrential rain. In no time at all the camp would be turned into a quagmire, and tents would be blown down by severe whirlwinds.

There had been a strong rumour for some time that we would be moving to Southern India, and this became a fact when a move to Bangalore was announced. I have no idea why we moved, but it does seem likely that the main reason was the impending monsoon. The south west monsoon brought very heavy rain in the months of July and August to Delhi, and then to Calcutta which is near Ranchi, where the rains persisted well into October. So a move to Bangalore for training would be advantageous, as the rain in the south was much heavier in May, though we would not escape the storms altogether. In the meantime, preparations proceeded apace in the camp, trenches were dug around the tents and large quantities of bricks supplied, so that we could build walls inside the tents for further protection. The weather was now hotter than ever, and the humidity made life uncomfortable.

The advance party and our vehicles left Dipitali at the beginning of July, and I was part of the main party left to tidy up. We did our best but the rain made life very difficult indeed. On Sunday, 11th July, I went in to Ranchi for the last time to the evening service in the cathedral, but I did not stay for a meal afterwards as all the eating houses had been closed due to a severe outbreak of cholera in the city. Luckily, we had been given a booster injection at the end of June when the epidemic was first suspected. Finally, two days later we packed our kitbags and decamped in Indian transport and headed for the railway junction at Bakakana. We had been at Dipitali Camp for almost nine months.

7

The Die is Cast

By now, most of us had become used to long rail journeys on Indian trains, but this next trip was certainly the worst that we had encountered. The overall journey was 1,300 miles and it lasted a full seven days. We were cooped up in third-class accommodation, and the compartments were not as spacious or airy as the military troop coaches. The weather was hot and humid, and the washing facilities were primitive, small plugless handbasins at the end of each coach. In addition the water supply ran out twice for around twenty-four hours each time. The toilets became blocked and the whole carriage stank.

Unlike the American troops who we came across parked in a siding near Tatanagar Junction soon after we started, like most British troops, we were very passive and accepted the situation with just a few grumbles. The Americans were sitting on the platform and refusing to board until toilet paper was available for the lavatories. They may have waited a long time, because the Indians themselves did not use this commodity which would have to come from the nearest US stores in India.

After the first two days, our route closely followed the eastern coast of India, and we had expansive views of the Bay of Bengal. As was usual in troop trains, we made very slow progress, giving way to all other traffic, and spending many long hours in station sidings. Our first long delay was at Kharagpur, but by the third day we had made better progress, and crossed several long bridges spanning the delta of the River Mahanadi at Cuttack. During the next few days we continued south west along the coastal strip, through Berhampur, Vishakhapatnam and the even wider estuary of the River Krishma at Beswada Junction. Beswada is now known as Vijayawada.

The weather continued to be very hot, wet and sticky, and although there was much grand scenery to appreciate, we often became bored and played cards or slept to pass the time. There was plenty of water along the coastline. The River Krishma had been dammed, not only for irrigation but also to operate a large generating plant that supplied electricity for the district. After another hundred miles, the flat paddy was replaced by miles of sandy coastline, almost desert country with large cactus bushes and palm trees lining the track. At one point we ran quite close to the sea, and with a great deal of imagination it reminded me of the railway line in England between Torquay and Paignton.

After five days of travel, we skirted the city of Madras and began the serpentine journey inland through the hills, in a westerly direction towards our destination of Bangalore. This involved a climb from sea level to over 3,000 feet in just two hundred miles. It took us a full two days. Around the half-way point of this ascent at Jalarapet Junction many of us had the wonderful opportunity of an unofficial shower under the station water tank while the engine was changed. It was our first real wash for days.

Eventually we arrived at Bangalore cantonment station at midnight. Transport was waiting to convey us to the new camp, thirty miles from the city. On arrival, we dumped our kit and lined up for a meal of the usual bully-stew, and even at 0230 hours in the morning, it tasted delicious. Our accommodation was in 'bashers', soundly constructed bamboo huts, the framework and roof of which consisted of two-inch diameter poles, lashed together with sisal ropes and thatched with very thin bamboo twigs, laid in bundles, looking very much like straw. The walls were also made of bamboo, split and woven into matting.

After a late reveille at 0800 hours the next day we spent our time sorting out our kit, reading the mail which had preceded us and finding our bearings in the camp. We also found out very quickly that the bashers leaked, so we had to spread our groundsheets over our beds and belongings. In fact, the huts were old and within the first week, the local natives rethatched them and made other repairs.

We had previously experienced the destruction that termites could cause, but we now learned another of their skills, which was to eat through the panels at the sides of the shelters without leaving any visual effect on the bamboo weave itself. As they chewed away, they left their excrement behind, which hardened like brick and left the panels looking the same, but any object leant against the wall would cause the whole side of the hut to disintegrate.

On the next day at 1500 hours, we paraded as a regiment for an important announcement by the CO, Colonel Trotter, who disclosed that we would now commence training for action with a large force, for combat against the Japanese. This prediction on 21st July must have been in response to a directive from GHQ India to keep us on our toes, because I later discovered no firm plans had by then been made to involve the 70th Division in battle.

The next morning, I was called to attend CO's orders for an interview with Colonel Trotter. The directive came out of the blue and my imagination ran riot. Actually, it was to advise me to withdraw an application for a commission, which I had submitted nine months earlier and forgotten about! Our CO was a fine soldier and I was ready to accept his advice. The only possibility of being accepted for training at OCTU would be with an infantry commission application but not one from the Royal Signals. I did not need a great deal of persuasion. In the Arakan at this time, second lieutenants were not surviving the necessary six months service before being entitled to their second pip.

We continued our day-to-day activities in much the same way during the month of August, while on the other side of the world, plans were afoot that would completely change our future. Back in England in early August 1943, Winston Churchill was preparing to leave for Quebec with his chiefs of staff on the *Queen Mary*, to attend the Quadrant Anglo-American Conference. On 4th August, Churchill had an interview with Brigadier Orde Wingate over dinner. Wingate, who had already distinguished himself in Abyssinia, now Ethiopia, and jungle fighting in Burma, had been summoned home by Churchill, in order, as he explains in volume five of his account of the Second World

War, 'to meet him and have a look at him'.

The British people had become tired of war, due to our reversal of fortune in the Far East and the continual postponement of the second front in Europe. Although Wingate's first Chindit operation had achieved minimal military success, his exploits had captured the imagination of the populace and the press release had ensured that he would become something of a national hero. Churchill was more than impressed with Wingate so he commanded him to travel to the Quadrant Conference in Canada, in order to expound his military theory to the delegates. When Wingate expressed his regret at not being able to see his wife during this short visit to Britain, Churchill arranged for her to be collected and they sailed together the following day with the military entourage on the *Queen Mary*, arriving in Halifax on 9th August.

Wingate felt encouraged to explain his plans at length to the British chiefs of staff on the voyage. At the Quadrant Conference, most of the participants became enthusiastic regarding his outline of the principles of Long Range Penetration. If anything, the Americans were very much more impressed and supportive than the British chiefs of staff. Subsequently, his ideas were accepted and the die was cast. During the conference, the details were discussed and deliberated, and signals for the required action went out to General Sir Claude Auchinleck, Commander in Chief in India. This was the first that GHQ Delhi had heard of the whole proposition, which at first was most firmly resisted. There were indeed many reasoned objections but on the 26th August, the British chiefs of staff signalled to Auchinleck, leaving him in no doubt that these orders, however unacceptable, had to be accepted.

Included in the requirements, was the specific command that the 70th Division, one of the most distinguished and successful formations of the British Army, was to be broken up and reformed as Chindit columns. This order to disband the 70th Division as a fighting unit, and transform it into Long Range Penetration columns was received with incredulity and bitter resentment by the GHQ India, and many of the top brass never forgave Wingate. He was to meet much opposition and cussedness from the beginning to the end of the ensuing campaign.

The news of the new role of the 70th Division was eventually made known to the regiment at a special parade on Tuesday 7th September, when the divisional commander, Major General Symes spoke enthusiastically about our future. We were stunned of course, almost to disbelief. Indeed we were dumbfounded. After training for two years as a mechanised unit, we were to revert to infantry, to drive the Japanese out of Burma. That day, Major General Symes hid what must have been a bitter disappointment with his enthusiasm, because unknown to us, he already knew that he would be losing his command to General Wingate, a much junior commander. The only sweetener for him could have been the chance to see some action again, after the long stagnation as commander of a reserve division in India.

Since that day nearly fifty years ago, when General Symes addressed us and gave us the outline of our future, I have had plenty of time to read and research the many articles and books written on the Second Chindit Operation. To obtain a balanced picture of Orde Wingate as a military leader they should all be read. In the political military jungle of GHQ Delhi he had many critics, but he has also been praised, his final accolade coming from Winston Churchill soon after Wingate's death. In the House of Commons in August, 1944, he said, 'There was a man of genius who might well have also become a man of destiny ....' (See Appendix 2).

When Major General Symes left the 45th Reconnaissance Regiment on 7th September, after delivering his bolt from the blue, we naturally expected an acceleration and fresh approach to our training. After all, we now had to march instead of ride, but nothing new happened. I have searched my diary for clues from that date, until we left on 13th October for our new training ground in Central Provinces. Admittedly two route marches were scheduled, the first on Monday, 27th September, was cancelled due to torrential rain, which was not a very good excuse for fighting troops, and on Thursday, 6th October, when we marched all of three miles with rifles but without any webbing, water bottles or haversacks.

In fact, life was easier at this time than ever before. We had another sports meeting and the hockey, soccer, cricket and rugby matches continued. There was more frequent evening leave to Bangalore, guard mountings, musketry training, wearing gas masks and three separate days on the firing range. These were our hardest tasks during that period.

War Office records show that the 45th Reconnaissance Corps was officially transferred to Special Force, the new designation for the second Chindit Operation, on the 16th September. However, in retrospect, the whole programme seemed designed to keep the unit in limbo, to await a change in plans. I also wondered what our CO, Colonel Trotter knew of the overall situation. (See Appendix 3).

Amongst ourselves, there was obviously much talk about our future as infantry. One evening, several of us were talking about marching and the subject of footwear cropped up. We had always found that army socks caused a problem, especially as new issues were rare and our efforts at darning led to uncomfortable ridges in the soles. One of our despatch riders, Bill Key, reckoned that no one could march without socks anyway, and in the ensuing discussion both Ray Scully and I stuck our necks out, and we bet that we could and would. We hated to be proved wrong and in spite of the odd blister, we stuck to our claim. In a couple of weeks, my feet hardened and I found it quite comfortable to manage without socks, as did several of my companions. Later in Burma, this resolve was to prove an absolute blessing, especially when continually tramping in and out of streams all day.

So we began the task of sorting out and packing all remaining stores for loading at Bangalore cantonment station. We finally left camp and boarded the troop train on Wednesday 13th October.

8

Survival of the Fittest

Just after midnight on 13th October, we pulled out of Bangalore, leaving Mysore State. After travelling all night, we breakfasted at Jelarapet junction, where three months previously, we had enjoyed the delightful platform shower. We had already descended 2,000 feet and the weather became hotter. During the early evening we reached the coast, as we skirted Madras. The suburbs and the city were in total darkness. They were experiencing a blackout, probably due to Japanese submarine activity off the coast of the Bay of Bengal.

We followed the coast through Nellore and Angole for several hundred miles, back the way we had come from Ranchi, but on Saturday 16th October, after reaching Beswada and recrossing the River Krishna, we took the branch line inland towards Warangal into Hyderabad Province, reaching Wardha early the next morning. By midday we were in Nagpur Junction, crossing the main Bombay–Calcutta line to continue our journey north. During the long wait at Nagpur, we were lucky enough to find a Salvation Army free canteen for a cup of char. The regiment had been exactly one year in India.

By mid-morning the next day, we stopped in Bhopal, and by a strange coincidence part of our divisional convoy passed overhead on the road bridge, making its way, like us, to the new training area. We travelled quite fast after leaving Bhopal, passing through Bina Junction and Talharset, and arriving at Jhansi just before midnight. But this was not quite the end of our rail journey as we stayed in a siding overnight and at around 0400 hours we were on the last leg of our 1,400 mile journey. We got off the train at a very small station called Jatpur in the early hours of 19th October, and were transported in Indian three-ton lorries to the new camp, some sixty miles east of Jhansi.

In Central Provinces, we caught the tail-end of the monsoon and it poured with rain without respite for the next two days. To make it worse, there were eighteen of us to a small bell tent, with hardly room for ourselves, let alone our kit and rifles. There were no drill parades, and we spent our time in the signals marquee, sorting out the wireless sets for handing back to the Quartermaster's stores. We were to be issued with updated versions in the new setup. In the end, we were so wet that we lit several large bonfires and were able to dry some of our clothes. In the evening, we were actually issued with a rum ration.

Sadly Friday, 22nd October marked the end of the 45th Reconnaissance Corps as we had known it for the past two and a half years. Our CO, Colonel Trotter, the Second-in-Command, Major Acland and Company Commander Major Boileau, as well as several other ranks, left the regiment without ceremony. Anyone over forty years of age was deemed too old for the coming operation. Colonel Trotter had been well respected by us all and held in high esteem. In our early days in England, soon after formation, he had circumvented rules and regulations. He went out of his way to allow married men to be billeted out with a ration allowance, whenever wives were able to visit, so that they could spend time together. I wrote in my diary 'This is the end of an era, things will never again be the same.'

On Sunday, 24th October, the regiment was reorganised into two guerilla columns later to be known as nos 45 and 54, and those of us operators who had passed the recent regrading examination packed our belongings and moved over to the brigade signals. We were still in the same brigade and would be considered for transfer to 16th Infantry Brigade Royal Corps of Signals. At this time we were told that all the brigades in Special Force were to be flown into Burma behind the Japanese lines by American Dakotas and gliders early in the new year.

Most of the personnel in 16th Brigade had served in the Middle East. We joined them, together with a group of Royal

Artillery gunners, thus making up the total number. New information circulated by the hour. Our new Commander was to be Brigadier B.E. Fergusson DSO, of the Black Watch. He had been a column commander under Wingate on the first Chindit operation. We would be split up into eight columns as follows:

2nd Battalion: The Queen's Regiment.
No. 21 and 22 columns.
2nd Battalion: The Leicestershire Regiment,
No. 17 and 71 columns.
51/69 Royal Artillery,
No. 51 and 69 columns.
45th Reconnaissance Regiment, Royal Armoured Corps,
No. 45 and 54 columns.

These column numbers were haphazard for security reasons.

We soon heard through the grapevine amongst other rumours, that we would not be flown into Burma, but instead were expected to march all the way. There was much debate as to which was the lesser of the two evils but one thing was certain, that we would have no choice. The following day, we moved over to the Royal Corps of Signals' lines, and immediately felt more cheerful. We were comfortably housed, with six to a bell tent, and immediately noticed the difference. Not only was the food much improved, but we were now amongst professional tradesmen and instead of playing soldiers on spit and polish parades, we could at last spend most of our time improving our sending and receiving of Morse Code.

Next we were given our new address for mail and we met the new officer, Captain Moon, a regular soldier from the ranks, having already done a stint of eight years abroad since 1935. He gave us an interesting and very informative talk regarding our future in the Royal Corps of Signals, and found time to talk to each of us individually. What is more, he was one of the fastest operators on the key, much better than any of us. He went on to outline the expected role of the Royal Signals in the coming operation. A sergeant operator would be in charge of each column wireless, with two further operators and an electrician. We would have four mules and four muleteers to carry our equipment. He stressed that his main objective was to ensure that over the next few weeks our operating skills were improved to match those of the Royal Corps of Signals personnel.

The next two weeks were entirely devoted to intensive signal training, transmitting and receiving messages, and the exacting procedures of the clerical work. Every other day, we had a test and our improvement was remarkable. Meanwhile, the rest of the units were training as columns, which would have a contingent of around 450 men in each. Each would be made up of four rifle company platoons, a commando platoon for demolition and booby traps, a support platoon with Vickers or Bren guns and three-inch mortars and a reconnaissance platoon who would mainly be Burmese, and I later discovered there would also be flame throwers. The column headed by the commanding officer would include among other specialists, the administration and transport officers, the intelligence, cypher, signal and medical sections.

It is safe to say that the despatch riders, transport drivers and mechanics of the regiments involved, had the biggest jolt and initial feeling of frustration, when the force was formed. The military, rightly or wrongly, decided that maintenance of vehicles was very similar to animal husbandry and the care of mules, so they became so to speak, 'saddled' with the job. Many of my friends, including Ray Scully, became muleteers.

By now, our day-to-day routine had already changed, and we were in for yet more surprises. Our respirators, which had been part and parcel of our equipment were to be handed in. That was rather satisfying because we had cursed their very existence many times, when we had to wear them for gas drill and even to carry them when on leave. We threw them on the pile without shedding a tear!

Later in the day, we handed in not only our pith helmets, but the steel ones as well. The former were no loss at all and a welcome riddance, but the latter had given us a feeling of comfort, especially in our early service on the Kent coast. Our headgear was now the Australian bush hat, and we wondered what protection, if any, it would give in the action ahead. It had a chin strap, and what we first thought were spare leather laces round the crown. After the issue we were told that they were indeed laces, but for use as tourniquets for constricting arteries and staunching the blood if we were wounded.

We were also issued with much larger packs, like the haversack used by mountaineers, because soon all our belongings would be carried by us on the march. Also all our underclothes had to be dyed a dirty green, colour 19 SCC, whatever that meant. Three steaming vats were provided and in went the vests and pants. Observing the articles that were thrown in, some were of a dubious colour, and really needed no camouflage! Luckily, the weather was now dry and in the hot sunshine our underwear soon dried out. There was now no canteen and little chance to spend our money, but we could lose it playing cards, so at the next pay parade, when I had the option, I decided to leave it in the care of the army paymaster.

On the 5th November, the first batch of no. 22 wireless sets arrived and next day we began training. They were an improved version of the no. 11 set but they looked rather flimsy. In practice however, they were excellent and gave us good service. Like the no. 11, it was a general purpose transmitter-receiver, with radio telephony and carrier wave (Morse) facilities. Built before the use of transistors, it had altogether twelve of the old type valves for its various functions. Officially, its range on carrier wave was approximately forty miles with a long thirty-four foot static aerial, but in Burma we used a different method which I will explain in detail later. On listening-watch, it used two amps per hour and on sending carrier wave, nearly five, so in operation the twelve-volt, forty-eight ampere-hour accumulators needed charging every day.

There was one major improvement in the no. 22 set, it was what the technicians called a transceiver, and this improvement over the old no. 11 set was to prove vital in long distance communication. On the old set, we had to tune in to the incoming signal on one dial and then set another dial for the outgoing transmission. Now, the two dials were locked so that once the incoming signal had been tuned in, the transmitted signal would be spot on the same radio frequency.

During the following days, training proceeded apace, involving both fresh intakes and some of our officers. Obviously my knowledge of the new set was limited, but by reading the instruction manual overnight I had not time to forget before applying my new-found knowledge.

The lightweight infantry pack no. 38 set for short wave radio telephony, had now been replaced by the no. 48, which was an improvement. It incorporated a dry battery, and in theory could be operated on the move by two men, one carrying the set on his back and the other behind, operating it. It was used for communication from column HQ to the fighting platoons. I had trained operators initially, but now the training would have to be carried out by the signallers who had not qualified to join the Royal Corps of Signals.

On the 8th November, Captain Moon, who had now been promoted to Major, called me to his office and very formally asked me to sit down and discuss the future. I had passed my signals examination and was now promoted to full sergeant in the Royal Corps of Signals. There was an additional pay rise for us as corps troops and an even higher one for me as a sergeant. More money but nowhere to spend it! In the forthcoming operation I would be in charge of a column wireless detachment, probably the sole means of communication with Brigade and Rear Brigade Headquarters. As we would work on the set as a closely knit team, I was given the chance to choose my own operators. Therefore, I chose the two best men on Morse, Denis Elkins and Eric Nightingale who had been friends and companions for a long time in the old unit. My electrician had not yet arrived. I had to make a further choice, I could go to 51, 69, 45 or 54 column. I decided to join 45 column as I knew many friends from the old Reconnaissance Corps. Better the devils you know, I thought.

We were introduced to our mules and began the experiment of loading equipment. Because of the heavy loads, we had been allocated the very large mules which came from Argentina, and were much bigger than those we had previously seen in India. The mules must have been

128

warned about us because they certainly won the first round. All that we had heard was true. They were obstinate, they could kick harder than a horse, and they were most intelligent. First of all, the muleteers affixed the saddles and tightened up the girths underneath their bellies. The mules would then manage to pull away from the load as we lifted it to attach it to the harness with the hooks provided. But after a while, the mules realised that they had a job to do and settled down to the job on hand. Silence was essential in jungle travel and all the mules that we came upon in Special Force had been 'de-brayed' by having their vocal chords cut under anaesthetic.

Very soon, we realised how important muleteers were, and that animal husbandry was indeed very much akin to vehicle maintenance. Even the hardiest mule could quickly be reduced to immobility by carelessness. The muleteers had to ensure that the webbing girths were correctly fitted, checking periodically for slackness, that the buckles did not chafe and that the specially constructed saddles for the loads were clean, before being placed in position. They also had to check that the bits and harnesses were not causing damage to the gums or teeth.

Any failure to check quickly caused sores and galls and could put the mule out of use as a means of transport. The muleteers fed, watered and groomed their charges and as time went on, we realised what wonderful creatures mules were, much more companionable than three-ton lorries. In fact, mules and men worked together as a team, and often became inseparable. At this time none of our equipment for the operation had arrived, for instance we had not yet received either special containers for carrying petrol, nor the charging unit nor the special panniers for carrying the signal message pads.

The mules had specially adapted carriers for the unusual loads.

Mule no. 1: The no. 22 set on one side.
            Spare set to balance on the other.
Mule no. 2: The battery charging unit (chorehorse).
            Two petrol cans (when a two gallon tank was empty we filled it with water to balance the load).

Mule no. 3:   48 amp hour battery on each side.
Mule no. 4:   Pannier on each side.
                These panniers were made of thick solid leather. 3ft x 1ft x 1ft.

The loads varied in weight so we rotated the loads after every stop. Officially the panniers carried the electrician's kit, oil for the charging unit, water and acid for the batteries. Auxiliary equipment for the no. 22 set, including earphones, keys for sending, aerial, rope and spare copper wire, message pads, pencils, operating light for night work and a groundsheet. The latter was essential in heavy rain, Not only to protect the set but to ensure that the messages we wrote out were legible. Unofficially, they carried a few comforts, which was especially useful when one of my signal team had health problems. A blanket in the pannier instead of in the back-pack was a great help. With experience, we became expert on balancing the loads.

Before we had even started on our first big exercise with the mules I had lost one member of my original detachment. On Friday, 12th November, Denis Elkins, who in spite of being an excellent cricketer and soccer player, discovered that he had varicose veins, went sick and was excused marching. So he was sidelined to Rear Brigade Signals for the coming campaign, and a newcomer, Bill Quinn took his place.

During the following weekend, I went swimming, played the organ for the 9 a.m. church service, checked my new equipment and put strips of 'sorbo' rubber inder my big haversack shoulder straps. Monday morning dawned and my section reported to 45 Column for our first exercise and a taste of the task ahead.

We took enough rations and kit for the next four days of initiation into living rough and sleeping in the open, exposed to the weather, the jungle and the mosquitoes. My diary on the 17th November made interesting reading: 'Up at 4 a.m., loaded mules, shouldered packs and rifles and marched two hours in the dark before breakfast. Off again at 0700 hours, weight of pack real purgatory, and all I can see, now it is light, is the backside of one of our mules and the scrub and bamboo each side. This is already the hardest day of my life. Column halt from 1200 to 1500 hours, mules unloaded. Contacted Brigade Signals and passed messages while most of those around us had a sleep. Then off again until 1800 hours. Unloaded mules for night. Passed more messages all in cypher. Completely shagged out but writing up diary.'

From now on, exercises became monotonous and tiring, to say the least. Generally, it was a long trek behind the same mule for hours on end, and one had plenty of time for reflection. The reason that we usually marched for two hours before breakfast or even a cup of tea, was that Wingate considered marching was easier in the early morning when the cool was too precious to waste. We certainly got used to the routine, and enjoyed the eventual breakfast break.

The shape of our future offensive now began to appear. We began our training by marching for fifty minutes before taking a ten minute break, but soon it became established that we marched for a full hour before the halt. We now also realised that we would have a harder job than many on the columns. The three-hour breather in the middle of the day and the bivouacs at night would be working time for us. We sometimes worked well into the night, when atmospherics and interference from other radio channels made communication almost impossible. Also, maybe surprisingly, we really did not get to know our muleteers very well, and spent little time with them. On the column march, we were just behind or just in front of the mules and their handlers, but on arrival we were separated by bivouac routine.

The four mules would be unloaded in line, and once unloaded they would be led away by the muleteers to the designated area for supervision by the column transport officer. In a later account, I read that the handlers were the only members of the column who were not expected to unload the mules. Whether it was expected or not, our lads always helped, maybe so that they could get away sooner.

When we finished our first training march, we arrived at a new camp. Everything we had left behind had been transported by road. This was to be the new Brigade HQ. We were on a hilltop overlooking the River Ken and the Gongau Dam. It was roughly 100 miles from Jhansi in a south-easterly direction. This part of Central Provinces was really beautiful country, with marvellous views across the dam, and the river which wended its way through the valley. The thick scrub and bamboo forest around was the nearest thing in India to the rain forests of Northern Burma.

After a short break here, we were off again for three more days when we had our first practice supply drop. The site had been chosen by the brigade commander to train the column in collecting supplies after a drop. This was our first 'stage performance' in sending actual messages to obtain rations for a whole column. We already knew that all the supplies we would need in Burma, such as food, equipment, clothing, fodder and ammunition, or in fact replacements of any kind, would have to be supplied from the rear base in India and dropped by parachute at supply drops.

In order to reduce paperwork and speed up the whole operation, the quartermaster's administrative staff at Rear HQ had produced a photostated booklet in code, which was issued to all columns and put in the charge of the column administration officer. This booklet listed pretty well all our possible needs, from boots to communion wine, under the appropriate headings. Against each single item there was a four-figure code number. Included in the coded message, of course, were details of where and when the column would prepare the dropping zone.

There was also a code number for what was called a standard drop. This covered the basic needs of a column for five days; mainly food and fodder. Extras could always be added to the basic request, which was based on a column strength of 450 men. Having sent this message code named a 'QQ' to base, we would await the reply. The acknowledgement of the request giving confirmation would be the signal for preparations to be made for the drop. This return signal was known as a 'QK'.

The site for the supply drop would have been pre-selected before the request left the column. Very often, the site had to be chosen from a study of the ground as shown on the map, probably miles away. Ideally an open space, like paddy or thin scrub would be chosen. It needed to be at least a quarter of a mile in length, which in practice was very often hard to find and as we experienced, a great deal of the supplies were lost. Indeed, some missed the area altogether and many parachutes were caught up in trees, when either time or inaccessibility precluded any recovery before having to be on our way. There must have been times during the coming operation when the Naga and Kachin tribes thought it was manna from heaven!

It was also standard practice and economical to drop some items like fodder for the mules, boots and clothing without a parachute, and consequently there were casualties. To assist the planes, wood fires in the shape of a letter L were prepared and lit when the planes were identified. Detailed squads with mules formed the recovery party, and they would go into action as soon as the last plane had left. Supplies would be collected and taken back, and sorted in a central dump for distribution to the column. From this point on, we would now be called Special Force or the 3rd Indian Infantry Division. The reformed division now consisted of six brigades, of which ours was code-named Enterprise. Actually, there was not one Indian unit in the whole new division, unless one included the Gurkhas of Nepal who are Mongolian by race, and who are by tradition professional soldiers, though Hindu by religion. Possibly it could be that this title of 3rd Indian Infantry Division was another sly tilt at Wingate by the planners in GHQ India. They knew that he had no faith at all in Indian Regiments. He had refused the help of an Indian parachute brigade, and even the use of the best muleteers, the Punjabi Muslims of the Indian Army.

There is no doubt that one of the alternative proposals, mooted tentatively in Cairo at the Sextant Conference was for a parachute brigade to be flown in to capture Indaw, to reinforce the Special Force Operation, and that this plan had become anathema to Wingate. In GHQ Delhi, Wingate had acquired the surreptitious nickname of Tarzan, and knowing his fixation, they called the project 'Tarzan'. This concept was one of many that never left the planning stage.

Day by day, our training became harder. Contrary to popular belief we had no volunteers from the rank and file, and very few amongst the officers. Those officers that did step forward had either been on the first operation and promoted, or they had been summoned by Wingate or simply by the call for adventure. The bulk of the infantry were from British regiments, formally part of the 70th Division. The wastage was high, and evolved through a process of elimination. It became very apparent that many troops had been passed A1, when in fact they had only been given a cursory examination, to swell the ranks and make up the numbers required for wartime service. All officers and troops over forty years of age were automatically excluded and were quickly joined by those who had any problems at all in marching. These soldiers were all left behind in India. I certainly got the feeling at this time that any excuse would do, and many went sick in the hope of unearthing bygone ailments. Now that we were close to action, many, like the Earl of Warwick in Shakespeare's Henry VI were aware that 'Rumour doth double, like the voice, and echo, the number of the feared.'

As I have said before, we were now approaching the time when we would have no base at all, and all we needed would be carried on our persons. The list of items was long, and we did in fact start off with all the items listed:

Dark green shirt.

Dark green slacks (Shorts were out for obvious reasons).

Short puttees (Very necessary, especially to combat leeches).

Socks, three pairs (Now quite unnecessary for me).

Pants, dark green. Two pairs.

Vests, dark green. Two pairs.

Housewife. (Green darning wool and thread. 5 Needles. Thimble. Green Plastic Buttons).

Boots (Renewed later.)

Army groundsheet, dark brown.

Lightweight American blanket, dark green.

Large haversack and back fitting, green.

Water bottle, dark khaki.

Mess tins, aluminium.

Green mug.

First Field Dressing. (Bandages. Gauze.)

Webbing belt, green (Plus attachment and straps for bottle and pouches.)

Pouches for ammunition, two (containing 25 rounds and two grenades).

Bush hat (Australian Type, chin strap and spare boot laces).

Rifle (No. 9989) or sten Gun.
Washing and shaving kit, toothbrush.
Compass. (Officers and sergeants only).
Rations (30lbs maximum.)

Anything extra was a matter of choice! The total weight of the baggage when we started was quite 75lbs. Other items were issued, such as 'panic map' and silver rupees.

At the end of November, we had another five-day exercise, similar to those we had previously been on. We brought wireless sets, full kit and rations for the five days. This ration was an experiment, provided by the American forces. We only had five packs to last the exercise, and they were initially meant as a ration for paratroops on landing. To be fair, we also carried tea, powdered milk and five small packets of army biscuits. Each meal was in a thin cardboard container labelled 'Food Packet Individual Assault 1A'. Inside there were two tins two inches deep and three inches in diameter and a small package. The first tin contained 'B Unit Crackers Cookie' and the second contained 'beef and pork loaf' which weighed six ounces. The first tin was manufactured by the Carr Consolidated Biscuit Company in Chicago and the latter by Otoe Food Products in Nebraska. The accessory packet contained cigarettes, matches, candy, chewing gum, coffee, sugar, water purification tablets, a plastic spoon, a miniature can opener and of course, being American, toilet paper.

On this exercise, we also practised for the first time the method used to break track for security reasons, as we marched along in single file. A whistle blew to halt the column and everyone turned left or right through ninety degrees, according to instruction, and then at the next command, they left the track into the jungle for five minutes. Then, at the sound of the next whistle, we turned and again, fell into single file once again following the man or mule in front. This ensured that the previous track had been lost, and that there would be no link with the new one. This procedure was most essential, when we left the track at the end of the day to form our nightly bivouac.

Training, of course, is often rather different from the real thing. This precaution was executed much more easily in the scrub and woodlands of Central Provinces, than it could be in the almost impenetrable jungle of Northern Burma.

On 6th December, while we were back in camp, resting between training, we heard that a tragedy had hit the mortar platoon of our sister column, the 54th, when five men were drowned in the Gangou Dam. One of the officers had commandeered a couple of flat-bottomed punts to practise landing attacks with mortars, but things went very wrong. Maybe the boats leaked or were wrongly loaded, but one boat overturned well out in the lake. Strangely, all the drowned men were good swimmers who had probably tried to help those who were unable to cling to the half submerged craft.

This accident was a great shock. I had recently played rugby football for the old regiment with one of the men, Lance Corporal Pugh, and although we were on active service, deaths like these were not expected in the comparative safety of friendly soil. The first body was recovered almost at once and the funeral service arranged for the next day. There would be full military honours and the Brigade Padre asked me to play for the service at the military cemetery in Nowgong.

I had not known this particular soldier who had died, but his name was Trooper Egbers. The chaplain conducted the service at the graveside and I played two hymns, *Rock of Ages* and *Abide with Me*, on the small portable harmonium. There was a salute of twenty rifles and a bugler played 'the last post.' It was a sad but fitting goodbye which I still remember vividly, although it is over fifty years ago. The other four men whose burials I did not attend, were Troopers J. Fleming, F.W. Lord, F.J. O'Brien and Lance Corporal Pugh.

Out on the exercise the following day, we witnessed another supply drop on another column, and as we were not involved this was a welcome respite. We then marched eight miles with full kit to Brigade HQ for a demonstration of Direct Air Support (DAS). The idea was that the RAF wireless detachment marching with the column, could call up Rear Brigade and ask for direct air support against the Japanese forces in the area.

When the planes arrived, the attack could be directed by smoke bombs, or by short-wave radio instructions from the ground. We sat on the gently sloping hillside looking down

Dominion Monarch (Shaw Savill line).
Service: London and Southampton to Las Palmas, Cape Town, Fremantle, Melbourne, Sydney, Wellington and return, three-month round trips. Commissioned February 1939. Made record passage from London to Fremantle in 23 days. 17 hours.
Reproduced by kind permission of the National Maritime Museum, London.

Signal Troop. 45th Reconnaissance Corps, India 1942.

Back row : Troopers Strange, Gilborn, Hubbard, Cresswell, Griffiths, Rogers, Upton.

2nd row : Troopers Snell, Powell, Capel, Hartley, Moffat, King, Nightingale, Bell.

3rd row : Troopers Tibbles, Hyde, Brown, Key, Gale, Gillian, Bell, Birket.

4th row : Trooper Brockhurst, L/C Popham, Sgt. Hocken, Sqd. S/M Channon, Lt. A.D.H. Musselwhite, Sgt. Stringer, Cpl. Sharpe, Cpl. Scully, Trooper Farrimond.

Front row: Troopers Shales, Slade, Gummer, Towell, Bennet, Wooley, Jarvis.

The author, *Charwallah* Ali, Trooper Farrimond.

Ray Scully, the author.

Airgraphs could be forwarded to: U.K., Eire, Canada, Newfoundland, Australia, New Zealand, Fiji, New Hebrides, Tonga, Gibraltar, British West Africa (Nigeria, Gold Coast, Sierra Leone, Gambia), R.N.A.F., C.M.F., M.E.F., and British forces in Iceland. Cost was three annas. Each airgraph had to be unit censored before despatch.

The author in the hills near Ranchi, October 1942.

Watermanship course with Royal Engineers of 70th Division at RATU, November 1942.

Dipitali camp, Ranchi, November 1942. Road building by local villagers.

DRIVING VEHICLES ACROSS INDIA FROM BOMBAY TO RANCHI,
NOVEMBER – DECEMBER 1942.

Typical main road – hardcore, stone and sand surface.

Camel train resting.

Performing bear and attendant. They shared a tin of our bully beef.

Performing monkeys.

Elephant transport.

Sasaram, Sher Shah's mausoleum.

DRIVING VEHICLES ACROSS INDIA FROM BOMBAY TO RANCHI
NOVEMBER – DECEMBER 1942

Cawmpore, Christmas Day. Cresswell on left next to Sgt. Chapman. Author in turret.

Entrance to Allahabad city. Route taken in error. Photograph taken before we turned back as city banned due to riots.

Dufferin Bridge over Ganges at Benares, vehicles crossing. Interesting milepost at bottom right hand corner. Calcutta 418, Delhi 467, Karamnasa 25, Sasaram 69.

The author in Humber wireless truck, 'Harmonic'. March 1943.

Thatched shelters built by Indian villagers. Three of them took less than a day and they charged one half rupee (roughly 7½p).

LEAVE IN BOMBAY APRIL 1943

Train to Bombay. Trooper Towell, the author, Trooper Nightingale. Note *chagulls* hanging from door. Slow evaporation cooled the water.

Approach to Victoria terminus, Bombay. Beggars all with only one arm.

Y.W.C.A. tennis courts, Bombay. Marker and *chokras.*

Victoria railway terminus, Bombay.

Breach Candy.

Malabar Hill,
Bombay.

Back Bay, Bombay.
The author and Ray
Scully with naked
Indian urchins.

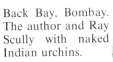

Traffic policeman. White umbrella to reflect sun. *Chaplis* on feet. Most Indians walked barefoot unless Europeanised.

Churchgate reclamation. The Eros cinema, which showed mostly American and English films.

Meeting with my brother, Cyril. I wore 'civvies' as officers were not allowed to be seen out in the town socialising with other ranks.

Lt. A.D.H. Musselwhite, in happier days training in India. An excellent officer killed in action 18 April 1944.

Athletics track in India. Not so good on the outside lane!!!

Pice coin used extensively as a very cheap washer.

The author training in Central Provinces just before March. From Ledo Road to 'Aberdeen'.

Chindit shoulder badge. The name was derived from the Burmese *chinthi* or *kyinthe,* the mythical animal, half lion, half gryphon, that guards the Buddhist temples. The name thus signifies guardianship of the pagodas and the Chindit badge consists of a *kyinthe* and a pagoda, gold on a blue background.

Refuelling L5 light planes, 40 gallon drums in foreground. These planes evacuated wounded from temporary airstrips to be flown back to India from the 'Aberdeen' runway.

Casualties. Two C47 transport dakotas, one American Army Airforce, one R.A.F., cleared to edge of airstrip. Ammunition boxes in foreground.

Sikorsky R-4 helicopters under test in America before delivery to Europe. These were the first helicopters to be successfully used under combat conditions in Burma.

45th Column Signals and Cypher personnel
Back row: Bert Fennell (Bristol) Operator R.C.S., Bob Aplin (Somerset) Cypher, Hedley Chapman (Yeovil) i/c Cyphers, Bill Warbutton (Manchester) Electrician R.C.S.
Front row: The author (Bath) Operator i/c Section R.C.S., Bill Webb (Somerset) Cypher, 'Buck' Buchanon (Northumberland) Operator R.C.S.

Four members of Rear Brigade Signals and two muleteers.
Back row: Sgt. Stringer, Dennis Elkins, George Bell (all R.C.S.)
Front row: Wilf Rogers (R.C.S.), Harry Foreman, Bill Farmer (both muleteers).

on a large flat area of paddy, behind which in a real situation, the enemy would be dug in. To the left was Column 17 of the Leicesters, complete with a ground to air detachment from the RAF. Then, right on time, eight Vengeance dive-bombers circled overhead and dive-bombed the target. Explosions erupted roughly in the spot we had expected, though I thought rather too close to the friendly troops for comfort. We were told it had been a successful exercise.

Much later, I learned that these planes were from 84 Squadron based at the airfield in Gwalior. They were the only British aircraft in India with sufficient range, that would be suitable for the coming Burma operation. Luckily, Wingate was assured of the support of the American No. 1 Air Commando under Colonel Cochrane. This had been agreed at the Quadrant Conference. The B25 Mitchell bombers and the P51 Mustangs had a far greater range than the Vengeance dive-bombers, so they became the spearhead of the highly successful close support dive-bombing during the 1944 Chindit Campaign.

Training now proceeded apace, and those who did not fall by the wayside were fitter than they had ever been before. Those who persevered had what is now known in slang as 'bottle', and had resisted the temptation of reporting sick in the hope of a soft job in Rear Brigade Headquarters. Make no mistake, none of us enjoyed the prospect of the physical hardships and the dangers ahead. We were now sleeping on the ground without any mosquito net protection so we were given a course of mepacrine tablets, three a day for five days every three weeks. According to the column pundits, the tablets were liable to give a yellow tinge to the skin, and inhibit sexual drive. My skin was not affected, and as for sexual power, chance would have been a fine thing!

Our activities now included crossing the River Ken representing the Chindwin in Burma. There was no let up in our marching with full kit. We continued to move off before dawn, covering the ground for two hours before breakfast and halting for three hours at midday. We were now sending and receiving messages at well over twenty words per minute. Rations varied, but we had begun to improvise. One of our concoctions we called 'burgoo', a mixture of water, powdered milk and biscuits. The flavouring varied, we used sugar, cocoa, soup powder or bully beef to give it a varied taste.

We actually crossed the River Ken in three different ways during the various exercises. Twice we waded across up to our middles, holding our weapons above our heads, the mules retaining their loads and crossing without protest. It was planned for us to arrive for the midday break, so we would be able to strip and dry our clothes in the warm sunshine on the other side. Both times we lit fires under the shelter of trees, it was not a security risk, because in Burma the natives lit fires all the time, so that rising smoke, within reason, was in order.

We also crossed three times, stripping to our underclothes and floating our belongings as we had learned on our watermanship training back in Ranchi. We built rafts of bamboo to float over the equipment but it took rather longer than we had planned. Some of the mules in the column were a problem but once one was persuaded, in most cases the rest followed like sheep. Luckily with a column of over four hundred men there was always help and experience at hand.

Finally, just once, we crossed in comfort in flat collapsible assault boats with outboard motors. As we only had three for a whole column and equipment it took just as long, but we enjoyed the luxury. The mules again went over under their own steam, several being held at the rear of the boats by their bridles. Although we were not told details of our future role at this stage, there was now a very strong rumour that we would not be flown into Burma like the rest of the brigades, but that our brigade under Brigadier Fergusson would march in and cross the River Chindwin.

Out on yet another march, we saw a demonstration of the American No. 1 Air Commando light plane. This was called an L5, which had originally been manufactured for use as an artillery spotting plane in the American Army. It was very small with short clipped wings held to the body of the plane by struts, very much the same as a bicycle frame. The struts continued down like a figure X to the bottom of which the small landing wheels were affixed. This biplane had a small squat propeller, and it looked like a Heath Robinson construction. But it proved a life saver in the coming campaign, saving hundreds of lives when casualties built up in the jungle operations. Flimsy as they looked, they were more than tough, and could land and take off on a very short landing strip. Furthermore, they could negotiate very bumpy ground hastily flattened out of paddy. In fact, during the demonstration, a genuine call came from one of the columns for help with a seriously injured man who had been kicked by his mule. A landing strip was hastily prepared, the plane flew off and we later heard that he was in a military hospital within an hour of the call.

Back with the Royal Signals at Brigade HQ, we spent 24th, 25th and 26th December in camp at the Gangau Dam. There was a midnight service in the mess tent early on Christmas Day, and communion at 0900 hours in the morning. Later, we had an excellent Christmas dinner and a free bottle of beer, and we made the best of the break. There was a feeling of expectancy in the air, that it would not be long before we left for Burma.

During the afternoon, we released some of our pent up energy in a game of soccer between the tents. Everyone joined in from time to time, including some of our officers, the ball was often picked up and at one period something like fifty a side joined in. As there were no goalposts, the direction of play was rather vague. During the late afternoon, another of the American L5 planes landed, and word soon spread around that it had brought General Wingate on a visit. He went straight to the officers' mess and we did not see him. The operators at Brigade Signals had sent out a message to recall our Brigadier, who had been visiting each column in turn to talk briefly about the coming action. Brigadier Fergusson then arrived in another light plane half an hour later to discuss plans with Wingate. When we returned to 45 Column on the 27th December, Brigadier Fergusson in a short talk confirmed that it had been decided that the Brigade would in fact march into Burma from somewhere in Assam.

In early January, both my operators went sick and were pronounced unfit. Bill Quinn had succumbed to the rigours of training and was pronounced anaemic, and Eric Nightingale had been diagnosed by the medics to be suffering from flat feet. Their replacements were men of a different breed, like all Royal Corps of Signals who had seen action before.

Their names were 'Buck' Buchanan and Bert Fennell. They were both first class wireless operators.

Buck was a tough short wiry Scotsman from Glasgow, hard to rouse in the pre-dawn morning starts, but tireless when static and radio interference kept us working well into the night. Bert had a dry sense of humour, and came from the village of Easton-in-Gordano between Bristol and Clevedon in Somerset. The name of the village was new to us and at first we thought he was making up the whole story. The final arrival was Bill Warbutton, my electrician, a Mancunian, very quiet, and if anything rather a pessimist. We quickly settled down as a team and a harmonious and compatible existence developed. This was just as well, as thrown together, we were to experience and share the coming hardships in a closely knit companionship.

An RAF wireless detchment joined the column at this time, operating on an RAF set no. 1086, which was very cumbersome and was nicknamed the 'barrel organ'. They were answerable to Rear Air Base in Sylet, India, for calling for air support and for directing close support bombing. Although we sent our operational messages back to Rear Brigade Special Force at Imphal, when communications built up, it was possible for them to send on some of the traffic for re-routing. We were not able to work together for security reasons. The loss of one set would have been a calamity, the loss of both methods of contact with the base in India would have meant complete isolation. Nevertheless, in training we became firm friends with the RAF personnel, Sergeants Bill Bouverie and John Hircock.

Lord Louis Mountbatten, now Supreme Allied Commander, South East Asia, arrived from Saugor with General Wingate on 12th January, to visit 16th Infantry Brigade. He visited each column in turn and after two hours, he eventually drove up to our column in an American Jeep. Standing on the bonnet, he spoke for ten minutes without any amplification, but in a semi-circle, we had no difficulty in hearing every word. 'The war was going well, the Middle East was won and soon a second front would be launched to free Europe from its bondage. Ours was to be the final drive to clear the Japanese from Burma.'

This speech confirmed, if confirmation were needed, that we had reached the point of no return, we were ready to go. Before our last exercise manoeuvre, we made our final preparations for the imminent encounter with the Japanese.

During this final exercise, we were given the chance to write letters for collection the following day. It was explained that due to the operation we were to take part in, almost certainly behind the Japanese lines, there would be long delays before mail could be collected for despatch, but we were told to ask those at home to continue to write letters, which would be dropped to us regularly by parachute when we had our supply drops.

To allay to some extent the fears of our loved ones at home, a special airgraphed letter card would be sent to our next of kin from Rear Brigade in India every month stating that 'Your son, husband or other, is fit and well but owing to operational reasons, will be unable to write as usual.' It also requested that they should continue writing to us as before. I also read afterwards, that every man was given the opportunity to make a list of birthday and anniversary dates so that a special telegram could be sent at the appropriate time. We were certainly not given this chance in 45 Column, and I fancy it was an invention by an over enthusiastic journalist. Sending these special letters once a month was a marvellous idea in theory.

If you normally wrote home regularly and eventually came out safe and sound, then no harm was done. However, due to the type of guerrilla warfare we were engaged in, casualty figures were often delayed and lists could be incorrect. A column might have to disperse, and it could be weeks before the stragglers could be accounted for. Added to this, we would often be out of communication with Rear Brigade in India for days on end. So in some cases, the letter card would continue to arrive after the man was injured, missing or even killed in action. Furthermore, quite a number of the men I knew hardly ever wrote letters. It must have been quite a surprise when their nearest and dearest received a regular monthly letter card.

141

Later in the day all ranks were issued with a bright orange piece of silk, measuring about four square feet. On one side was a map of North Burma, and on the reverse most of Central Burma, both printed in black. The original had been produced in France and the references (legends) were in French and English. It had been heliozincographed at the Survey of India offices onto the silk. I was never able to find out the story of its origin. We were informed that it had two uses. Firstly, several laid out in the shape of a letter L could be used as an emergency guide for planes, either landing to pick up casualties, or making a supply drop. Secondly, troops lost, cut off or stranded in battle, could use it to find a way back to a previously agreed rendezvous or friendly territory.

The square was known as a 'panic map' and most troops wore it as a neckerchief. After a few days, I folded mine up and stored it in the bottom of my pack. It survived to become a souvenir. Worn around the neck, the material soon became grimy due to the elements, perspiration and handling, so it quickly became quite unreadable. Even in mint condition, it would not have been an ideal aid. The scale was very small, no contours were shown and without knowledge of Burmese, Naga, Kachin or other dialects, progress in this unfriendly country would have been most difficult. This silk map was definitely a boost to morale at the time of issue. However, I never experienced its use at a supply drop, or heard of it being used to aid escape to friendly territory. Admittedly, my observation is limited to my stint with one column in a vast force, and there may well have been instances when this 'panic map' was used to guide planes to a supply drop, or to save lives.

Our final exercise ended on 24th January, when we reached our last bivouac in India. Since leaving the Gangau Dam, the pattern of our training had varied little. Marching for long distances with heavy packs had now become almost second nature. We loaded and unloaded the mules with few problems, radio communication with Brigade HQ had become routine and my squad worked as a team. However, it was with enormous relief that we shed our packs to enjoy a few days rest before beginning the long train journey to Burma.

Rations during this spell had been very basic and we were continually hungry, so it was with great elation that we noticed the splendour of the mobile field kitchen at the camp. For the next few days we luxuriated in cooked meals of fried bread, baked beans and bully stew which had never tasted better. Some of the columns had already left when we arrived, and the following day all the mules, their loads and the muleteers, left us to go ahead by special mule train to the starting point in Northern Burma. Apparently as the brigade was already behind schedule, to save time it had been decided that the order of march in Burma would be governed by the arrival here from the last exercise. Columns 21 and 22 of the Queen's Regiment, columns 17 and 71 of the Leicestershire Regiment and columns 51 and 69 of the 51/69 Field Regiment RA had already left. Brigade Head-quarters's personnel left, while we were in the camp resting. They made up quite a small party of around one hundred, consisting of a number of administrative officers including Major Moon, who would be serving in Burma.

Our turn to board the train came on Friday, 28th January, which left only our sister column number 54 to follow. We shouldered our packs and arms, and marched the short distance to the railway siding at Teharka station, which was twenty-five miles east of Jhansi. Once the last two columns had left, Rear Brigade with their transport and field kitchens would pack up and make the long road journey to rear base at Imphal.

We now experienced yet another six days of travel by train, this time in a more sombre mood. The atmosphere was tense, an intangible cloak of expectancy hanging over us. We were strangely subdued, with inner thoughts of the future ahead. Once again we journeyed through Allahabad and Benares, before the train branched north east through Patna, Kalihar and Rangpur. Then we went along the northern valley of the River Brahmaputra, below the distant high mountains bordering Bhutan. At Rangia we changed coaches for the narrow gauge railway which continued this side of the river. The main line turned to cross the Brahmaputra at Gauhati. This was the major rail route for supplies maintaining the needs of the British, American and Chinese troops fighting in the very far north of Burma, which is probably one of the reasons we were re-routed.

We travelled two hundred miles with the towering mountains of North Assam on our left, beyond which were the frontiers, at between 14,000 and 22,000 feet, of Tibet and China.

On the morning of Wednesday, 2nd February, we reached the small station of Pathalipani, where American Studebaker lorries were waiting to transport us the forty miles to the ferry crossing opposite Dibrugarh. The Brahmaputra was still very wide here, despite being five hundred miles from the Bay of Bengal. We crossed the river in the flat-bottomed ferry boats, skirting the massive sandbanks and evading the river traffic in the main channel. On the other side, we marched to the railhead in Dibrugarh and scrambled into the coaches awaiting us. It had been a long and tiring journey which, with all the changes, had seemed endless, but at last we arrived at Ledo and found ourselves in a siding, completely enveloped in the surrounding jungle.

The army objective was to keep this massive troop movement secret, and from now on we would only move forward in the dark. We only had our packs and equipment plus arms to worry about, so we were soon off the train and marching half a mile through one foot-high undergrowth and thick jungle to some old native huts. We lay down here to await the night, as the rain poured down.

We now found that we had become victims of the leeches which abounded in the damp scrub. We were soon hard at work removing these blood sucking worms, but as it was our first experience, our efforts were not very scientific. As a result, some of the troops looked as if they had just come off a battlefield. Later we soon learned that a dab of salt or a lighted match end would ensure that they let go without damage. We soon realised that as we walked, even on a short journey, our boots and puttees became covered in leeches, which in some cases would enter through the laceholes in our boots. Later these were the least of our problems, but some suffered more than others.

No meal was provided and we had run out of rations so we were cold, wet and miserable. This was the jungle that we had read about or seen in films, but which we had not experienced. Tall trees towered above solid bamboo thickets, thick elephant grass, banana plants and huge ferns, all seemingly bound together with a network of creepers which hung down from the trees in a solid mass.

Just after midnight, we received the order to march which came as a relief. The rain still came down and we felt cold, though the weather was quite muggy as we footslogged back to the siding. There was an overall smell of damp sodden rotting vegetation everywhere. A fleet of giant American lorries waited in the siding. The canvas coverings over the chassis were supported by curved stanchions, which made them look like the old covered wagons seen in American Westerns. We stowed our kit and clambered aboard, thirty men to a vehicle, and as we left the siding we noticed what appeared to be masses of stores covered with tarpaulins.

The convoy was soon on the road leading to our concentration area, the engines grinding as the wheels ploughed through the deep mud on the road.

We had a long journey ahead, not so much because of the fifty mile journey to Tagap Ga at the foot of the Patkai Mountains, our starting point for the march, but because of the climb and the viscid mud on the road. American engineers had been building the Ledo Road through the Naga Hills since early 1943. They had ultramodern road-making machinery shipped from the USA. It was a wonderful feat of engineering but needed constant maintenance due to the weather and the constant traffic.

The highway had been cut in a deep furrow through the jungle, rising and falling like a switchback. It needed thousands of tons of rock, rubble, and specially kilned bricks to form a base, and innumerable tree trunks laid and lashed crisscross, to form bridges and platforms over the myriad streams and ravines. It was not tarred and the surface was always deep in mud. As previously recorded, we travelled by night for security reasons so that the assemblage of this vast army of almost 4,000 troops would be a complete surprise to the Japanese. Our convoy slowly clawed its way up the rising and falling gradients, the chains on the wheels gripping the solid surface beneath the mud and leaving deep channels. We passed gangs of workers, toiling under suspended arc lamps, as they carried out repairs, taking advantage of the lull in overnight traffic.

Chinese and Negro labourers formed the bulk of the work force. We noticed several of their large camps; the huts set in open spaces carved out of the jungle and a couple of rough hewn ranch-style eating houses with illuminated facias. These had been established as restaurants by the enterprising and omnipresent Chinese.

This transitory journey was depressing, and it instilled a feeling of hopelessness. Like ships that pass in the night, we would soon be worlds apart from these artisans. Hungry, cold, damp, stiff and tired, with the future uncertain, we would have gladly opted to change places with these workers, and slaved away as happy labourers.

Early on the journey, caution regarding the chance of air-attack, seemed to be ignored, but as the lorries neared the end of our climb we were swallowed up in the misty drizzle and utter darkness. The objective in building the road was to eventually link up with the China-Burma road, which ran as far as Myitkyina, so that supplies could be sent along it to China and thus relieve, to some extent, the need to airlift all supplies for the American army under Stilwell and the Chinese forces who were with him.

When we reached Tagap Ga, the road progressed a further one hundred miles to Shingbwiyang, Stilwell's advance HQ. But due to the continuing landslides and maintenance coupled with the extended land supply route from India, it was never more than an alternative to air supplies over the 'hump'.

We arrived at our destination while it was still dark and raining hard. Military police disguised as American troops, guided us to some rough shelters, where we dropped our packs and slept. The weather was exactly the same the next morning, which would have been no surprise to any meteorologist.

The whole of this region, where Assam is bordered by Burma, Tibet and China, is treated to a minimum yearly rainfall of one hundred and twenty inches, rising in places to over four hundred plus. Often twenty inches, where recordings are made, fall in just one week. This is in comparison with the yearly London average of twenty four inches. The precipitation is caused by the warm breeze

146

from the Bay of Bengal meeting the freezing winds sweeping down from the Himalayas, the only real respite occurring during the months of December and January. Here, every day was wet, varying from a heavy downpour to a merciful drizzle.

Our spirits were low as we viewed the scene, brewed our char and shared tins of bully beef and biscuits issued at first light. We were in a long, low valley, the surrounding hills presenting a tangled mass of green leaves, creepers and bamboos. The rain poured down and everything we touched was wet and clammy. Near us, at the bottom of the slope we could see the bend of a fast flowing stream. We would certainly not be short of water.

Later, we were introduced to the American 'K' ration. In fact it was only intended as a temporary field ration for paratroops and patrols, until permanent army kitchens could be established, but it was to be our basic food for the next three months. The ration consisted of three meals, labelled on the outside as breakfast, dinner and supper, measuring roughly 7 in x 1½ in x 4 in. The inner carton was impregnated with wax for easy lighting. At this initial issue, we were instructed that the carton would burn without smoke, which it did, and that the resultant heat would last sufficiently long to heat a mess tin of water, which it did not. The contents were:

Breakfast:	Small tin of chopped ham and egg (with pull tag), fruit bar, chewing gum, two packets crackers, five cigarettes, sachets of coffee, sugar, plus milk powder, salt and water purification tablets.
Dinner:	Tin of pasteurised processed American cheese (with pull tag), dextrose tablets, lemon powder, chewing gum, two packets crackers, sugar, five cigarettes.
Supper:	Corned pork loaf (with pull tag), candy bar, bouillon soup powder, chewing gum, two packets crackers, five cigarettes.

Each carton weighed exactly one pound, so five days'

rations meant an extra fifteen pounds to carry in our packs. I was one of the minority of non-smokers, so could always find someone to swap my cigarettes for the fruit bar, candy bar or the dextrose tablets.

We were impressed by the novelty of this ration at the outset. It was certainly a well balanced menu and though not substantial, it proved adequate. Now and again we managed to get extra biscuits and some rice, so our evening burgoo was possible. But even at the best of times, although the ration was enough to keep us in action, I cannot remember when I was not hungry. Later, the time came when the same meal day after day became absolutely monotonous, especially the corned pork loaf. It had a fatty insipid taste, and some men, even at the expense of genuine hunger, could not stomach this item. The 'K' ration would have been fine as an alternative life saver for a few days at a time.

I have recently read Admiral Lord Louis Mountbatten's edited diary, covering the period when he was Supreme Commander South East Asia. The volume was published in 1988 by William Collins. He makes a reference to the 'K' ration on page fifty-six. It was Wednesday, 12th January, when he visited the American Air Commando Base at Lalitpur with General Wingate. He quotes:

'We stopped on the way and had luncheon off one of the American 'K' rations which are issued to this unit. It was excellent.'

Fair enough, but maybe he had enjoyed a wholly substantial breakfast before setting out, and would certainly eat well in the evening when he was to be the Guest of Honour at the Special Force Training Centre at Saugor.

Unknown to us at the time, the political conflict between the war leaders concerning strategic plans and policies still continued to rage, and our future role was still in the balance at this late stage. Stalin had been urged to enter the war against Japan, but he would only agree if all Anglo-American efforts were concentrated on the second front in Europe, at the expense of the Burma operation. Chiang Kai-shek however, would agree to continue the war in North

148

Burma only if the allies carried out an amphibious operation against the Japanese in Southern Burma, the Adaman Islands, or Sumatra.

Churchill's imagination had been fired by Wingate when he had presented his plans at the Quadrant Conference in August, 1943, and had agreed that the Long Range Penetration operation should have prime choice of men and materials. However, since then he had been having second thoughts, due to the conflict of strategy between East and West and now favoured an amphibious attack against Sumatra as the main priority. Very recently, this and other seaborn landings had become doubtful, due to the lack of resources and especially the return of large numbers of landing craft to bolster the Mediterranean theatre. All that was now at all possible was a landing behind the Japanese lines on the Arakan coast.

Roosevelt had also been excited and impressed by the soundness and feasibility of Wingate's proposals. Also, he favoured the opening of the land route from India to China by the completion of the Ledo Road between India and China. As far as he was concerned, the proposed Wingate infiltration behind the Japanese lines would be of great benefit to the American and Chinese forces operating in North Burma under General Stilwell. Success in pushing south would expedite the completion of the land link. Furthermore, backing any assault on the Japanese in North Burma would ensure that Chaing Kai-shek would agree to the establishment of American air bases on the Chinese mainland, to attack the Japanese held islands in the Pacific, including Formosa and the Philippines. To complicate the issue still further, the Chinese leader also wished to cultivate his friendship with Stalin by urging the British to advance the timing of the invasion of Europe.

This then was the overall situation which had become a web of political intrigue between East and West. This difference in strategic demands had quickly filtered down and been mirrored in the various commands. South East Asia Command was no exception. When Lord Louis Mountbatten had been appointed Supreme Commander at the Quadrant Conference, a major sea invasion of Japanese held territory had been very much on the cards.

Mountbatten never really believed that a land offensive through Burma was the best option. His view, probably influenced by his naval career, was that the land battle should be contained, and subsequently by-passed by seaborn forces.

There was friction between the American and British commands in India, as to who should give the operational commands, and this was really never sorted out. Partly because of this, Wingate was kept very much in the dark. Initially he had been promised large back-up forces, which he continually tried to augment, to exploit his anticipated successes. This included a division, provided by General Slim, to be flown in once Indaw was captured. But that was withdrawn in the planning stage, and it became a continuous battle to maintain even his original establishment. In fact, since the formation of SEAC, no definite strategies had evolved. Plans and counter plans had been formulated, amidst much procrastination, and then shelved. Added to this was the opposition and, in some cases outright hostility, towards General Wingate by the top brass in GHQ Delhi, which had started on the very first day that he set foot in India after the Quadrant Conference. As mentioned earlier, the combined chiefs of staff's orders to GHQ Delhi, to break up the 70th Division into three long range penetration brigades of eight column each, was blamed on Wingate. He was never forgiven. Urgent supplies were held up, and it was a continual fight to maintain the momentum of the build up.

On the 5th January, 1944, Wingate protested to Mountbatten at the lack of support given him by the 11th Army Group and threatened to resign. He protested again as late as the 25th January, because of a change of mind in the strength of the garrison troops already promised by General Slim. Each time his resignation was refused by Mountbatten. Wingate was treading on very thin ice, but there must have been good reasons why his resignation was not accepted.

His resignation would have enraged Churchill, because he had promised full support, and the heads of those responsible for upsetting Wingate would have rolled. Politically, Roosevelt also wanted the Chindit operation to go ahead. It is possible that Mountbatten had words with those responsible for causing Wingate to take umbrage. Finally on this subject, there is no doubt that by this time, British and American intelligence had obtained very clear evidence that a major attack on the Burmese-Indian border was imminent. In the absence of any concrete plans for the defence of India, there must have been a sigh of relief that Wingate's columns were trained and ready to disrupt the Japanese supply lines.

Much further down the command echelon, our own brigadier, Bernard Fergusson, offered his resignation to Wingate on the 16th January. He had found out that the promised military backing to consolidate gains would not be forthcoming, and he feared a repetition of the isolation, suffering and loss of life which had befallen his column on the first Chindit operation. Wingate's reply, however it was phrased, must have contained some assurance that garrison troops would be available in a follow-up capacity, and influenced Fergusson's decision to retract his request and continue with command of 16th Brigade. What was actually said is still open to debate.

Even as late as 11th February, at the Axiom Mission held in London, no firm policy on future Far East policy had been finalised. On the 25th February, Roosevelt sent a personal note to Winston Churchill urging an all out drive into Burma. In his reply, Churchill assured Roosevelt that 'No forces will be withheld from the North Burma Campaign for the sake of seaborn operations.' Up to this time there was a very firmly held belief in SEAC Headquarters, that the Chindits would never be committed to Burma.

Even the High Command had little faith in Wingate's plans. As late as 22nd February, Sir Alan Brooke recorded in his diary that 'There is no definite objective and large forces of long range penetration troops are being launched for no express purpose.' It is significant that it was not until the 28th February that Wingate was at last able to issue his final orders to the brigade commanders of the 77th and 11th brigades at the fly-in base at Lalaghat.

But we have got ahead of my story, so back to the first days of February, when our column was waiting at the start point at Tagap Ga, seventy miles along the Ledo Road. It is still raining. We were to have a few more days wait here for the mules, muleteers and our radio equipment. They were struggling up the road through rain and mud, travelling only at night time for security reasons. Our shelters leaked, but we improvised with thick plantain leaves and our groundsheets and were reasonably comfortable.

During the latter part of our training and here in this laager, we slept fully clothed, which had now become second nature. Washing facilities were primitive and there was no chance of a shower, though the very hardy among us bathed in the stream. We had also been instructed that from now on we need not shave. Beards were to be the order of the day which, considering our future task, was most sensible. Living rough, shaving had become a difficult and time-consuming chore, and after initially feeling scruffy, I soon became accustomed to the change and I grew a lush largely unkempt beard.

It was certainly better to have a beard than periodic growths of stubble, to be removed only when the opportunity arose. So at once, almost without exception, all razors, shaving soap, blades and containers were discarded. They were the first of our so-called essential items of equipment to be dumped in order to save weight. Beards thwarted the mosquitoes to some extent, but we were still bitten, and there was little else we could do to escape their constant attention. Mosquito cream would have been impracticable in Burma, as we would have needed to carry tons of it. However we were now being issued with the suppressive tablets of mepacrine, which delayed the effects of malaria until it could be treated in hospital.

Once we began the march, we would have to be prepared to move at a moment's notice. At night, I only removed my boots, and with the soles turned sideways and outwards I used them as a pillow. My bush hat acted as a cushion over the boots, and if there was no hollow for my hip bone, I fashioned a hole with my *Dah*, which is similar to a machete. The big problem was whether to sleep on or under the groundsheet in the ceaseless rain. I usually lay on the ground, groundsheet over the top. The thin woollen lightweight American blanket was surprisingly warm, although at the present height of under 2,000 feet the nights were comparatively mild. However, even here we were always damp and conditions would get much worse. Leeches abounded in the undergrowth, and we were continually removing them from our lower legs and sometimes more intimate places. Fortunately we found that they did not invade the comparative dryness of our shelters.

My greatest dislike, which bordered on an irrational fear, was the night-time creepy-crawlies and the myriad flying insects, not forgetting the mosquitoes which revelled in the darkness. During earlier night-time exercises I had devised a practical method of keeping my face clear at night. It was a mini-mosquito net, with a small section just big enough to cover my head and tuck the ends into the blanket. Propped above my head with two short sticks, it worked amazingly well as the netting had no weight but it collapsed quite often during the night, leaving me at the mercy of the barrage. However, rather like a child's nursery nightlight, it gave me a feeling of security from the invaders.

The first mules to arrive from the road journey bore strange loads, resembling giant tubas from a military band. We had seen nothing like them before. They were actually the very latest in flame-throwers, the first of a newly manufactured weapon to arrive in the Far Eastern war zone. They were officially called lifebuoys, because the oval fuel container looked very similar to the real thing. Many years later, I read that they had arrived late because the initial shipment had been routed to the naval stores in Bombay. That same evening, the flame-thrower operators gave a demonstration to all the brigade officers present, and we watched from a distance out of curiosity. With the lifebuoy strapped on his back, the operator trained the nozzle towards the river bank. Suddenly an awesome jet of burning fuel leapt ahead across the narrow river, turning the opposite bank into a fiery mass of flames, smoke and steam. The pools of liquid in the river floated downstream in great plumes of fire. The demonstrations continued for some while and we noticed that on two occasions the jet of liquid failed to ignite, which must have caused some embarrassment to all concerned.

153

So the unit was not foolproof. The flame-thrower was controlled by two button switches on the module. One activated the supply of compressed air, which ejected the jet of napalm fuel, and the other completed an electrical circuit, which heated the ignition coil at the nozzle. No doubt in this case the damp had shorted the electrical contacts, so that the coil was not red hot.

Overall, the flame-thrower was of dubious value on the coming operation. It was cumbersome and an awful mule load, and had we either come upon, or expected, Japanese resistance, they could have been dropped from the air with supplies. Furthermore, the size of the unit, measuring around 4ft x 3ft in addition to its weight of 70 lb plus, made it difficult to use as a surprise weapon. If the operator did not bag his quarry first time, a red hot bullet hitting the lifebuoy could burn him and any adjacent troops to a cinder. The flame-thrower was dangerous to operators and enemy alike, as was made evident later in the campaign.

By the next morning, on the 10th February, we were once again in radio communication with Rear Brigade Headquarters, now back in Imphal and I recognised the keying style of Eric Nightingale, who had so recently left us. It was most amazing how a combination of Morse dots and dashes could be sent quite precisely, but in slightly different styles. In between the official messages, we exchanged brief personal snips. HRU meant 'How are you?' and OKU 'Fine, and you?' and so on, but we obviously kept these asides to a minimum.

During the morning, the first two columns in the brigade, the Queen's Regiment nos 21 and 22, set off on their way towards the hills and the River Chindwin. Surprisingly, I had never actually watched a whole column pass by in single file before, a long chain of heavily laden men and mules pressing on in the ever-present steamy drizzle. There were frequent hold-ups in their progress, and it was over two hours before the last of the 900 men in the combined columns disappeared into the tunnel of jungle.

The order of advance of the columns of the Queen's Regiment followed the general pattern of Chindit marching, when in single file, described as 'column snake'. A reconnaissance platoon, usually made up of men from the

Burma Rifles, led the way, as they had personnel who could converse with any natives met on the way. They were followed by one of the infantry platoons, and close behind, so that he could have control in the event of trouble, was the column commander. As was obvious today, when the danger of any large Japanese patrol was minimal, he would be accompanied by his staff and the specialists in the column, which included the RAF and Royal Corps of Signals, intelligence cyphers and medical men. If trouble was expected the 'soft belly' would be positioned further back towards the middle of the line.

Next morning the R.S.M. read out an official communication issued by Brigadier Fergusson to each platoon or section in turn.

Special Order of the Day, 3rd February, 1944.
'We are going into Burma to hit the Jap and hit him hard. We are going to hunt him ruthlessly and without pity. We belong to what may be the best brigade in the history of war, and we are making history with every move we take. We are all together in an enterprise which the world will marvel at. May God prosper it. When in doubt go for the Jap.'

Brigadier Bernard Fergusson.

The same day I was issued with thirty silver rupees, which were to be kept in my care until needed. This was part of a large sum spread throughout the column to be used in emergency to reward Burmese for information about the Japanese movements, and also to purchase supplies of food if the need arose. I stowed them safely at the bottom of one of our leather panniers until they might be needed.

I was also issued with a half inch map covering the initial part of our march, and just one glance gave a warning of what was to come. Published by the Government of Burma under the direction of the Surveyor General of India, 1932 edition, these maps were printed on green-backed paper, possibly intended as camouflage, with contour intervals of 100 feet. The first map was number 92 B/SW and apart from the south east corner where the Tarung Hka looped through

155

the plain, it was a mass of tight contours. Our route was along the watershed of the Patkai hills, which we would have described as mountains at home. In some places, we would have to climb to well over 5,000 feet.

At one point, Sergeant Chapman who was in charge of the intelligence section, came over with messages for Rear Brigade and told us that serious problems had been encountered on the first mile of the march. Due to this, all the columns were behind schedule, and our start would be delayed for at least another day. From now on, we would see even more of Hedley Chapman and his two cypher operators, Bob Aplin and Bill Webb. All wireless traffic had to be coded, and they were in charge of the cyphering and encyphering of all messages. They were also the only troops with a camera and film, although I never saw it in use.

We entertained them with the usual cup of char as we sat and talked. Hedley told us,in confidence, that there had been real doubt as to the feasibility of the route, though why that was in confidence was strange as we had no one to tell. Then as if to substantiate what he had said, General Wingate, Brigadier Fergusson and the column commanders of the Leicesters and Royal Artillery hurried past us on the way to the start point. This was the first time I had been near enough to obtain a close look at General Wingate, and though I had no idea then, it would be my last. Looking very pale and haggard, in ill-fitting jungle green and with muddied boots, he had a groundsheet slung over his shoulders to ward off the pouring rain. If it had not been for his usual tropical khaki topee, certainly a most bizarre headgear for these condition, he would certainly have gone unnoticed.

All this time, all most of us knew about Wingate was that he had commanded the first Chindit Expedition, and that Brigadier Fergusson had served under him as a major in charge of one of the eight columns. Very few had heard about his previous service and his outstanding military successes in Palestine and Ethiopia. This was firstly because we had had little contact with those who had taken part in the first Chindit campaign, including Wingate, and secondly because the extensive world-wide publicity surrounding his success had not filtered through to us in detail.

Regarding the first reason, the initial campaign in 1943 was small, and consisted of just one brigade. These 3,000 troops made up of eight columns, did their training in secret under the guidance and omnipresence of Wingate, and they knew him well. After a long gruelling march, high endeavour and gallant endurance, just over two thirds of his men returned to the safety of India or China. Continually hounded by the Japanese during the return, they lost most of their mules and equipment. The rest were killed, captured with dire consequences, or in the case of the Burma Rifles, allowed to jettison uniforms and return to their villages for anonymity and survival.

Those officers and men who escaped, almost without exception, needed long hospitalisation and rest to combat malnutrition, malaria, scrub typhoid, sprue and many more less serious ailments, such as jungle sores and foot-rot. These troops were naturally glad to escape with their lives and felt that they owed this deliverance to Wingate, and this engendered a deep respect which in some cases amounted to hero worship. Only a handful of these men were fit enough for another toil in Burma, and the few who did take part in the second operation were mainly officers. I personally knew of no one else in our whole brigade except our commander, Bernard Fergusson, who was actually taking part in the march for the second time.

We were, of course, a virtually new force, vastly larger in numbers, with the equivalent of six brigades consisting of over twenty-five columns, mostly made up from the former 70th Division. So in the optimal circumstances, we could not have expected to see much of General Wingate. In actual fact, he had been busily occupied in planning and co-ordinating supplies for the coming campaign at GHQ Delhi, against the closed ranks of opposition, but with more furtune in dealing with the American Air Force at Gwalior HQ. Afterwards, he had been seriously ill with typhoid while we were under final training, and had been in hospital from early October, until resuming command of the Division on the 1st December, 1943.

The publicity surrounding him in Britain and the allied world, where the press had praised him in glowing journalistic terms, had given Winston Churchill a golden opportunity to uplift the spirits of the people at home, with an heroic account of the Chindit operation. Since the beginning of hostilities, they had suffered from uniformly depressing news, which included reports of military and naval losses or withdrawals. This had been especially true of the Far Eastern theatre, from whence had come a melancholy tale of shattered morale and defeat.

So Churchill exploited this first Chindit operation to the full, and Wingate was heralded as a national hero. He received a second bar to his DSO and the Royal Asian Society awarded him the Lawrence of Arabia Memorial Medal. The media of Britain hailed him as the new 'Clive of India' and were encouraged to embellish the tales without mentioning the losses, making every soldier a 'man of the hour'.

Certainly, we had heard reports of the Chindits on the BBC Overseas Service via Delhi, and read something in the forces' newspapers, SEAC or Contact, plus the few newspapers we received from home. But in fact, what we had read had been considered as just another wartime campaign, with no direct relevance to us. Overall of course, security had become the watchword and we soldiers at column level knew very little of the strategies and battles in other theatres, or how the war was actually progressing overall. At this time, our thoughts were occupied with much more basic feelings as we waited for the march ahead, with little to look forward to and much to fear.

We were just an isolated pocket of troops, very wet, uncomfortable and with a feeling of deep despondency. We would even have welcomed the spit and polish and the rifle parades of India. All we had here was the depressing prison of damp overhanging jungle. In fact, there was too much time to think and compare our lot with those of our comrades who had been considered unfit for marching. They would be enjoying dry beds, regular meals, duty shifts and a canteen and money to spend on luxuries. We did not need money as there was nothing to buy. In signals, we were luckier than most, as we had a job to do in radio communication which staved off the soul-destroying emptiness of the present regime, but quite frankly we were bored and began to wish we could begin our journey whatever the consequences.

Eventually, we watched the two Leicester columns 17 and 71 march away, followed next day by 51 and 69 of the Royal Artillery, and then followed on Saturday, 12th February, by Brigadier Fergusson and Brigade HQ. The camp now looked very deserted, and of course once we and our sister column 54 were on the way, it would be abandoned. There were no more troops to follow us, and in a short time the jungle would cover up all traces of our sojourn.

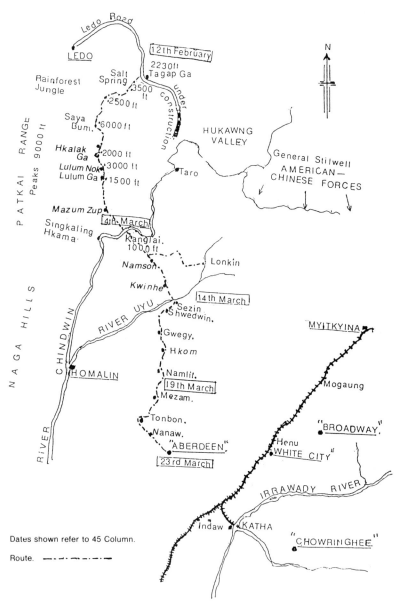

16th Infantry Brigade. March into Burma 1944.

9

Hannibal Eclipsed

On Saturday, 12th February, our turn came to move at last. At first light, after a quick brew up and 'K' ration breakfast, we loaded the four mules, shouldered our packs and rifles and moved off along the well-trodden jungle path, soon emerging and crossing a section of paddy, once part of a long deserted settlement.

We had not marched any real distance with a loaded pack since our training stints back in India. Furthermore, the burden of over 75 lb weight of kit was augmented by seven days of 'K' rations and the rainwater which penetrated our webbing and clothing. Even crossing this flat abandoned rice field, the poundage bore down on us, and made just lifting our feet over the water-retaining ridges an energy-sapping exercise.

Half-way across the paddy field we crossed a wide, fast running mountain stream by means of a recently strengthened bamboo bridge, and very soon we came to a halt at the foot of our first climb. I had already studied my half-inch map section and thought the route would be hard whichever way we went, but this climb ahead looked ridiculous. However, there was ample evidence left by the preceding columns that it was possible.

Originally a narrow footpath used by the Naga tribes, winding a tortuous path through the matted jungle network of bamboo, thorn bush, vines and tropical vegetation, it had been hacked away on either side to form a tunnel, wide enough for men and loaded mules to ascend. We could clearly see the beginning of the track before being swallowed up by the mass of greenery. Steps and traverses had been carved into the steep incline, lengths of bamboo laid down and secured with short timber pegs to form a staircase. But as we got nearer we realised that the passage of the previous columns had created chaos. In their efforts to climb the zigzag ladder, the mules had kicked away the steps and underpinning on the rain-sodden slope, and it was just a slippery mud slide.

Our infantry platoons leading the column had downed arms, packs and equipment and were now busily re-cutting the steps and footholds, and replacing the timber and bamboo supports on the traverses. We halted and had a long wait until repairs had been completed, so we enjoyed the break with the customary 'brew up'. Survival manuals insist that you must learn to light a fire anywhere under any conditions, and that it is not enough just to know about all the methods, you must be expert at their application. Expert or not, to light a fire without matches, would have needed at the least a miracle, or at least the chance of finding some dry tinder.

However, we had devised a much quicker and easier method to obtain a fire, and so we were very popular with our fellow travellers. Attached to one of our mule saddles there was a small tin can, half-full of sand. Bill Warbutton placed this tin on the ground, added some petrol from our supply, and without removing the batteries from the mule's back, attached two thin wires to negative and positive, touching the other ends over the tin to jump a spark across the gap. In seconds we were heating our water, it was one of the few advantages we enjoyed.

While drinking my tea, I had another look at the map and the dotted line which I had previously dismissed as an impossible route. Our present height was the same as Tagap Ga, 2,236 feet above sea level. On the way up the hill, the path would cross twelve contours jammed together until we reached the ridge at the top, a climb of 1,200 feet in just over three quarters of a mile. A formidable task. At the foot of the map, it stated that contours were approximate, which is not surprising. The first edition had been published as late as 1932, reprinted in 1942 with major corrections, and again in 1943 with minor corrections. The cartographers were improving but with later experience of the information on offer, I felt that what they really meant was 'we are not really quite sure about this part of Burma at all.' But there was certainly no doubt about the hill that towered above us as we moved on to tackle the climb.

We made the first level without much difficulty, but then the trouble began. Our mules had some of the heaviest and most awkward loads, and although strong and determined, they were beaten by the slippery mud and the steps and terraces which had been kicked away by animals on previous ascents. The mule carrying our wireless sets proved the exception, partly due to the fact that the muleteer dumped his pack and almost ran the mule to the summit. In actual fact, the combined weight of the two sets at around one hundredweight was far less, in proportion to the mule's strength, than the seventy-five pounds we carried on our own backs.

We had no alternative other than to unload the other three mules, but even without their loads, it was a battle for the muleteers to get them to the summit. We struggled to the top, crawling on hands and knees up the verticals, levering ourselves upwards by the protruding branches and getting lacerations from the edges of the split bamboo. Bert Fennell was in a state of collapse when after two hours we eventually reached the ridge, which was 3,500 feet high. The muleteers tethered the mules while we dumped packs and webbing and stacked our rifles, leaving Bert in charge. Then all seven of us went down again to collect the loads and one pack. The return was little easier than the ascent, as we were wet, muddy and exhausted. We cursed everything and everyone, including the mules. We dragged the charging engine, petrol tins, batteries and the two heavy panniers up the slope, stopping more and more frequently to regain our breath and strength. The whole unit was in the same situation. We worked away like explorers on an expedition, helping each other to the summit. Altogether I went back down three times to help rescue other loads left at various points on the way up. We had had a prolonged and exhausting day.

By the time all the loads had been manhandled up the hill and the column had regrouped, it was almost dark. The climb had been a shambles and we were completely exhausted. None of our training experiences had been remotely comparable to those of today. Bert Fennell, now recovered, had a fire going and one of his special burgoo porridges was almost ready. In addition to the rations we carried our packs, we had a hidden store of army biscuits, powdered milk, sugar and tea, stashed away in one of the leather panniers. This cache was the only extra luxury we enjoyed, and we topped it up when the opportunity arose. But later even this larder became bare. We had nibbled into our 'K' ration all day and were already into tomorrow's ration. From now on, the pangs of hunger were always with us and we progressively lost weight.

One temporary consolation was the fact that the heavy rain had eased to a faint drizzle, though at this height the temperature had dropped to a bitter chill. Wet and miserable, we fashioned a framework of bamboo and covered it with two of our groundsheets. Under this shelter, we spread the other two waterproofs in readiness for the night. In conditions like these, we slept together for mutual warmth. Individual privacy was a thing of the past. Building the cover for the night, my thoughts went back just a few years to the days when my mother had taken me to task for going outdoors in the winter. 'Do not blame me if you catch your death of cold,' she warned when I refused to wear a vest. The opportunity and the situation had dramatically changed.

Tired and chilled as we were, we still had a job to do. Out came our direction aerial of copper wire, extended with the thin rope tied to an unprimed grenade. We took a compass bearing on Rear Brigade at Imphal in India and then Buck, who had the best throwing arm, lobbed the grenade in the correct direction through a conveniently forked branch. He was not always so lucky the first time and further attempts were necessary. The sections around us soon learned from experience not to bed down in the direction of Imphal. By now, they knew how important it was to maintain communication, so they were always ready to give us a hand, even if it meant climbing a tree with the rope. As will be appreciated, because of the difficulty of finding a suitable accessible tree, we sometimes had to move the set location to accommodate the correct aerial length.

Special Force radio network had been precisely designed

for the campaign. The bulk of our communication from now on, would be through Rear Brigade Signals at Imphal. Spread along the ridge, the leading columns of our Brigade would be miles ahead and almost certainly out of wireless range. The no. 22 sets carried by the eight columns of the Brigade and Advance Brigade HQ, good as they were, only had a short dependable range of up to twenty miles in carrier wave (Morse), often greatly reduced by mountains, jungle, interference and static. Furthermore, communication between the columns and Advance Brigade could only take place when both were in laager, so all messages were routed through Rear Brigade Signals, for onward transmission. Here, powerful sets could pick up the signals and transmit back to the columns in the field when they were operative. In fact, Rear Brigade acted very much like a *poste restante.* Another advantage of this system was that with the end-fed directional aerial, we could beam our transmission back to Imphal via the 'Heavyside' layer. This stratum, named after the scientist who discovered the electrical field, exists in the upper atmosphere at a height of between fifty and 150 miles, and bounces the electro-magnetic wave of a transmitter back down to earth, at an angle relative to the original direction. The height of the layer varies, due to the variance in day- and night-time temperatures, and fading is often experienced. Nevertheless, due to this phenomenon, our signals were often stronger when they were picked up at Imphal, 200 miles away, than when received by another column a few miles along the route. Rear Brigade Signals used the Army Sender no. 53, one of the most powerful transmitters in use at that time. Its power supply unit functioned on a 1,500 volts high tension rectifier, and anyone touching the aerial as signals were going out would receive a nasty electrical shock. In the quiet of the night, its powerful beam was a joy to hear in the headphones, as the carrier wave cut through the maze of static and radio interference.

Bill Warbutton had to put the batteries on charge nearly every evening, but by now the rest of the column realised that this noise was essential, for their contact with the outside world, and the 'pop-pop' sound of the two-stroke charger was accepted. In any case, like sleeping on a long train journey, one soon got used to the background noise. Furthermore, noise was absorbed in a very short distance by the heavy surrounding jungle foliage, and lost in continual night-time chorus produced by the cicadas, frogs, jungle fowl and tribes of monkeys screeching continually, as they chased each other at tree-top level. There were also a variety of birds which chanted and warbled all night. When off duty, we operators used to find ourselves, trying to read the signals. We called one of them the 'toto' bird because it continually sent out single and treble dashes. (- --- - ---: T O T O).

Operating at night when all activity had ceased was an eerie business. With headphones clamped over our ears and the shaded night-reading lamp plugged into the set, we worked away over the message pad, oblivious to all else. We could not even hear the clicks from the key, which gave evidence that we were still working. Sometimes I was so absorbed that a touch on the shoulder would make me jump.

We woke up next morning, to find that most of us were bloodstained from the leeches, which had fastened on to us the day before, feasted without our knowledge and attempted to slide away when satiated. However, we got used to this blood letting. The bite cannot be felt, and the big danger was infection or jungle sores, caused by careless removal. Salt or a cigarette end would do the trick, but there was not always time to organise leech hunting. Once sated, they fell off leaving hardly any trace. Ticks were much worse, because they burrowed under the skin, but luckily, for some reason, they did not fancy me.

For a long time now, hygiene would become primitive to say the least. Column commanders who wrote books about troops marching through almost impenetrable jungle, dodging the Japanese, refrained from mentioning how calls of nature were performed. The answer was with embarrassment and some danger. Peeing behind a tree was no problem, but squatting down in the scrub in semi-privacy, doing a balancing act was no fun. I say semi-privacy because instances occurred later when troops seeking seclusion were never seen again, or were fired upon by their own comrades as they returned. For long periods on the first part of the march, washing was out of the question, though we later made the most of any opportunity to have a quick bathe, when water and time was available. As we set off this second morning at daybreak, we could still hear the roar of the traffic, as the lorries battled through the mud of the Ledo Road. The jungle dropped away steeply on both sides of the ridge, but for the first hour we had no real problems. The gradients were reasonable, but because of the mule loads we often had to make detours down and back up to the ridge, to pass large trees and regain the path.

We had our 'K' ration breakfast at the first halt, but were already becoming weary of the same diet. The rain became heavier again, and we hastily fixed temporary shelters with our groundsheets. Dead bamboo abounded here, and we were never short of firewood or supports for shelters. There was no restriction on fires. At the moment there was little danger from Japanese patrols and in any case, smoke from jungle fires looked the same whether lit by natives, the Japs or by us. But we did have to be careful with bamboo and make sure we split it before lighting up. Unsplit bamboo bursts in the heat, with a crack like a rifle shot, similar to the noise of a sten gun being dropped, which usually made them fire. Consequently untold panic could ensue.

It seems almost unbelievable but although the rain was almost constant, at this altitude we had no water. The rain ran down the watershed and all the streams of reasonable size ran far below. Luckily this morning, although our water bottles were already empty, nearly everyone still had the canvas water bottles we had obtained on arrival in India, and these were slung on the mules' saddles, but the muleteers had to struggle down hundreds of feet to obtain water for the mules, before we pressed on. Towards midday, we came to the end of the ridge and started down the escarpment to a stream which ran through the ravine. There was no chance of a halt; we just had to keep going. Descending was almost as difficult as the climb of the previous day, due to the slippery worn tracks.

Towards the bottom of the ravine, the ground flattened out and the jungle thinned as we arrived at a large flat area almost clear of trees. This was our laager for the night. The commanding officer had chosen his tree, and the column would be circulated around. Infantry sections would be left to block the path we had just travelled, and advance some distance along the track we would follow the next day. A clear, deep and fast moving stream flowed through the middle of the clearing, and further troops guarded up and down stream. The clearing was marked on the map as Salt Spring and the river, the Jum Hka. This jungle clearing might well have known habitation some time in the past, although the Naga tribesmen usually lived in stockaded villages high up in the hills. There probably was still a salt spring here, but there was no time nor chance to explore.

As usual, we were positioned quite near to the command post, with the intelligence and cypher sections, as all worked very much together. The mules were halted, we unloaded the wireless equipment and the animals were led off to the mule lines well down stream, to be fed and watered. They drank their fill and fed on the plentiful young bamboo leaves and wild rice grass along the river bank. This greenery was almost sufficient, though they enjoyed a special treat when hay was included in the supply drops.

After two days of hard backbreaking toil in these atrocious conditions, climbing up, along and down the first ridge, we had covered just six miles from the roadhead start at Tagap Ga. In a direct line, we were just four miles away with impenetrable jungle between the two points. A further glance at the map showed that this was just a minor sample of what awaited us as we pressed ahead. We faced a mammoth climb next day out of Salt Spring, to reach the elongated ridge which would take us south for many miles and reach a height of well over 5,000 feet in many places.

The river here had been swollen by countless streams running down the south side of the ridge, while on the northern edge, another river, the Tahkam Hka, gathered torrents from the other side of the watershed. Well past Salt Spring, they joined forces and eventually became yet another tributary of the Brahmaputra. Here at Salt Spring, we were able to replenish our water supply and enjoy a hasty wash just down stream. The rain stopped as we arrived and the sun shone briefly.

We had just begun to set up our transmitter, when we witnessed a party of five Naga hillmen coming towards us.

They were all balancing a pile of blankets on their heads, and carrying a variety of spoils in cloth bundles which had been jettisoned by the columns ahead. Exhaustion had supplanted greed and the desire for so many creature comforts, and those in the lead had realised the difference between excess and essential. Many had taken extra blankets, shirts and underclothes, and these had in spite of the cold nights, been dumped along with personal possessions and other dispensables.

During the next few days, many in our column would follow their example and lighten loads even further to the absolute bare minimum. The Naga tribesmen passed us silently, unsmiling, almost fearfully, glancing neither to the left nor the right. They need not have worried, no one wanted their loot. Almost certainly, they had never seen white men before and probably not even mules.

Deep down in the ravine and blotted out by the hills around we were unable to contact Rear Brigade at Imphal, though we heard their signals very faintly. Luckily, our sister column 54 were still behind, high on the ridge bringing up the rear of the brigade. They took our messages and relayed them back to India. We did not immediately realise that communication might be the weak link in future operations. Now and especially later on, we were adjacent to the cypher operators and often we worked together late into the night. Nearly every day, Rear Brigade Headquarters produced a SITREP, which as the abbreviation suggested, contained a situation report of the whole of Special Force. We watched the cyphers decoding the message and I was absolutely astounded at the subject matter. The bulk of the contents appeared to be quite extraneous to our operation, though no doubt our commanding officer, Lieutenant Colonel Cumberlege enjoyed his daily forces newspaper!

Considering that we were a brigade operating away from the rest of the force, this daily SITREP could have been sent just to Brigadier Fergusson at Forward Brigade HQ, thereby saving signallers much toil. The fact that we had to work after a long tiring heavily laden march, while others rested or slept would have been more easily accepted, had we thought that all the messages were vital to our operation. Signal traffic should have been limited to that required by a guerrilla patrol in the field.

Our third day's progress was a physical nightmare and on reflection, it was by far the worst climb of the whole campaign. As we set off across the stream, knee deep in the fast flowing water, the heavens opened and the torrential rain returned. The experience of our first day's climb had given a warning of what to expect, but this ascent proved far more perilous and longer.

In spite of the effort that was being made by our advance infantry platoons to repair previously created damage, they had a hopeless task. The fact that steps and lateral traverses had been prepared through the dense jungle foliage, made it easier for the rain to create a fast, muddy waterfall down the steep hillside to the ravine below. The underpinning gave way on whole stretches, as the mules struggled to obtain a foothold. We continually had to halt because of trouble ahead, and standing immobile with heavy wet packs was much worse than making the effort to climb.

Before long, we unloaded the mules so that they and the muleteers could negotiate the inclines unhindered. As before, stores and equipment lined the route, a further hazard to our progress. There were no official halts, and sections leap-frogged each other as the day wore on. We unloaded and loaded many times, dumping packs and going back to drag our heavy signal equipment up the slopes.

The same pattern continued all day. From time to time, we halted and pulled to one side for a quick brew up, while others passed. Then, late in the afternoon we came upon the bulk of the column, laagered for the night in one of the few semi-flat areas Once unloaded, the mules and muleteers stayed with us. Exhausted, we sat down on the mule loads, lit a small warming fire, brewed up and ate the same unending 'K' ration. No messages were received from the column. Afterwards we each rolled up in our single blankets and groundsheets to seek warmth and sleep. The rain, heavy and insistent, added to our misery and we slept fitfully, waking up long before dawn, cold and shivering.

The next few days seemed unending misery. The rain, solid and unbroken, gave us no respite. It was an awful toil, soul destroying monotonous torment and muscle-tearing

170

labour. The fact that every man, from the commanding officer down to the lowest rank was involved in this challenge against nature and the elements, gave us some measure of self-discipline and willpower. Only the sheer determination engendered by our army training kept us on the move. Each platoon made their own way, halting from time to time to assist a muleteer whose charge had come to grief. Often, the mule had to be unloaded so that it could regain its feet, the girth readjusted and tightened, the saddle checked, cleaned and replaced until ready to proceed.

Sometimes, the way ahead would be completely deserted as we lost ground, but there was only one dark tunnel along the well-trodden track, and no chance of being lost. Certainly there was no danger from Japanese patrols attacking the flanks. Climbing the almost vertical sides of the ridge here was out of the question. Apart from the forest of trees, the matted clumps of bamboo, thorn bush, vines and dank decaying vegetation made an impenetrable wall. We were without doubt taking the route which offered the best prospects for surprise and secrecy. On this first stage of our journey, we had now reached a height of over 5,000 feet. The night-time temperature dropped to a bitter chill, despite this being sub-tropical rain forest.

Continual dampness pervaded our uniforms and equipment. A sense of humour was a bonus in these conditions, as when we received another superfluous directive from Rear Brigade Signals on wireless set maintenance. This message, an extract from the signal training manual, All Arms, 1938, Chapter X, reminded us of the need to keep batteries, leads and sets dry. It ended: 'Before the set is put away after work, everything must be clean and dry.' Unbelievable! We had waterproof covers on the sets, but water inevitably penetrated the inner cases from time to time, in these atrocious conditions. However, the wireless sets proved exceedingly robust and completely reliable. Luckily, a certain amount of heat was generated by the old fashioned valves when the set was operated, and this helped to ward off most of the dampness.

In spite of our mounting problems of fatigue on this first stage, my signals team worked well together, sharing maintenance of radio equipment as well as sending and receiving messages. All messages, of course, were encoded in letter or figure cypher so that extra care and concentration was required. Had our communication been in 'clear', the words, phrases and sentences would have been recognised and recorded much more easily. Once in contact with Rear Brigade, the first dual exchange would be the abbreviation QTC, which meant 'How many messages have you to send?' That at least gave us some idea of the task ahead. We used the 'Q' code a great deal, such as QRM (interference is bad), QRN (atmospherics are bad), QRS (send more slowly), QSM (repeat the last message).

We also often had to resort to the QSR procedure, which mant that each group of letters or figures would be immediately acknowledged before proceeding. The one signal we really looked forward to receiving was QRU, which meant 'I have nothing for you', but this would be rare. Message recording and timing was now vital, unlike our training days and everything was written down and timed on army form C 2130. We checked our watches at nearly every transmission, sending the code QTR, meaning 'What is the correct time?'

Although this duty involved long hours and application, it certainly gave us less time to contemplate our future. We, and indeed the whole bedraggled unit depended very much on successful communication with our former companions now manning the sets back at Imphal. Without communication, there would be no food, ammunition, equipment, drive or direction for the whole column.

It must be admitted that we were becoming rather envious and even more resentful towards these 'base wallahs' who had been weeded out to remain in India due to their flat feet, varicose veins, other medical problems or just evasive skills. Housed in comfortable bashers with real beds and mosquito nets, thcy were enjoying regular cookhouse meals and when off duty, a canteen, sunbathing, swimming, entertainment, films and mail from home.

These feelings increased, when wet through, tired and hungry, we crouched in front of the set, our chilled hands tapping out the call sign on the key with no response from India. In our mental state, we conjured up vivid pictures of the operator lounging in comfort, probably dozing with the headphones off, or listening to Vera Lynn on the radio, meanwhile reading his latest mail and sipping char. However, in reality, our former colleagues did a marvellous, conscientious job, making sure that listening watch was maintained without fail throughout the twenty-four hour watch.

Ninety-nine per cent of the problem was not their fault, but caused by well-known problems such as thunderstorms, atmospherics, static, other transmissions, gaps in the Heavyside layer and the deep valleys and intervening mountains. Later, towards the end of March, a vital error in forward planning by the administrators in Rear Brigade, Special Force, resulted in panic and ensured complete disruption of signal communication for nine whole days. It was to have severe repercussions during the future battle for Indaw, in which Brigadier Fergusson was left without contact with his columns, and thus unable to conduct a co-ordinated action.

The jungle certainly had a special way of shaping a man's desires which were now very basic: a prayer for dry clothes, sleep, a proper ration and an end to the leeches, ticks, fleas and mosquitoes. The latter were now an ever present pest and gave us little respite, though I was more than pleased with my small night-time protective net.

We had a plentiful supply of mepacrine, and were now taking three tablets every day. High up here in the hills, far from human habitation, it was possible that these mosquitoes were not infection carriers. In any case, many of us would not know for a long time whether we had contacted malaria. Mepacrine was a synthetic drug which did not cure, but only suppressed the eventual outcome. But even this ability could be questioned, as Bert Fennell amongst other, who had always obeyed orders and taken the tablets, suffered several malarial attacks, as we marched deeper into Burma.

During this stage of our march, there was not the slightest chance of evacuation for even the severest of casualties. Back in our training days around Jhansi, we had witnessed impressive demonstrations of mercy missions by the L1 and more modern L5 light planes of the American No. 1 Air Commando. However, they needed a reasonably level strip

173

approaching 300 yards, to be able to land and take off. Up here, there was no terrain within miles suitable to land a helicopter, let alone an aircraft. So there was no chance of evacuation for those whose malarial sufferings would have meant instant hospitalisation in the rear areas.

Similar, but very much worse than influenza, first shivering, then a high fever followed by excessive sweating, the malarial symptoms usually cleared up in just over a week. A man had but two options; the first was to grit his teeth and soldier on, aided by aspirin or quinine if available and the help and support of his comrades. The second option was to give up. A few did just that. They lay down and were left to fend for themselves, in the hope that eventually they would recover and catch up with the column or make their way back to Tagap Ga.

On our fourth day's march, we struggled past a group left behind by one of the columns ahead. They lay exhausted in the wet jungle and all we gave them was a glance. There was absolutely nothing we ordinary soldiers could do. We had a job to do and problems enough of our own. That night, we awoke in a frenzy, burning all over. We had unwittingly bedded down next to a resentful colony of red ants in a thorn bush. These little creatures, although minute, had a vicious bite and we lost precious sleep beating them out of our uniforms, before moving to an adjacent spot in the hope of some respite. For several days we suffered the effects of this encounter. The poison formed patches of red blotchy skin, and the itching added to our discomfort.

We now realised that although there are better things to view and contemplate than the rear end of a mule, they were extremely intelligent animals. By this time they had accepted the burdens placed upon them and they no longer lashed out or attempted to dislodge their loads. Furthermore, it was now absolutely safe to grasp a mule's tail to avoid stumbling, or even to hang on for help up a steep incline.

By the fifth day, we had begun to fall back into a more regular routine of progress. We rested for ten minutes after each hour's marching, and enjoyed the three-hour halt from midday onwards. These breaks were not co-ordinated throughout the column. Sometimes, just as we caught up

174

with those in front, they moved on again having had their requisite ten minutes. These delays often meant that our long break was curtailed. Like vehicles in a road convoy, those towards the rear suffered the worst disruption.

In an attempt to eliminate these gaps, a newly invented portable communications item had been issued to all units in the Brigade. From America, this 'walkie-talkie' officially called the SCR 536, was crystal tuned to identical frequencies and carried by officers in the column. One would be carried by the leading platoon, others were carried at various distances along the line and finally one carried at the rear. At first, it was a welcome addition for control and reducing gaps in the column, but like most new toys its popularity waned.

This hand-held radio bore little resemblance to the modern mobile telephone used fifty years later for crowd control, and its range was very limited in jungle country. It was a bulky item, a large dry battery, a sizeable speaker and microphone and the outer case measured 12 inches long and 4 x 4 inches wide and weighed over two pounds. As an additional piece of equipment, it received rather rough treatment, being dumped with packs and other encumbrances at halts on the wet ground, often getting filled with water which resulted in corroded contacts and shorted batteries. This additional maintenance chore annoyed Bill Warbutton, and he had much to say regarding the officers' lack of care. Luckily he never voiced his candid remarks in the hearing of the culprits.

We kept a supply of batteries in one of the two panniers, but usually all these instruments required was a good clean. Long before we reached the River Chindwin, requests for repair mysteriously ceased, probably like other non-essential equipment, they were conveniently mislaid. We eventually dumped the batteries for more practical necessities.

In spite of the appalling conditions and imposed hardships, which now formed part and parcel of our existence, there was a bond of togetherness and disciplined helpfulness throughout the 45th Column, due no doubt to the fact that the majority had previously soldiered and trained together for over two years, as a mechanised unit in the 45th Regiment Reconnaissance Corps. However, it must be made quite clear at this early stage of the operation, that we were very much aware of the violent and archaic code of discipline that had been legislated by General Wingate before we left India. It later transpired that this order had not even been discussed with, let alone sanctioned by the higher authority in Delhi.

This dictate from Wingate, passed down the chain of command verbally, ruled that a man found sleeping on guard or stealing rations, either from his comrades or during a supply drop, would be given a severe flogging in front of his platoon. Should he transgress again, he would be given a rifle and five rounds of ammunition and banished from the column to fend for himself. Furthermore, all officers had been briefed that in the event of the slightest sign of mutiny or cowardice amongst the men, the offenders would be shot without exception or hesitation.

As far as desertion was concerned, this was most unlikely to be a problem. Leaving the column in Burma would invite almost certain capture, followed by torture for information, either culminating in a horrible death or a battle for survival as a prisoner. Of course, we fully realised that the normal procedures for punishment laid down in King's Regulations would be quite unworkable in the present circumstances. Putting a man on a charge to be followed by a court martial, involving witnesses, escort and accused was out of the question. Apart from being unworkable, it would certainly have been no deterrent to any would-be transgressor.

Indeed, the thought of a trip back to India for trial, followed by a long term of imprisonment in the safety of a detention centre, might well have encouraged delinquency. Such punishment would have offered a most welcome alternative to humping a pack weighing over seventy pounds in pouring rain, constantly hungry and with the Japanese lurking in the wings, but we had accepted this code without question because as far as we were concerned, the die had been cast when we left for Burma. Now we needed this discipline and commitment to help us fight the Japanese and give us a chance of survival.

However, there will be more to tell of this decree unofficially devised by Wingate, because soon after we

176

crossed the River Chindwin, discipline weakened due to mounting mental and physical pressures.

We were now well behind our projected schedule of progress. Two nights before we had sent out a 'QQ' signal for a supply drop on the route ahead, and Rear Brigade Signals had sent the required 'QK' in acknowledgement. But this plan had had to be postponed, when during the fifth day we had managed to struggle barely three miles uphill towards one of the peaks along the ridge, only twelve miles from our start point at Tagap Ga. So that evening, we were still four miles short of the previously agreed dropping zone at map reference 588662.

An alternative was to have the planes re-routed to our present location. The spot was clearly identified on the map by a trigonometrical point confirming our height at 5,249 feet and the figures stood in splendid isolation surrounded by thick jungle, with only a conglomeration of tributary streams and tight contours to keep them company. However this recourse would have been a complete disaster, the parachutes would have drifted sharply away on both sides of the ridge and landed way down in the valleys either side, so that night we sent off a revised time at the previously agreed location, a daylight drop at midday the following day.

We set off early at 5.30 a.m. with four miles to march to the dropping zone. Luckily, the going was much easier than had been expected. Although there were no really level stretches, the track went almost straight along the ridge with little real deviation in height. We were now very hungry indeed and completely out of rations, except for some tea and the dregs of our powdered milk. However the expectancy of rations later in the day, coupled with the probability of a longer rest than usual, while the stores were collected and distributed, gave us a new lease of life and spurred us on. The rainforest was thinner at this level but we had no view at all, as today we were enveloped in thick cloud. The misty vapour crept up the slopes from the west, and fell away down the other side. We trudged on resolutely, the drizzly haze muffling the scraping of our boots and the clatter of the mules' hooves on the bare rocky outcrop.

The column administrative officer had a very difficult job

in planning the supply drops, as the half-inch maps of this area had already proved suspect. The choice of a site two days' march away, needed information from the columns ahead as well as a great deal of guesswork. Coupled with the difficult selection of a suitable drop zone, was the need to ensure that the troops could traverse the intervening jungle in the time available.

We arrived at reference point 588662 well before midday, and laagered near the proposed dropping zone which in fact was a large marshy area, caused by an extensive natural depression, quite unexpected at this height of over 5,000 feet. We had a great deal of signal traffic to clear during the halt, so we did not see much of the supply drop operation, though we heard the planes and saw some of the parachutes floating down. Now and again there was an additional thump, as a free drop, mostly fodder for the mules, came down without a parachute.

However, we soon heard that even on this comparatively flat area, the supply drop had been something of a disaster. Many of the loads had floated away some thousands of feet into the depths of the valley below and loads dropped without parachute plugged in the marshy ground. The pick-up and distribution went on for most of the day and we eventually received six packs of 'K' ration each, sufficient for two days instead of the expected five. There was also tea, sugar, powdered milk and three packs of hard army biscuits to divide between four. The one special treat was a battered tin of pears to share. As the muleteers could not be left out, being part of our team, the eight of us had a half pear each and some syrup straight out of the tin. Bert Fennell broke up all the biscuits into a large tin, added water and a packet of bouillon soup from a 'K' ration and brewed it on the fire. This soup was very salty on its own tasting something like marmite. Our hunger had been acute, and this broth tasted absolutely delicious.

From now on we collected empty tins after a supply drop, threaded them with wire for a handle and hung them from either our packs or the mules' saddles and discarded our mess tins which were bulky and difficult to balance on an open fire.

Hunger will warp a man's sense of morals and loyalty

towards his fellows, and evaporate all fears of detection and punishment. Now at the bottom of the barrel in any regiment, there are always some troops who will steal from their comrades without hesitation. Indeed, it was at this early stage in the operation that X platoon retained a parachute that had failed to open, quite close to them down the slope of the ridge. They absolved their conscience by deciding that, had the drop fallen a further twenty feet, it would have been lost anyway. Not even the Naga tribesmen would venture down the slope in these areas. This was the first instance that was uncovered, and the one NCO involved was reduced to the ranks, and all were deducted one day's ration at a later date. However, the incident was kept very quiet, because there is no entry in the official War Diary.

Our advance was very much a case of follow the leader at this stage. Six columns plus Advance Brigade HQ were ahead, and our sister column was at the rear. At least, two columns, approximately 450 men, had organised supply drops ahead of us on the marsh, spending the night nearby. As we left, we went past one of their overnight halts, instantly identified by its vile stench. However much one hated this tropical rain forest, it did at least smell sweet and fresh. As we went by this trampled patch we were hit by the nauseating fetid stench of stagnation and excrement left by our predecessors. It truly did stink to high heaven, but like all the previous laagers it would soon revert to its pristine splendour, and evidence of our passing would be lost for ever. We certainly felt we had no grounds to judge or disparage the hygienic dispositions of our leading columns.

In our present condition, none of us would have passed muster for cleanliness. Our bodies were dirty, our garments sweat-stained, damp and muddy. Furthermore, all were suffering to some extent from the unending forays launched by ticks, leeches, insects, ants and lice who gave us no respite.

Heavily loaded, we leaned forward, following the man or mule ahead, and for most the time passed desperately slowly. Frequently I found myself counting my steps up to one hundred, then two, then three, like a prisoner notching up the hours and days on the wall of his cell. Then the temptation to steal a glance at my wrist-watch would reveal that a bare ten minutes of the one hour stint had elapsed. Often, my thoughts drifted ahead towards the luxury of the evening sojourn. The joy and relief of dumping my pack and equipment, to stack my rifle and stretch full length on the ground, even if at night I only had my boots as a base for my bush hat pillow.

Even these musings were often supplanted by contemplation of the conscription and enforced circumstances that had brought me so far, and I was overwhelmed with pangs of nostalgia. The happy family life with my parents, two brothers and sister had been taken for granted. Hostilities had meant the end of my job, my leisure days of rugby, cricket and music. Now, miles away from home, the old way of life was just a memory to cherish.

By marrying during the first year of the war, like most couples, Mollie and I had expected some separation, but like many others we had fostered the hope that the war would soon end. For over two years, reasonably frequent leaves in England had been eagerly awaited and enjoyed, but since embarkation, letters had been our only link for a similar time span. Even that connection had been severed. Mollie wrote long frequent letters, but mail would at present only arrive in batches, if at all.

That night we reached Saya Bum, a high peak at 4,966 feet above sea level, after a long tiring switchback, six miles without a level stretch. On the upward gradients there was the continuous downward drag from our heavy, wet packs, (admittedly around twelve pounds lighter due to the supply shortfall) and from our pouches with grenades and ammunition, waterbottles and rifles or sten guns. Whilst descending, the whole weight thrust us forward, straining our legs and thigh muscles. We did our usual late night stint of communications, but fit as we were, that night we were terribly cold. Our bodies even now were still attuned to the heat of the Indian Plain around Jhansi, and the dampness chilled our bones.

When we set off the next morning on the eighth day of our advance, it was through yet another heavy downpour. Since the start, we had not had a day without rain. The track gradually descended but was still undulating and winding. We did not have our customary midday halt, and in the early afternoon the rain ceased. As we looped around the downward slope, the jungle tunnel suddenly thinned and the sun shone, and we came upon a most wonderful and unexpected scene.

Down below in the valley, there was a picture postcard view of an inhabited Naga village. Smoke rose from the solid log-built huts and formed a haze along the line of the well thatched roofs. Built on a rise in a large jungle clearing, there was activity everywhere. Above and around the houses there was a panoramic view of line upon line of green summits to the mountains beyond. All the time we had been expecting to bump into Japanese patrols, but here was what appeared to be peaceful civilisation. We hastened down the steeply sloping trail, our tiredness gone and our spirits high.

This was Hkalak Ga, actually an allied outpost turned into a stockaded fort and manned by Chinese troops. But to us, as we approached, it looked like heaven and we felt that surely the worst of this awful journey must be over. It had taken us nine days to cover just thirty-five miles. The columns ahead had already rested and were now on the way again. We rested at Hkalak for two full days and it gave a wonderful lift to our physical and mental health.

Frequent supply drops had been in operation, and we enjoyed the luxury of bully beef and tinned tomatoes to supplement our full ration of 'K'. Of course, no field kitchen was available, but we cooked our individual meals with great delight. Also mail had arrived here at last, my first for five weeks, six letters and some newspapers, three letters from Mollie and three from the rest of my family. Fresh medical stores were dropped and we were able to renew our supplies of mepecrine and water purification tablets. Best of all, was the chance to wallow naked in the stream near our laager and wash our clothes.

There was no landing strip at Hkalak Ga, so none of our sick could be evacuated. However, there was a Chinese field hospital and three men from our column were left to recover from serious illness. One of our officers had sustained a severe knee wound from a machete cutting his way through a bamboo thicket, so he joined several other seriously injured men from the advance party in the hospital. These men had pioneered the way, cutting steps in the sheer slopes and widening the previously foot-wide jungle tracks, and had been the victims of booby traps. Very likely however, these traps had been left not by the Japanese, but by our Chinese allies to protect their security.

Setting up these explosive devices was often an essential and effective exercise. They could delay the progress of a following enemy, protect the surrounds of an established stronghold or delay the repair of demolished installations. But in this type of warfare, especially later when our own columns repeatedly crossed and recrossed the same tracks, the idea was quite insane.

Unfortunately, there was no opportunity to reply to our letters, as no mail could be lifted from this outpost. However, I took some comfort in the fact that those at home would now know the reason why my letters were not arriving. Mollie had already received one of the special postcards despatched by the War Office each month, informing her that 'Your husband is fit and well but owing to operational reasons is unable to write as usual'.

During this brief respite at Hkalak Ga, we had luxuriated in the chance to rest, to satisfy our acute hunger and cleanse our bodies and clothes after the long initial nightmare of a march. Nevertheless, this was but a short breather. At 2 p.m. on Tuesday, 22nd February, we left this fortress outpost, and like packhorses back in harness, we shouldered our burdens, resuming our journey to the River Chindwin without enthusiasm and just a trace of reluctance.

Once on our way, we soon threw off this despondency, and were in better spirits as we made nightfall, six miles further on at the deserted village of Ringhkau Ga, at reference point 520028. This was not the first time we had come across uninhabited villages on our way through the Patkai hills and the reason for this abandonment was not the wartime situation.

The Nagas, like other Burmese tribesmen had moved because they had over-exploited the surrounding land. They therefore departed, lock, stock and barrel, setting up another hilltop village some distance away on fresh fertile soil. They still had the warlike tendency of their ancestors and were still head-hunters. Every hilltop village was a stockaded fortress. There was no dry season up here, so they had no problem with water for agriculture. Even so, the women thought nothing of descending many hundreds of feet to fill up their pots with drinking water.

Probably because the Pighkau Ga shown on our map had been deserted some time, there was no easy way down for water. We had to scramble two hundred feet down the steep slopes through thick undergrowth to find a suitable spring. Once again our arms, legs and hands were scratched and lacerated, as we hauled ourselves through a porcupine-like thicket of thorns, bushes, bamboo and vines. For the muleteers, the numerous journeys were real purgatory as they lifted sufficient water for their charges. As we walked on, the midday sun, though masked by the overhanging branches, made the tropical jungle steam like a Turkish bath. We rejoiced in the unexpected warmth and realised that we had left the mountain country behind. Even so, the going was still formidable and the terrain at an altitude of over 2,000 feet was still dense jungle. We were now moving in a south westerly direction, though eventually we had to travel east. Of course, the direction was dictated by the leading trailblazers and any detour would have wasted even more time and further exhausted both men and animals.

Even though the way ahead had been well trampled and widened by preceding columns, there were frequent delays. The fast growing undergrowth had to be re-parted or trimmed back, to create a wide enough tunnel for the broad mule loads. Infantry sections took turns at the head of the single file to clear the track, but it was always an interminable struggle.

The map showed no obvious route through this jungle barrier. The whole area was a maze of tight contours and interlocking streams. All that could be confirmed with some certainty was that our passage to the River Chindwin would be predominantly downhill. The wide river valley, where we had to eventually find a suitable crossing point was a 1000 feet above sea level, half the height of our present position.

The legend, 'Path follows bed' repeatedly appeared on our

map sheet, and in these narrow river valleys it meant just that. We had often crossed streams and rivers during our training back in India, but today was an exhaustingly new experience, as we travelled a good three miles along a river bed. Once committed to this track there was no alternative. The banks on either side were sheer, gouged out over centuries by the watercourse. Stretches of sand had formed opposite the deep channel on alternate sides of the bends and the jungle hung over the edges. We frequently had to cross the main stream up to our waists in water, in order to reach the next stretch of sand.

Making headway in these conditions was very demanding on our stamina. The bed of the stream was solid enough, but stones and small boulders below the surface caused problems and several early baths. The alternative of ploughing through the sand of the banks was even worse. Our boots sank into the dry loose grains and filled our boots with grit. We were glad when this initial ordeal was over and the track took us uphill away from the valley.

From now on, we often marched for long or short periods through or along these stream beds, and this added a further health problem to many of my companions. In a few cases the constant damp caused foot-rot, though in the main it was the combination of wet shrinking socks and particles of gritty sand that aggravated already inflamed blisters, causing a multitude of problems and suffering. The previously mentioned challenge that Ray Scully and I had taken up in our early days in India was now paying a dividend. The bet to prove who could wear boots without socks the longer was never settled, but in my reckoning we both won hands down.

My feet were now as hard as nails which was an absolute bonus. When we had marched non-stop in and out of streams, my feet and boots dried more quickly at the end of the day. I had less to carry, no socks to dry or mend, and certainly no blisters. I had last seen Ray at Ledo in our sister column number 54. He was serving as an administrator with the muleteers, and continued throughout without wearing socks and without having foot problems. However, Ray suffered badly from malaria and dysentery and was never fully fit again. Like all our ex-despatch riders he bemoaned the need to march and tend mules instead of riding and tinkering with his beloved 350cc Norton. The only advantage of the marching that day, was the chance to fill our water bottles and chaguls, and let the mules drink their fill, before we camped eight miles further along, just past the village of Nawsing Nok. Here, the villagers watched us with vigilant curiosity from behind their plantain leaved doorways.

On the evening of the 25th February, we arrived at Lulum Ga. During the previous year, the Chinese Army had commandeered this hilltop village and established a stockaded outpost, but now they had departed and the Nagas were back in habitation. It was indeed a beautiful village, typical of those we had passed through over the Patkai hills. Perched way up on the hillside, the huts were built on stilts, a good six feet off the ground. Many had a wide platform in front of the entrance, and bamboo had been used throughout in its construction. Smoke from the open hearths in the centre of the huts filtered its way through the windows and chinks in the palm frond and plantain thatched roofs. Dogs, goats, chickens and pigs occupied the space under the huts, milling around beneath the raised habitations.

The villagers were bolder in their approach, probably because they had experienced the previous upheaval and would have made some resistance against a repeat forced exodus. The men, barefooted, wearing only loosely fitting loincloths, armed with spears and dahs slung round the waist, came forward, squatted on the ground, and watched silently as we filed past. I wondered if these tribesmen really were the fearsome warriors, renowned throughout Northern Burma as savage ruthless headhunters. They were indeed, but their warlike nature was directed at rival tribes in the Naga community.

The gruesome display of a severed head was sure proof of successful conquest in battle, and the numbers acquired gave due status to a warrior in his village community. In addition, the Naga religious belief was that the head contained the soul, the matter on which all life depended. The Naga tribesmen had no doubt at all that his soul would be rewarded in the life hereafter, commensurate to the number of heads accumulated during his sojourn on earth.

I wonder what their reaction was, when the first of our troops in the brigade, the Queen's Regiment arrived from the surrounding jungle. Just like us, they were a frightful sight, a heavily bearded band of scruffy warriors with dusty torn apparel. The children had no reserve and came up to us laughing and chattering without restraint, though like us, they did not understand a word. But as always, actions speak louder than words. Without doubt they were looking for gifts of cigarettes and especially the American 'K' ration fruit bars. Running alongside, they waved the empty wrappers of previous gifts.

On arrival at Ledo, well before the march had begun, permission had been given for us to grow beards. Previously, even a hint of stubble would have been conduct to the prejudice of good order and military discipline. So without further bidding, we had jettisoned our shaving kit and slowly cultivated a variety of barbarous shaggy growths. The order was sensible with many advantages. The weight of a shaving mirror, soap and razor, though minimal, would nevertheless have been an added burden. The daily task of maintaining a stubble free face would have meant the regular cleansing of soapy tins after shaving, in order to brew our char, and the wastage of hard earned water. In addition, shaving every morning would have meant losing at least ten minutes sleeping time, which would eventually have added up to many hours.

Although we had been hungry or very hungry for most of the expedition, our bodies had become hardened and very tough due to the endless marching. We certainly had no excess fat and our rib cages were by now very prominent. The majority of us had survived the constant dampness, the cold and the eternal attention of the mosquitoes, leeches, ticks, flies and the multitude of other poisonous pests. No doubt our youth, previous fitness and medications had played a major part. We had received numerous injections before the start, and we were taking mepacrine malaria suppressive tablets. Also, when we remembered, we used our water purification tablets.

However, by now we had a small nucleus of quite serious

186

cases of malaria and two cases of real dysentery, not the less glamorous diarrhoea. They were being diligently shepherded along by the medical orderlies in the hope of eventual evacuation. Once again, on arrival at Lulum Ga, we had virtually no rations at all and we awaited an evening supply drop. However, the planes did not arrive because of operational problems, so the drop was postponed until the following day, and once again we were forced to waste precious time.

Later that evening however, we had a very welcome bonus. Earlier in the day, the administrative officer had collected five silver rupees from the thirty which had been issued as we set out. It had been spread between the senior NCOs in the column as a safeguard against total loss in one fell swoop. Apparently the villages had a large store of rice which they were willing to sell. We were agreeably surprised to receive a very adequate quantity, probably around one pound in weight to share amongst the four of us.

Before we could soak and cook the rice, we had another offering. There were several horses and ponies with the column for use in commincation and to carry seriously wounded men, but unlike the mules, they had not survived the long march, and had begun to weaken. Two had either died or been shot. The carcases had been carved up by one of the troopers who claimed to have been a butcher in civilian life, so we were presented with small chunks of non-prime questionable meat. Luckily, Bert volunteered to do the cooking, and we eventually shared the result. However, in spite of my hunger, I could not stomach the meat which was gristly and unpalatable, but the fatty gravy tasted much better than it looked. We had the rice to follow as afters, and this was absolutely delicious and satisfying, flavoured and sweetened with a 'K' ration fruit bar and powdered milk which Bill had been saving for an emergency.

After a good night's sleep, the next morning we moved a mile down the track before the supply drop for security reasons, and practised creating a secure and secret bivouac, which because of the previous terrain had not been easily possible. A halt was called and we turned to face the left hand jungle; then we plunged forward at right angles to the track for about five minutes, and formed up again in a single line. In this way, we had covered our tracks, and would be safe from patrols in deep undergrowth. Colonel Cumberlege led us on by compass into the interior for about two hundred yards, and then selected his command post. The soft belly of the column, which included us, would be near the centre, with the rest of the troops spread around like the spokes of a wheel, with the infantry platoons around the rim.

The chutes landed over a wide area, and we spent the rest of the day picking up the supplies. Parachute silk was now in abundant supply We tore it into strips for neckerchiefs, cleaning rags for the wireless equipment, and stored a long length in our wireless pannier. The lengths of nylon cord were used as belts and wound round our bush hats for future use. There was obviously great benefit from the day's rest, but we found our limbs were stiff as we set off very early the next morning. However, we managed to cover a further ten miles.

Monday, 28th February was the busiest day of communications we had experienced. We had a long SITREP to record and a string of messages both ways.Late in the evening, we were told by the cypher section that the Leicesters had reached the Chindwin. One of the messages we received was the famed and often quoted message from General Wingate, 'Well done, Leicesters. Hannibal eclipsed.'

The surprise to me was that I had understood that the two Queen's Regiment columns were leading the Brigade. Apparently, back at Hkalak Ga, the Leicesters had leap-frogged the Queen's to give the latter a respite. Of course, we operators only learned the contents of our coded communications when we were able to listen to gossip from the cypher section.

The following day was very hard going, but for some reason the news had given us mixed feelings of excitement. Crossing the River Chindwin would be an adventure, but would bring us into the Burmese territory occupied by the Japanese. The next three nights, we laagered at map reference 368455 (Masum Zup), 339380 and 353305, each evening bringing further news of the arrival of the preceding column at the Chindwin. We left the village of Kawala, full of expectation. According to the map, we had about five miles to go before reaching the river.

Our eyes focused with expectation on the panorama ahead, as each bend revealed yet another sandbank and overhanging greenery. Then, suddenly there were no more bends, just a vast expanse of water ahead, with the broad sandbanks on either side. In the far distance, blocking the lower horizon, was a solid bank of low dark green jungle below a misty grey sky. It was the far side of the River Chindwin.

10

On to the Stronghold

We soon left the stream, trudged wearily up the sandy bank and melted into the shadowed obscurity of the high protective trees and thick scrub near the Chindwin's edge. We were surrounded by a buzz of activity which was not yet visible. Our laager area had been mapped out in advance. We quickly dumped our packs and equipment and unloaded the mules in the now well established pattern, while we awaited orders. The time was 1600 hours on Saturday, the fourth of March, and we were at map reference 355210. The first stage of our long march was over.

We had negotiated some of the world's wildest virgin forest, a wilderness of high peaks and deep valleys, endured almost constant rain and sometimes bitter cold. Our seventy mile journey had taken twenty-one days, due to the terrain and frightful conditions, and also because of the diabolical supply drops. An extract from Brigadier Fergusson's report in the War Diary, now held in the Public Records Office, sums up our ordeal:

> 'This march was the heaviest imaginable. The rain was torrential and almost continuous; the gradients were often one in two; no single stretch of level going a hundred yards in length existed between Tagap and Hkalak, and few thereafter. Many mule loads had to be carried by hand up steep slopes, and the path had to be remade, or the traverses rebuilt, two to three times during the passage of a column. The cold was intense, particularly at bivouacs over five thousand feet.

The 70lb which men were carrying were greatly
increased in weight due to saturation with water. A
dry bivouac was practically unknown. Leeches,
which were innumerable, were the least trying of
the conditions . . . . Wireless communication was
difficult, and the supply dropping on the whole
was atrocious, up to forty and fifty per cent of the
supplies dropped, falling hundreds or thousands
of feet down the cliffs and becoming a dead loss.
Columns averaged nine days to cover the thirty-
five miles from roadhead to Hkalak.'

It was now five days since the leading elements of the
brigade had reached this bridgehead on the Chindwin, and
daily supply drops had been organised. We were able to
draw five day's 'K' rations, powdered milk, tea and sugar for
the journey ahead. In addition, we had an extra issue of
bully beef, jam, biscuits and rice for a special meal in the
evening. Some replacement kit had been dropped, and at
last I was able to get new denim slacks and a shirt which I
had asked for some time previously. At this time we knew
very little of the organisation behind this crossing of the
Chindwin, but as usual Hedley Chapman, column
intelligence sergeant filled us in with some of the news.
    General Wingate had already flown in by light plane to
inspect progress, but had now returned to Imphal.
Apparently the Brigade had been forced to follow the only
passable route to the River Chindwin, the original planned
direction had proved to be through impenetrable jungle. We
had reached the river five miles further downstream than
had been intended, and much nearer to the Japanese
stronghold of Singkaling Hkami, now ten miles to the south.
Patrols from another unit had been landed in that direction
by glider to create diversionary tactics, and keep the
Japanese busy well away from the main operation.
    Sections were allowed to take turns in bathing under the
trees at the water's edge, and it was absolute bliss for me to
step into clean garments. We were amazed at the feverish
action around us and at the water's edge. The troop crossing
was in full swing. Fifty yards away a long line of men and
animals waited patiently on the shelving sand. Actual

outboard motor boats plied back and forth across the river, the mules were unsaddled and loads, saddles, kit and equipment transferred to the boats. The men scrambled over the sides, the mules swimming behind while the muleteers held the reins, and the boats chugged away from under the overhanging branches to cross the river.

This really was an amazing sight and a huge relief. Since our extensive training in India, we had had the daunting prospect of crossing the River Chindwin at the back of our minds. To us, there was only one conceivable method to be used, as up to now, river crossing had meant bundling arms, equipment and clothing into a buoyant laced up ground-sheet package, launching it ahead of us with some trepidation, to half swim and half float across the water.

Under the massive greenery above us, we walked along the bank to watch this operation. The laden boats made landings on a broad sandbank adjoining the far shore, probably formed and left after the monsoon rains. It was fully a quarter of a mile long and about the same distance away. In between, the broad sluggish river, would have presented a formidable barrier had we attempted to cross using groundsheet floats. But with this method no time was lost. The lone sapper engineer in each returning assault boat, steered an elliptical sweep, slightly downstream back to our side.

The first column of the 51/69 Field Regiment Royal Artillery was crossing, both columns of the Leicesters and Queen's Regiments had already gone on their way. At one end of the sandbank, a glider stood forlorn and conspicuous, a sitting duck for Japanese reconnaissance aircraft. Meanwhile, two Stinson L5 liaison and light transport planes were being manhandled and pulled to the shelter of the far bank. We were absolutely fascinated by the happenings around us, but hunger overcame our curiosity and we returned to our bivouac area. Instructions had arrived that our crossing would commence at 0700 hours the next morning, and until then the time was our own.

Forward Brigade Signals were covering communication at the bridgehead, so we had no need to set up our transmitter, but we did listen for a while to the BBC overseas news, via New Delhi. Apparently, the war was going well, as always.

The German and Italian armies were being driven back from the recently established Anzio beachhead, whereas, in fact they were hanging on grimly. The battle in the Arakan had apparently been brought to a victorious conclusion, which was later substantiated. There was no mention of us of course, but in any case, when Special Force did make the headlines, it was always referred to as 3rd Indian Infantry Division for security reasons.

The fact is, we had no Indian soldiers at all. All the thirty odd Battalions were British, except three Gurkha, three Nigerian and one Burma Rifles. In some of the strongholds formed later, we had British gunners, with 25-pounder Howitzers and Bofers 40mm Anti-Aircraft guns and in the overall operation, the vital extensive support of the No. 1 American Air Commando. They operated Dakota C47's, B25 medium bombers, P51 Mustangs and Stinson L5 aircraft. In total there were something like eighty planes, an additional two hundred Waco Hadrian gliders and two experimental helicopters. There were also the two RAF Squadrons which had dropped some of our supplies.

As darkness fell, we feasted and enjoyed the extra and agreeable variation from our normal 'K' ration. As we sat round our fire, we had the welcome surprise of a visit from our Brigade Signals Officer, Major T. Moon. He was a professional soldier who had risen from the ranks, a first-rate signal operator who talked our language, with whom we could discuss the communication problems to date. Major Moon was leaving by light plane in the morning to return to Rear Brigade HQ Signals at Imphal, in order to make plans for an improvement in communications. His second in command, Captain Kesting, had been flown out in his place, to 'rough it' with Forward Brigade Headquarters. Major Moon stayed talking for half an hour, shared a cup of our 'crash can' treacly char, we wished him a safe journey, and jokingly asked if we could join him back at Imphal.

Mail from home had arrived that afternoon and was distributed. We were informed that letters written tonight would be collected in the morning and flown out by light plane. It was short notice, but there really was little that we could say except that we were well. (That was difficult for some). I wrote to Mollie and my parents knowing it would be a wondeful bonus for them to get a letter. Quite a number of my immediate colleagues had now become very lethargic and did not make the effort to write.

Although we had to be away and across the river very early in the morning, the day had been different from the previous long slog, and we were still excited by the river crossing operation. Despite our tiredness, we decided to have another look at the goings on before going to sleep. The outboard motors continued to chug across as the assault boats ferried the rest of the Royal Artillery columns across. Aldis lamps, operated by the RAF detachment brought in by glider for the manoeuvre, winked across the water. A thin mist drifted over the river, the moon had not yet risen, and we could barely make out the further shore.

On the sandbank, the makeshift landing strip was in use and several light planes landed and took off, almost silently at this distance. We were about to leave when we heard the unmistakable drone of an aircraft overhead. We could not see it but recognition lights were flashed, so the plane must have been established as friendly. At first, we expected to watch a supply drop, but as the plane continued to circle overhead, two tiny blue lights appeared at the end of the sandbank low on the ground, and then another almost at the other end, further back. The noise of the plane overhead had faded completely and for a moment we were most puzzled, but then we heard it coming back noisily, swooping low along the wide river channel. The plane had its landing lights full on, and it was so near to the water that we expected it to land or crash. The suddenly the engines roared full throttle, it sped away climbing rapidly, with the blue light at the end of the sandbank following. As we followed the plane, climbing away in the moonlight we saw that behind it and under the blue light was a glider, almost certainly the one that we had seen earlier in the day. What we had actually witnessed was a snatch lift of an American Hadrian 225 glider by a Douglas C47 Dakota aircraft. The following year I was to have first hand experience of this operation, but the impossible, the totally unexpected, most audacious operation left an indelible imprint on my mind.

To clarify the actual method used I have drawn a rough diagram and explanatory text. All the personnel involved, especially the plane and glider pilots needed nerves of steel to take part in this very early venture. Back in the United Kingdom experimental snatches were still in their infancy, and this technique of lifting gliders from sandbanks or temporary landing strips by the American Air Commando in wartime conditions had never been attempted before. These pilots were volunteers from the American Transport Squadron and were highly experienced in all phases of troop carrier work. Glider snatches needed a high degree of skill. The Dakota C47 had to fly thirty feet off the ground trailing a hook which would connect with the nylon line stretched between the two bamboo poles. According to all the records I have been able to trace, this was not only the first instance of a glider pickup under combat conditions, but also the first in a night-time operation. After the war had ended Major General John Alison DSO, USAAF, joint commander of No. 1 Air Commando stated in a letter to Major General Derek Tulloch, who was General Wingate's Chief of Staff, that as far as he knew there were no night snatches in actual combat.

However, there is no doubt about the one I witnessed on the night of 5th March, 1944, and in fact another similar lift-off was carried out successfully on the night of 12th March, 1944. This night snatch was to lift the glider that had delivered river crossing equipment to 111 Brigade.

The Brigade, commanded at the time by Brigadier W.D.A. Lentaigne had, in fact, run into difficulties when attempting to cross the River Irrawaddy. They were discovered crossing by four Burmese police, whose commander, siding with the Japanese, had sent them to find out what was happening. The four Burmese were immediately arrested, interrogated, and sent back to India that night under guard in the otherwise empty glider. This supernatural method of transport must have been absolutely terrifying to these simple Burmese countrymen. Shelford Bidwell's account of this incident in the 'Chindit War' says:

'No one seems to have sympathised with the Burmese in their plight; subjugated by the British, reconquered by the Japanese; their country ravaged by the Chinese Army in 1942; bombed by

195

the Americans; and now carried off to India as "traitors." One can only hope that those unfortunate constables were one day restored to their homes and families.'

Method used to snatch lift the Waco Hadrian 225 glider by Douglas C47 Dakota aircraft.

This manoeuvre was used to relift a glider from sandbanks or short temporary airstrip after it had landed troops or supplies.

Two fifteen foot high poles were erected fifty feet apart, some one hundred and fifty feet ahead of the glider. At the top of each pole a special cradle was fitted to support the tow rope and a blue lamp wired ready for connection to a battery. The tow rope was then looped across the two supports on the poles and led back to the glider, where it was secured by fixing pins to the top of the fuselage above the pilot. Just behind the coupling was another blue lamp, which could be actuated by the glider pilot.

Radio communication was established by the ground crew with both pilots as the Dakota approached and the three blue lamps would be switched on.

The Dakota pilot then made his approach run, homing in on the triangle of lights, sweeping down low just above the posts. An extending self locking hook trailing below the Dakota would locate the elasticated nylon tow rope and the glider would be whisked up and away.

Very early the next morning, I could hear the muffled buzz of activity as the river crossing continued. There were just a few precious minutes to doze before the guard came to call our reveille. The light from a full moon filtered through the tops of the high trees, creating an eerie pattern of light and shade on the blanketed men around me. All too soon I heard the careful steps of the sentry, as he picked his way around the sleeping bodies. He tapped me lightly on the shoulder, I quietly answered 'OK' and reached for my hat and boots which nightly served as a pillow.

196

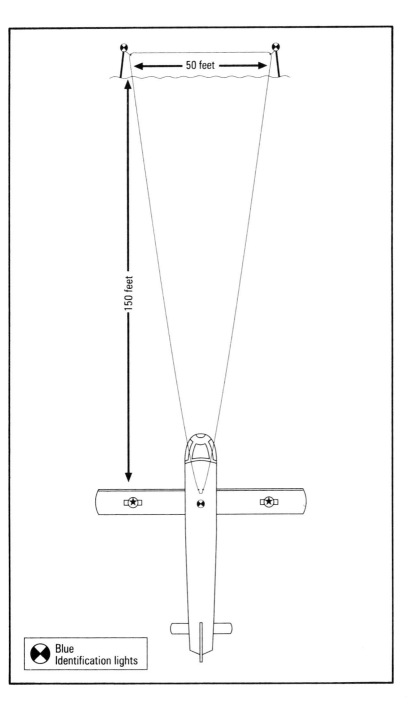

50 feet

150 feet

Blue
Identification lights

197

The bugle calls and cries of 'wakey wakey' had long since been mothballed. Stealth and silence were now our watchwords. Slipping on my boots, I awakened my companions before tightening the laces, folding my groundsheet and blanket, and strapping them securely to the top of my pack, with rifle and bush hat alongside. We breakfasted in front of our driftwood fire and brewed some char while consuming yet another 'K' ration. As usual, there was little conversation. Our early morning ritual was almost silent, automatic and predictable.

On the previous day, our morale had felt boosted. The first part of our slog was over, and we relished the change of menu, enjoying having full bellies for the first time since leaving our start point at Ledo. We had bathed in the Chindwin and donned fresh clothes. Furthermore, we expected the crossing to be much easier than we had previously thought, and we felt lifted and assured by the proficiency radiating in this secure temporary stronghold. But as the new day began, that euphoria suddenly evaporated and the outlook for most of us suddenly changed. However easy it had appeared yesterday, we still had to cross this wide river, and continue our march. Our baptismal taste of action could soon begin. We were leaving behind the no man's land between India and the Japanese-held Burma. Without doubt, the Chindwin was a major dividing line. Once across, we would have to be prepared to meet Japanese patrols and garrisoned villages.

We loaded the mules quickly in routine fashion, donned equipment and packs, shouldered our rifles and joined Column HQ, filing slowly towards the river bank. Our packs seemed very heavy and indeed were. With the full quota of five days' rations, most of us were carrying a weight which approached half our body weight. Luckily, the weather was fine and dry.

RSM Bamford was fussily organising the embarkation, and my Signal Section was allocated two assault boats. Since an unfortunate altercation during training, concerning the need to charge the batteries overnight, he began to treat my section with more toleration, accepting that we were a necessary, maybe even useful, attachment from the Royal Corps of Signals.

As the first of our allocated boats nosed bows-first on to the beach, we waded knee-deep into the water, carefully handling the wireless set and placing it in the centre of the flat bottom. Around this we placed one of the batteries, a can of petrol, the charging engine and one of the panniers. We had purposely split the radio gear in case of any mishap during the crossing. The saddles of two of the mules, four lots of equipment and packs followed before Bill Warbutton, Buck and two of the muleteers hastily clambered over the side. The boat reversed and turned towards the shore, as we led the two mules into the water. The muleteers grapsed the reins, the outboard motor accelerated and away they went.

In the early days of our training, all four of these large magnificent mules had been as obstinate as only mules can be, but now the first two swam off behind the boat without a murmur. We had now gained a great affection for them and the muleteers an even closer affection. Mules are very intelligent animals and the care, attention and kindness was certainly reciprocated. They were part of our working team and did not want to be left behind. We watched them distance themselves from us, heads bobbing up and down in the deeper water, their tails waving above the waterline.

Two of the muleteers, Bert Fennell and myself loaded the next boat across with the rest of our equipment and gear, losing no time in the process. The other two mules were good as gold, giving no trouble at all. But some of the mules in other platoons gave their handlers a great deal of trouble. Later in the day, one of them broke loose in mid stream, attempted to return to the start point, but was swept away and drowned down river.

On the way over, we realised that the Chindwin was a great deal wider and deeper than the impression given by our bankside view. Although only a tributary of the massive Irrawaddy, which it joins at Pakokku near Mandalay in central Burma, it is twice the length of the River Thames. The melting snows from the desolate northern mountains where China, India and Burma meet, as well as the tributaries from the rain forest, ensure that it remains a wide barrier throughout the year. During the monsoon period, the River Chindwin becomes a wide raging torrent, and the central channel is realigned, leaving new and completely uncharted sandbanks spread in its wake.

Aldis lamps continued the communication across the river, as we scanned the water up and down stream. Our rifles, like all the assorted armaments around us, were loaded and ready for action. We heard several muffled explosions at a distance and this added to our vigilance.

It was certainly most incredible that so many men and animals could be ferried across this river in Japanese-held territory without detection. The stratagem of landing patrols up and down river had undoubtedly been most effective in diverting Japanese attention. By the time our sister column, which was following us at the rear, had crossed, over three thousand men and nearly six hundred mules, ponies and horses would be safely over the River Chindwin.

Once ashore, we lost no time at all. Up to our waists in water, we rapidly manhandled the packs and equipment on to the sandbank. Still a long way from cover, the mules were saddled, girths tightened and loads affixed in record time, before we made a mad dash to the jungle edge, fully fifty yards across the energy sapping sand and shingle. Although the beach was deserted, we could not have missed the well trampled track, made by the hundreds of men and animals in the previous successful landings. Steps had been roughly fashioned, to help us scale the steep river bank and enter the sudden leaden silence of the friendly jungle camouflage.

Like vehicles at the end of a long convoy, we became separated from the rest of the column. We pressed ahead several hundred yards before rounding a bend and sighting the familiar but welcome rear end of one of our mules. As we regrouped to form into 'column snake', there was a monstrous deafening explosion just ahead. Sudden and unexpected, it sounded like the detonation of a mortar bomb on impact, and was followed by a single rifle shot. We froze, then dived for cover off the path into the undergrowth, prepared for the worst. With rifles cocked at the ready, we waited a seemingly interminable time in apprehensive silence.

A garbled message came back down the line ahead. One of our troops had sprung a booby trap. It had not been enemy fire. In fact, it soon transpired that tragically,

Sergeant Moore had taken a wrong turning and led his infantry section down a mined track. Many booby traps had been laid down by our own troops to protect the crossing, and it is likely he triggered one of those. Sergeant Moore was the only serious casualty, both his legs were shattered, and after hasty temporary first aid, he was hurriedly carried back past us to the river. Mercifully, the accident had happened when almost immediate evacuation was possible. He was flown by a shuttle service of American planes back to hospital in India that night. The rifle shot that we had heard quite clearly was never fully explained. However, as arms had been loaded at the time with safety catches off, it could well have been a spontaneous reaction from Sergeant Moore or one of his section.

This was the first gunfire and explosion we had heard under combat conditions. The fear of being ambushed was always with us, but we learned that day that silence was the best defence. Although this had been a minor incident in a now active service unit, it gave us a taste of events to come, and it caused a hold up in the column's progress while the evacuation was being organised. That night we camped near the village of Ningkau Ga.

During the afternoon we passed a large field of giant poppies. The petals had long since fallen, the leaves had withered, but the huge seed heads which had been left to mature and dehydrate, were ready for harvest. This was the first time we had come across evidence of Northern Burma's major industry, the production of opium and heroin. We already knew about the production of opium in this part of Burma, because the Naga and Kachin tribesmen were more happy to use opium for currency than the local coinage or Indian silver rupees.

Two days after we had crossed the River Chindwin, the two columns ahead of us, the 51st and 69th of the Field Regiment Royal Artillery, turned north to attack the town of Lonkin. Brigadier Fergusson had agreed with General Stilwell that these columns would attack and seize this Japanese stronghold, in return for General Stilwell's previous agreement that the brigade could make use of the Ledo Road as a springboard for our operation. This left a gap in the line of march, between the four columns of the

Leicesters and Queen's Regiments ahead and ourselves making up the rear, a divide that for reasons of fatigue and supplies, we were unable to close during the journey ahead.

When the two Royal Artillery columns eventually reached Lonkin, they found that the main body of the Japanese stronghold had fled, leaving the town virtually abandoned. After a brief skirmish with the enemy rearguard, in which a few casualties were suffered, they destroyed the dumps of stores and ammunition that had been left behind. However, by the time the stronghold had been cleared of Japanese, and they were on the move again, valuable days had been lost. In the event, they were never able to catch up with the brigade, and did not take part in the subsequent main battle for Indaw. In fact, apart from an additional minor skirmish by one of their patrols, they took no further part in the fighting.

This was certainly a great wastage of men and material. Previously trained gunners, battle hardened with the 70th Division in the Middle East desert, these 900 soldiers had been de-mechanised and trained as infantry and muleteers, in order to march hundreds of miles in the jungle wilderness, until they were worn out by malaria, illnesses and fatigue, and flown back to India.

While we were occupied with the Chindwin crossing, there was great military activity back in Assam. Codenamed 'Operation Thursday', the bulk of Special Force approaching 10,000 men and over 1,000 mules was assembled at the airfields of Lalaghat, Hailakandi and Tulihal poised for the strike behind the Japanese lines in northern Burma. D day had been finally decided for the night of Sunday, 5th March. The glider parties of engineers and bulldozers stood ready for the initial flight, to convert the landing zones into airstrips, which had to be long and smooth enough to land the C47 troop-carrying aircraft.

Zero hour for the first take off was 1700 hours, but half an hour before departure, an L5 plane landed at Lalaghat with a sheaf of photographs taken quite by chance, showing the proposed landing areas, code named 'Broadway', 'Chowringhee' and 'Piccadilly'. These revealed that the latter clearing had for some reason been blocked by tree trunks, making landing quite impossible.

This was a shattering experience for General Wingate, and indeed the rest of the British and American commanders present. Wingate felt that the whole operation must have been betrayed to the Japanese. A decision was hastily made by the American Air Force and British commanders on the scene. Presided over by General Slim, they decided unanimously to go ahead with the fly in, using only the Broadway and Chowringhee clearings. The decision was a most difficult one, especially for the commander of the joint USAAF-RAF Troop Carrier Command, Brigadier General William D. Old, who was directly responsible for the air armada. In the event, the Japanese were completely surprised, and the blocking of Piccadilly had merely been due to a routine Burma forestry operation. The logs had been laid out to dry in a convenient jungle clearing.

There is no doubt that the 9,000 men and over a thousand mules introduced by air, between the 5th and 12th March were an absolute surprise to the Japanese. In fact, it took them fully eight days to wake up to the fact that this great Allied Offensive Force had established a bridgehead in the middle of their military positions in Northern Burma.

At the time, many of us began to consider the absurdity of the hazardous march we were making. We were too late, ten days behind schedule with the prospect of a further one hundred and fifty miles to slog. Furthermore, it was to be over virtually unknown country, before we could reach our objective around Indaw in Northern Burma. In addition, none of us was completely fit. Some of us had nothing more than minor irritants such as blisters, insect bites and prickly heat, but many had jungle sores, foot-rot and the varying stages of malaria. We were all suffering from malnutrition, some men had lost a great amount of weight, and many were mentally and physically debilitated. It naturally followed that our fighting ability would be dulled.

The rest of Special Force were now either in battle positions or on the march to establish strongholds, just a few miles from their objectives. Admittedly for some, the couple of hours spent flying in had been uncomfortable and perilous, especially transport by glider. However, prior to take-off they had been well fed, with cookhouses and comfortable sleeping facilities, trained to the minute, and with high morale. The unfinished journey that had already taken us many weeks, had been achieved by them overnight. We had been told before we started that our march was to surprise the Japanese, but now the rest of Special Force had obviously stolen our thunder.

Nevertheless we had to press on. The route was still very hard going and though the hills were not as high as the Paktai mountains, we continually had to climb and descend heights of over 2,000 feet. By the evening of 9th March, we were again out of rations, though a supply drop was due at 1900 hours near the intersection of a track and a stream. However, things went very wrong. The five planes arrived on time but the handlers in the Dakota were more than slap-happy. It was maddening to watch the parachutes floating gracefully away from the dropping zones, some alighting high in the treetops, others missing the site altogether and finishing hundreds of feet down in the valley.

Although extra troops were detailed to salvage the containers, almost all were lost. The net result was less than a day's ration per man. Because of this, another request for supplies was ordered and it was after midnight before we were able to log the reply. Another supply drop had been arranged for the following day, but only a further two miles on. This, of course, was to create another unscheduled delay.

During the latter part of the night a violent storm broke out in full fury. Vivid and continuous flashes lit up the sky, and thunder rumbled around the hills. A solid downpour almost washed us away, and we were saturated. We were glad when it was light enough to sort out our belongings, and wring out our soaking garments. The rain had ceased as suddenly as it had begun, but as we prepared to move, water still spattered from the matted interlaced curtain of vines, thorn bush and bamboo. Our spirits reflected the surroundings. As we commenced our short day's journey, we spoke little, keeping our thoughts to ourselves. Fallen trees and upturned roots caused minor delays, making our sodden packs and equipment feel even heavier than they were. We trudged along, tempers short, moving like automatons through the endless narrow passage of the same design, a tangled mass of greenery.

Before the first halt, the sun in a now cloudless sky began to make us and the jungle steam. As the heat increased, the single column of men and mules ahead reminded me of a rugger scrum, with players wrapped in a cloud of vapour on a cold damp November day. By the time we left the trail just before midday and melted into the jungle, our equipment, clothes and bodies were nearly dry. We set up our radio on the edge of the large clearing selected for the evening supply drop, and were now pleased that today's journey had been so short. We took turns in spreading our belongings out to dry, and felt in much better spirits.

That night brought another setback. Only a solitary plane arrived, which meant only one day's ration for the column. We sent off several messages to Rear Brigade, and again we had to keep the set on the air until well after midnight. Eventually, cyphers told us all the traffic had been cleared. Apparently the stores and supplies intended for us had been dropped on a column ahead of us. From the air, we were in a very small area, and we lit the same type of recognition fires as the others. Unlucky for us, lucky for them. Even worse, the column had been told that the next possible date for a drop was the 14th. This meant we would have to exist on less than two days' rations for the next four days.

Sir Robert Thompson, a Chindit veteran, has been quoted as saying in praise of the air drop that:

'This air supply became so efficient that the troops relied on it completely. You could run yourselves down to one day's ration or less, you could go a day almost without rations and know perfectly well that if you demanded a supply drop at 10.00 p.m. one night, in a particular area of jungle, or in a paddy field alongside, you knew you were going to get it.'

This was brilliant praise and absolutely correct in theory. In practice however, there was no guarantee that supplies would arrive, due to many obvious reasons. The difficulty in radio communication, the nature of the country we were negotiating and not least, the shortage of aircraft available for the campaign were the main reasons. There is no doubt however, that troops in static positions fared reasonably well.

For most of the time the following day, we followed a dirty muddy stream down a long valley, continually crossing and recrossing the water. The weather was humid, and we were pestered by encircling flies and other winged pests. However some of the scenery was most beautiful, and the jungle in daylight always seemed less formidable. The monotony of the dense green slopes was relieved at times by a riot of colour from the cascades of white blossomed trees, hibiscus shrubs and large laburnums. As we marched through yet another deserted village, high poinsettia trees had filled the spaces between the huts with red and yellow foliage. Swarms of brilliantly coloured butterflies and dragonflies drifted from bush to bush oblivious to our passing. This could not be said of the baboons and monkeys, who seemed to follow us constantly. Always in the background, often out of view, they screamed and chattered as they leapt from branch to branch.

That evening, we laagered near the village of Namson. A light plane strip had been constructed by preceding columns, and the next morning two of our men were lifted out by the American Air Commando. One man had been suffering from sprue, an awful tropical disease of the intestine, and the other from cerebral malaria, which attacks the brain's nervous system and invariably proves fatal. Both men looked very ill and beyond care.

As we pressed on further, requests were made for supplies but to no avail as transport planes were at a premium. In fact, the promised date of the 14th was cancelled at short notice. In spite of our acute hunger, we now made good progress, marching ten hours daily. The weather and the land were now very dry and the midday heat intense. There were large areas of teak forest covering the undulating terrain. We ploughed through a thick carpet of dried leaves that had been undisturbed for years. They crackled and broke under our boots, causing a thick penetrating dust which lodged in our throats and nostrils. Luckily, water was not in short supply, though we had to ensure we filled our

206

bottles and chaguls at every opportunity.

We passed through one inhabited village, referred to as Kwinhe on the map, where the natives offered rice, which we gave to the few sick now struggling at the rear of the column. Modern travel manuals give comprehensive hints on jungle survival, but in our situation they would have been of little help. A game hunt to provide food for over 400 men would have been time consuming and the sound of firearms would have given our location away to the enemy.

On the 14th March, we reached the wide valley of the River Uyu, a large tributary of the Chindwin. This made a welcome change, as the going was flat for a long distance, though later we had to negotiate sandbanks as we continually crossed the river. On the next day we arrived at the village of Sezin, where we were surprised to see an airstrip constructed in the paddy and a platoon of the Leicesters guarding it.

One of the guards told us that the regiment had had a brief skirmish with a Japanese patrol, killing one and taking a prisoner whom they flew out. Later that day, there was talk of the prisoner being in fact a Gurkha who had been a Chindit on the first of Wingate's expeditions. At the time we dismissed this news as a tall story. But years later after the War had ended, this story was confirmed when I read our Brigadier's account of the incident in his book *The Wild Green Earth*:

> 'Below the village in the paddy, was the strip which the Leicesters had built to fly out their prisoner. He turned out not to be a Jap at all, but a Gurkha survivor of the first year's expedition, who had been pressed into the service of the Mikado. Shot in the leg, he had subsided cheerfully on the ground, beating his chest, smiling and shouting "77 Brigade! 77 Brigade!".'

This Gurkha had certainly been lucky. Firstly that the Japanese had allowed him to serve with them, and secondly that he escaped punishment for change of allegiance. Back in India, I doubt whether he was able to give much useful information. The Japanese, of course, could not understand why their opponents allowed themselves to be captured alive. Their rank and file had no instructions as to what information they might give if taken prisoner. It is an amazing fact that of the very few physically fit Japanese prisoners captured during the Burma campaign, not one was above the rank of Major. Within a very short time we were to have first hand experience of their fanaticism.

When we passed through Sezin, all was quiet and peaceful. We then hid in the jungle about a mile away, near another riverside village called Shwedwin. There was the chance at this halt to write letters to be collected and flown out from the strip at Sezin with another three seriously ill men. In the evening, at last we had our supply drop, in a clearing alongside the river, and almost all the five days' ration was recovered. In addition, extra treats were dropped such as bully beef, biscuits, canned fruit and extra cigarettes. I always looked forward to the latter because they had great exchange value. That evening, we enjoyed our first meal since leaving the River Chindwin, which included another of our special stews. We certainly had a feast and a brief respite from the monotonous 'K' ration.

It is hard to believe that our presence along this valley was unknown to the Japanese. The Japanese patrols were constantly around the villages in this area. The Burmese in the main were intent on living a simple peaceful life, working in the villages or on the surrounding paddy. However, if the opportunity arose, I am sure that they would have passed on information to either side for heroin or for money. Probably because we were such a large force, these small Japanese patrols, thin on the ground were wise enough to steer clear and avoid contact, especially as at the moment we were no threat to their supply routes. It should also be remembered that at this moment, the Japanese 15th Army, consisting of the 15th, 31st and 33rd Divisions, was massing to invade India by way of Imphal and Kohima.

Marching seemed easier when we began to head south across the marshy country, not only because of the almost flat terrain, but because our bellies were full. We passed several abandoned Japanese foxholes near the village of Gwegy and laagered that night near another named Mansein. We continued to make good progress during the

208

next three days, through thick scrub jungle or teak forest, but on an established well-worn track, taking short midday breaks to reduce the previous delays.

On the 19th March, we had another supply drop near the village of Mezam, but we had to leave half the rations behind with a guard for our sister column, the tail-enders of the Brigade. They had fared even worse than ourselves with supply drops. It was at this drop that a lance corporal and three men were caught stealing rations and charged. Certainly they were not the only party on collection who had done this, but according to the grape vine they had been suspected previously. Before we moved off, they were flogged by the CSM in front of their platoon, and the lance corporal was reduced to the ranks.

In *The Wild Green Earth,* our Brigadier made no mention of this, nor is it recorded in the 45th Reconnaissance War Diary at the Public Records Office, but he did say that 'Anyone found munching or filling pockets from a broken container was liable to severe punishment.' Indeed, there are few recorded instances of flogging in the records of the Special Force. However, two men of the Royal Artillery in Column 51 were caught asleep on sentry duty, and another man in the same column was caught pilfering rations after a supply drop. This was in March, when these two columns, the 51st and 69th were hurrying to catch up with us, after the diversion to Lonkin.

The column commander, Major A.C.S. Dickie, apparently after much soul-searching, had ordered both sentries to be flogged by the RSM with a bamboo cane. The man who had stolen rations was tied to a tree in direct sunshine for two hours during the midday break. After the War, questions were asked in Parliament about this and other instances, but only one case was ever judicially investigated. This involved the flogging of two men in the 2nd Battalion of the York and Lancaster Regiment in another brigade. The commanding officer was tried by court-martial, and quite correctly he was eventually exonerated. The evidence for the defence was that the men had consented to be punished in this way, and that the actual punishment was no more severe than that given by a schoolmaster. The men who received the punishment must have realised that they were lucky. In some armies at that time, they would have faced execution. Although flogging had been abolished eighty years before by the British Army, and field punishment after the First World War, it should be remembered that caning was the norm at schools up to this time as a disciplinary measure. In fact not many years before, I had been given 'six of the best' by my headmaster for sliding on the frozen school pond against orders.

During the next two days, wireless traffic increased and we realised that because of the strength of the other columns' radio signals, the brigade was converging on the area ahead. We passed through the villages of Taungbohia, Nanaw and Letpan in quick succession, and on the 21st March, we arrived at the much larger village of Tonbon, map reference 450740.

The natives here seemed very friendly, and they offered the column a very large quantity of rice. We were able to have something like an egg-cup full of rice each. This was only the second time that we had been able to buy enough for a whole column. Sergeant Chapman told us that the headman of the village had reported a large garrison of 300 Japanese troops ten miles away at Mansi almost due west. That seemed near, but this small town was behind us now, separated by thick trackless jungle and the Namsaung Range, with peaks in excess of 3,000 feet. We followed the Kalat Chaung the next morning down a beautiful winding valley, through Taungle where an airstrip was being constructed amidst feverish activity by troops from one of the Leicester columns. This airstrip later became the headquarters of the American L5 and L1 pilots.

Just before midday, we left the track and climbed a low hill overlooking the River Meza and the village of Kalat. Absolutely worn out by the long march of over 450 miles, it was with great relief that we were told this would be part of the new stronghold and our base for future guerrilla operations against the Japanese. The Leicester Columns had set out this camp, before moving to the other side of the valley. As the Brigadier's Forward Brigade Headquarters were here, we did not need to open up communication that evening, and we looked forward to a few day's rest.

Apart from an issue of rations, our one special pleasure

was the use of earth closets, proper latrines after six weeks of jungle squatting. It was here that three days previously, General Wingate had flown in and decided with Bridagier Fergusson that this was to be the 16th Brigade Stronghold and Airfield, code named 'Aberdeen'. During the afternoon we were allowed to bathe in the River Meza, in small armed parties. Later, mail was distributed, including English newspapers from the Red Cross.

Fortification of the base was going ahead at full speed. The Americans had arrived that morning in Dakota-hauled gliders, and their earth movers, bulldozers, trucks and jeeps were already in operation constructing a massive runway suitable for Dakotas and fighter bombers. This was certainly a beautiful setting. Where the two valleys met, the Burmese had created a fertile expanse around the rivers, clear of jungle one mile in each direction. We overlooked the village of Kalat, whilst on the other side of the Meza River, there was Naunghmi, half a mile to the east on the road to Banmauk. All the roads in this part of North Burma were constructed of beaten earth and rubble, very often potholed, and only motorable in the dry season.

The rest of the day passed quickly, and because of the activity around us, we felt much more secure than on the single file journey. We were able to read our mail, write letters, sort out our haversack contents, or just rest and do nothing. Little did we know that the next morning we were in for a rude awakening.

We were woken the next morning at sunrise and told the unwelcome news that we must prepare to leave for battle at once. Granted that as soldiers at war, it was our task to fight but everyone, including our officers, had expected at least a few days' respite after the gruelling march. In fact it is now quite clear from the records, that Brigadier Fergusson had protested on two counts. Firstly, that he was short of the 51 and 69 Columns, still way behind after the detour to capture Lonkin for General Stilwell, quite apart from the fact that the rest of the columns needed to rest. Secondly, because the method of attack on Indore was by direct assault. Our brigade of lightly armed troops were trained for guerrilla fighting, and not for the envisaged attack on strongly prepared positions. Having put his case to Wingate in vain,

211

being a regular soldier he obeyed his orders, having no other choice.

We were issued with five days' rations, ordered to burn letters for security reasons and at 1000 hours, we marched out of Aberdeen, heavily laden.

11

Disaster at Indaw

We were now well into the dry season, and as we left the stronghold in a cloudless sky, the sun beat down on the road, so that we marched in a haze of heat. Our boots raised a sandy, choking cloud which hung in the air, covering our garb in a film of dust, making our mouths dry and our eyes sore, even before we crossed the long narrow footbridge over the shallow and inviting Meza River.

We passed through the village of Manhton, before veering east on a gradual climb. We left the road for a narrow track through scrub which led us to a teak forest on the higher ground. At the first halt, we were warned of our nearness to Jap-held Indaw, and the need to move silently. Just before darkness fell, we crossed a stream, watering the mules and filling our water bottles and chaguls, soon disappearing into thick jungle for the night near the village of Nyauggon.

Soon after we had unloaded, we heard the unmistakable sound of battle not far away. We clearly identified the mortars and machine gun fire as well as the crunch of heavier shellfire, which continued well into the night. This puzzled us at the time, because we were comparatively lightly armed with mortars, machine guns, grenades, flame-throwers and small arms, so it could not have been any of the columns in our Brigade.

What we had in fact heard was the noise of the conflict between the Japanese and Major Calvert's 77th Brigade. This was one of the Brigades flown into Broadway from 5th March onwards. By now, they were defending a well-established stronghold commanding the road and rail routes at Henu near Mawlu. Heavy equipment had been

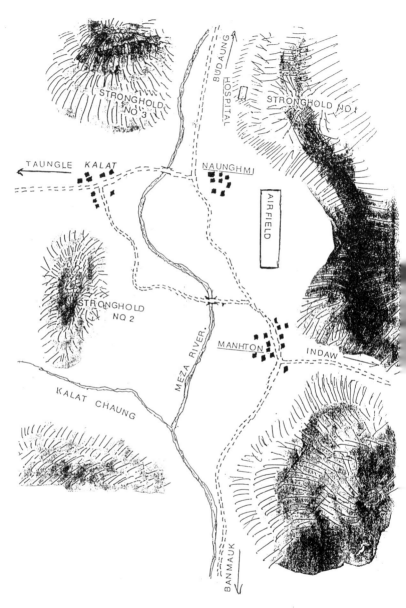

'ABERDEEN'

Air defence established with Bofors and Cerlikon anti-aircraft guns.
Ground defence by mines, Garrison troops and patrolling columns.

flown in by glider, including Howitzers and Bofors Anti-Aircraft guns, capable of firing 120 rounds a minute to a height of 12,000 feet. The story of Major Calvert's battle at the White City, so named because of the silk parachutes caught up in the surrounding trees, has since been much recorded, especially by Michael 'Mad Mike' Calvert himself, in his book *Prisoners of Hope.*

In India, the Japanese attack was sweeping forward almost unopposed. The road between Imphal and Manipur Road was cut, so Imphal could only be reached by air. The worsening situation dictated that non-combatant troops should leave. Consequently, Special Force Headquarters were flown out south to Sylhet. The big Royal Signals transmitters closed down, remaining silent for one full week. Admittedly, back in Sylhet, temporary number twenty-two sets began to operate, but they did not have enough power to be effective at a sufficiently great distance. All this, of course, was completely unknown to us at the time.

At Nyauggon, well into the night, we took turns on the set, transmitting our call sign, listening for replies, twisting the dials in frustration but to no avail. We could find nothing wrong with our set, nor with the fully charged accumulators. Frustration turned to anger, when the messages piled up. Eventually those with the highest priority were cleared by our RAF ground-to-air detachment, who opened up especially to help us out. We were most grateful for the support of Sergeants Bouverie and Hircock, though I doubt whether the messages via Air Base could have found Special Force Headquarters at that time, as they were on the move. For the next few days, my Signal Section with Column 45 were complete passengers. It could not have happened at a more crucial time.

There is no doubt in my own mind, whatever else is recorded, that Brigadier Fergusson's lack of success with the 16th Brigade, in his first and last battle, had been due to the original siting of Special Force Main Brigade at Imphal. GHQ India must have realised that the Japanese were preparing to invade India, and that the obvious route would be the move through the Manipur valley via Imphal and Kohima. It was certainly a military error to site rear communications so far forward. The airfields at Silchar,

Lalaghat or Hailakandi would have been much safer, because although the distance for telecommunication was further, there would have been no difficulty as the range of the American transmitters and wireless sender no. 53 had a range of up to 500 miles on the Morse code carrier wave.

Early the next morning, we moved a short distance nearer to Indaw, ready for the attack. The point was three miles from the village of Auktaw, near a double bend of the Ledan Chaung. Around us all seemed quiet, but the waiting was tedious. We opened up our wireless in an endeavour to contact Rear Brigade Signals but without success. We felt very useless and vulnerable, especially as we had no communication with our forward troops, and would not be in radio contact during the battle. Orders from the commanding officer to the forward column platoons were given on the smaller wireless set no. 18, and we had no responsibility for this network.

During the afternoon, we were briefed on the situation. The main object for the brigade was to capture the town of Indaw and the two airfields, Indaw West and Indaw East. Of the eight columns, the 51st and 69th were too far behind to take part. The 21st Column of the Queen's was already on the way, making a detour round the west side of Indaw Lake, in order to attack and secure the Indaw West airstrip. The other Queen's column was going even further west, to block the supply of men and supplies from Banmouk by road. So this left just four columns to make the main assault. The 45th and 54th Columns were to approach Indaw direct, capturing the village of Thetkegyin on the way. The 17th and 71st Columns of the Leicesters were to attack Indaw from the east in a pincer movement. During this briefing, on 25th March, we were told that according to intelligence reports, Indaw was only held by a small garrison, the bulk of which was the Burmese National Army, the traitor army.

The next day there was a long delay before we moved nearer to Auktaw to meet up with the two Leicester columns, just after 1100 hours. It should be made quite clear that we did not blunder into Auktaw, hoping to water the men and animals, only to find it held by the Burma National Army fortified by Japanese, as stated by Shelford Bidwell in *The Chindit War*. We and the mules were able to drink, water

216

bottles were filled, and at midday we were still on the banks of the Ledan Chaung, which was a wide clear stream.

The Leicester columns brought fresh reports from patrols. The information now was that Indaw had a reinforced garrison of over two thousand Japanese troops. Hardly had this fresh briefing concluded, when firing broke out to our right in a paddy field between us and the village of Auktaw. Who was fighting whom I cannot say, all I know is that we were not involved in the initial shooting. However, in the centre of the paddy field there were around a dozen enemy soldiers who were obviously ready to surrender. Two of them were waving pieces of white parachute silk. Nevertheless, several of the men began to fire at them, and one of our officers demanded my rifle so he could 'have a pot'. All of them were killed, except one who was taken prisoner by an infantry platoon of the Leicesters. This minor skirmish revealed a complete lack of discipline and inexperience of battle by those who fired. I now know that these were Burmese who had been pressed into service by both poverty and the Japanese, and led by one Japanese liaison officer.

Almost at the same time, but from a different direction, several shots were fired without any apparent reply. Standing around while all this was happening, with our four mules, and all the signal equipment, we were sitting ducks. However, within a few minutes of the shooting we were on our way.

We had become used to messages being passed along the column, but now a most unbelievable story was revealed. It was not an official communication, but started behind us in the rear defence platoon. The tale passed on by word of mouth was that a patrol returning to the column had been ambushed in error by the Leicesters. Two of our officers, Leiutenants Dickenson and Ryley as well as three of their men, had been killed and hastily buried at Auktaw. Maybe it was a rumour, but would certainly explain the second volley of shots we had heard.

Brigadier Fergusson mentioned this incident in his book:-

'It proved to be the luckless reconnaissance party I

had detached from the recce a fortnight ago, to have a look at Maingpok. Reaching Aberdeen and hearing that the battle for Indaw was imminent, they hurried on to join in the fun and walked straight into the enemy. Both officers were killed, and three of their men.'

He did not mention names. It would be interesting to hear from the survivors of that luckless platoon, as to whom they bumped into that day. As to the hurrying, I would think that after an extension of our long exhausting march, few officers or men would be likely to hurry to 'join in the fun'. It does sound rather like an outing to the seaside or a meeting of the local hunt.

Shelford Bidwell mentions in his book that two officers and three other ranks were killed in the skirmish with the Burmese Traitor Army. This was certainly not true. The firing came from an entirely different direction. It must be recognised that in this type of guerrilla warfare there was no front line. The easiest thing in the world was to run into another column in error, and identification was very difficult in the thick scrub jungle.

What was written in the Forward 16th Brigade HQ War Diary certainly remains a mystery. The record for the controversial month of March, 1944 is missing. It never reached the Public Records Office. Even more strange is the fact that the Operations Branch War Diary of HQ Special Force for that same month is also missing. The loss of communication, caused by the move of Rear Brigade Signals at this vital time, created confusion. Brigadier Fergusson was unable to receive intelligence reports nor was he able to keep wireless contact with his columns. The following entry for 24th March in the Leicester's War Diary highlights the problem:

'Heard that Rear Brigade HQ had moved to Syhlet. Spent morning on make and mend waiting for instructions re supply drop. Patrol contacted Brigade HQ and the two recce columns (45 and 54) moving south quite near our bivouac. We had no idea they had got so far and were alarmed to learn

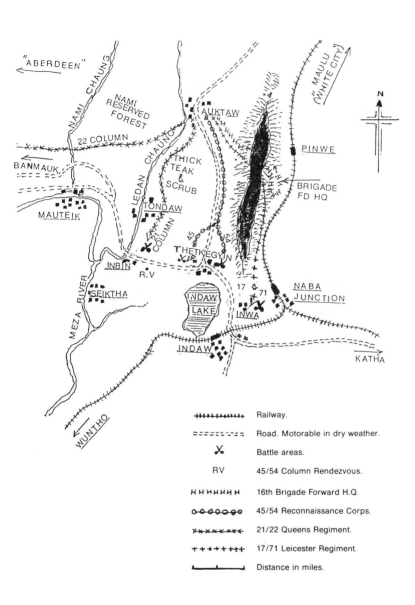

┿┿┿┾┿┽┿┽┿┽	Railway.
≠≠≠≠≠≠≠≠≠	Road. Motorable in dry weather.
✄	Battle areas.
RV	45/54 Column Rendezvous.
H H H H H H H	16th Brigade Forward H.Q.
○-○-○-○-○-○-○	45/54 Reconnaissance Corps.
×-×-×-×-×-×-×	21/22 Queens Regiment.
+ + + + + ++ +	17/71 Leicester Regiment.
▃▃▃▃▃▃	Distance in miles.

16th INFANTRY BRIGADE.
COLUMN ROUTES AT BATTLE OF INDAW.
MARCH 26th-29th 1944.

that we were late for the battle as planned. The breakdown was due to conflicting instructions we had received and the breakdown of W/T communications.'

As we pressed on towards Thetkegyin there was an air of foreboding. All was quiet around us and as the tension increased, the only sounds were the hooves of the mules as they scuffed the hard-baked track, and the odd nervous remark. The scrub became more sparse, the sun became unbearably hot and our shirts were sodden with sweat. No orders had been given about the possible scarcity of water, and many began to drain their water bottles to quench a mounting thirst. Drinking between halts was against orders, but because of the fact that up to now we had always been near water, discipline had become lax. Once we left the Ledan Chaung, the Auktaw forest was waterless. In March, the streams shown on the map became completely dry, except for the odd stagnant pool. Water could be obtained by digging deep in a dry watercourse, but not enough for practical purposes. The nearest water in quantity was either the Ledan Chaung, which we were getting further away from with every step, or the Indaw Lake which was on the way to our objective.

Historians have blamed Brigadier Fergusson for his failure to send reconnaissance ahead, to check on the availability of water. Firstly, there was obviously not time and secondly, he must have known the situation. He had in fact marched over this very area in March the previous year, as CO of number 5 Column on the first Wingate expedition, and would have been well aware of the situation in the dry season. Thirdly, he had been clearly ordered to take every risk to capture Indaw. This having been done, there would be no problem with water.

Progress was slow, and we had frequent hold-ups without being able to rest the weight of our packs. After two hours, we halted in the scrub on the edge of an expanse of paddy. We could see a dirt track road about thirty yards ahead. The map showed that this was the main road between Indaw and Banmouk, only passable in the dry season. At the other side of the paddy, we saw the huts of the village of Thetkegyin.

Column HQ were dispersed around us, but neither information nor direction was given, and we felt, and were, very vulnerable.

Almost at once, sporadic firing broke out to our left, and within minutes this became a fusillade of shots with long bursts, as machine gun fire was exchanged with the Japanese holding the village. We had a feeling that the attack was not going to plan when the admin. officer and a second lieutenant ran up. The former demanded to know where the CO was, and the latter yelled 'Why isn't your radio opened up? Get in communication.' Unfortunately, many of the junior column officers had the idea that we were like a telephone switchboard. Certainly, the RAF ground-to-air set quite near us had opened up, and Sergeants Bouverie and Hircock could have summoned air support and directed the attack if someone had been in command. Then everything seemed to happen at once.

Mortar bombs began to fall behind us, one exploded as it hit the treetops overhead with a deafening roar. Branches, leaves and shrapnel showered down around us. A hail of bullets whistled fan-wise overhead, ricocheting off the trees. We flattened ourselves on the ground, took up firing positions in the direction of the village and waited for the worst. Within seconds, more mortar bombs began to fall. They were now much closer and one exploded between our two signal mules. One was torn apart by the blast and the blood splattering all around us. Our wireless set was reduced to pieces of torn metal.

Simultaneously, two yellow lorries sped in a cloud of dust from the direction of Indaw, passing by us and pulling up no more than fifty yards away. How the Japanese failed to see us was amazing, because we were not in solid jungle. Jumping off the tailboards, they ran into the thickets behind us, presumably to encircle the rear of our column. I vividly remember that some had machine guns, and all were wearing white vests, jungle green slacks and soft P.T. shoes. They were huge fellows, nothing like the Japanese we had expected.

We felt doomed and without direction, when in the next few seconds there occurred probably the most fortunate moment in my whole life. Unbelievably, across the other

221

side of the road, Colonel Cumberlege was leading a group of men parallel to us away from the battle. Most of the HQ section around us were petrified, and I said, 'Let's join the CO.' As quick as a flash, Bert Fennell, Buck Buchanan, the two RAF sergeants and part of their section were with me. We unhooked grenades and threw them in the general direction of the village, as we tore across the track to catch up with the fast disappearing huddle of men with the column commander.

How the incessant cross-fire missed us as we raced over the open space still seems unbelievable, especially as we were hindered with our heavy haversack back packs in addition to rifles, ammo and grenades. Surprisingly none of the group seemed to notice us as we tagged on; all were intent on finding safety.

Colonel Cumberlege led us through thickly wooded teak forest in a westerly direction and after a short march we found a shallow depression where we collapsed on the ground, totally exhausted and drained. The dial of my wrist watch showed the time. It was exactly five o'clock in the afternoon, just two hours since our first brush with the enemy. The 45th Reconnaissance Corps had ceased to be commanded and no longer existed as an integral unit.

However, this was not in my thoughts at the time. Soon, a few more small parties joined us and I realised that we were at the rendezvous, chosen by the CO before leaving Auktaw that morning. At the start of the operation, Brigadier Fergusson had ruled that only officers were to be told R.V. whereabouts, though they could pass on this information to NCOs if necessary. I was never given this information but to be fair, our section was normally close to the CO when in laager. The reason for this rule was based on the assumption that NCOs and men were more likely to give away vital information, when captured and tortured, than officers. I doubt if this reasoning had a basis in fact.

Within the first half an hour of arrival, two officers, one of whom was Lieutenant Musselwhite, mentioned earlier, and a number of infantry from split platoons joined us, so that by now we were a force of some sixty troops. Although we had started the day with plenty of water, we were now very thirsty indeed. The heat had sucked the moisture from our

222

bodies. Our mouths and throats were dry and sore and our water bottles were empty. As we lay in this retreat, I suddenly realised that the left arm of my shirt was damp with blood, nothing to do with the stains from the dead mule. My arm had been gashed just below the shoulder with a piece of shrapnel, but I had not felt the wound. One of the infantrymen had a tube of sulphanilamide, which he lent me and after application and a bandage from my first aid dressing, I was able to forget all about it.

Colonel Cumberlege came round and talked to us in small groups. He was obviously very distressed, looking tired and haggard. He was one of the very few officers who had managed to evade the over-forty-years age limit, decreed by Wingate when the columns were formed. No doubt he had been physically exhausted by the privations felt on the march from Ledo, not to mention today's catastrophe. Colonel Cumberlege stressed that absolute silence was vital and confirmed that this was the rendezvous that had been chosen that morning in Auktaw before the approach to Indaw.

The map showed a stream leading to the Ledan Chaung, which was now completely dry. In fact, we were hiding in the dried-up watercourse. His plan was that at nightfall, we would go in search of water, leaving a small guard with the RAF wireless and three mules. It was essential that we left the latter behind, because once they smelt water they could be difficult to control and the noise would give away our position. Lookouts had been posted around our hide, and although a Burmese villager came very close while tending his cattle, we remained undetected.

Buck, Bert and I checked our equipment. We each had our rifles, plus fifty rounds and eight grenades between us, not a great deal if we were to continue as infantrymen. Our packs with blankets, groundsheets and 'K' rations for about one day were safe, but the bits and pieces of food we had hoarded, mostly rice, tea and sugar, were lost. That was our fault, because we had used the spare pannier on one of the mules to lighten our loads. Our chaguls had also been slung from the mules' saddles. This was a much more serious loss as our water bottles had long since been emptied. We could survive a few days without food but certainly not without water.

223

In the meantime, Sergeants Bouverie and Hircock were trying to get a message through to the RAF Rear Base at Lalaghat for transmission via Rear Brigade, to Brigadier Fergusson. Their batteries were low and the spares and the charging unit were lost, but in any case we could not have risked the noise of the engine in this situation. They did eventually manage to get a message through before their batteries petered out to the effect that Column 45 had withdrawn and dispersed.

Now, we were completely isolated, with no idea of what was happening to the other columns, or in fact, to the rest of the brigade. All this time, of course, we could hear the battle continuing to rage around Thetkegyin and Indaw. There was an almost incessant clatter of rifle and machine gun fire, and the intermittent crump of mortars. Soon after dark, we silently followed the commanding officer out of the hideaway towards the north west. Soon we were across the paddy going towards the Ledan Chaung. We were not the only parties seeking water, as the stillness of the night was frequently broken by the barking of dogs, distant calls, and now and again the noise of rifle fire. It all seemed too close for comfort.

We were certainly lucky. Only a mile away, just south of a very small village marked as Inbin on the map, and close enough to see their cooking fires, we found a track leading down to the Ledan Chaung.

We stealthily crept down in groups, while the rest kept guard. When it was my turn I lay flat on the sandy edge and drank greedily, dipping my head in the cool water before filling my waterbottle. After the ordeals and trauma of the day, the water tasted like nectar, though it was almost certainly polluted being so close to habitation. Just after the last of us had drunk, we contacted another section of 45 Column. They had been completely lost and they had two wounded men. We covered them while they quenched their thirst, before following the leader back to our rendezvous, taking turns to carry the cháguls and the several canvas buckets of precious water for the guard and the mules.

Colonel Cumberlege could have had no idea at all of the military situation, but early the next morning he had a hasty conference with the two officers who had reached the rendezvous. He decided to take as many infantry as possible, and endeavour to make contact with the Leicester Columns to the east of Indaw. It was a brave decision, but certainly a necessary one in order to preserve some of his credibility. His order to pull out 45 Column after only ninety minutes fighting needed a great deal of explanation. Obviously, the order to withdraw had not reached the majority of the unit, who appeared to be still engaging the Japanese.

A quick reshuffle of available troops resulted in the formation of two full infantry platoons, and they soon left with Colonel Cumberlege and one of the two officers to continue the battle. The officer left behind with us was none other than Lieutenant Tony Musselwhite. We were a mixed bunch, mainly specialist troops, administrative, cyphers, intelligence, RAF, Royal Signals, plus the sick and wounded. Our instructions were to make our way back to the stronghold at Aberdeen taking the three mules with us. We were to avoid contact with the Japanese, for which we needed no telling, though we were ready to put up a fight if required. Our first objective was to safely cross the Banmouk-Indaw road as we headed north. Lieutenant Musselwhite had lost his map case and maps in the fighting, but I was able to lend him the two maps covering our journey which took us to within two miles of the stronghold. It was certainly a great relief to be on the move, waiting around in the rendezvous had been nerve wracking.

We crossed the road without incident, but we put up lookouts for safety and to make sure the road was clear. In actual fact, no traffic of any kind came along, but crossing in small parties took a long time. We purposely avoided the main tracks, keeping to the patchy scrub. Luckily the terrain was reasonably flat. The distance from our rendezvous point back to the stronghold at Aberdeen was only twenty-two miles in a straight line, but our route would take us quite a few miles further. During later afternoon, we waded across the shallow Ledan Chaung somewhere between the villages of Tondaw and Hin-Ole, further north than our venture the night before. We once again set lookouts while we filled our water bottles and quenched our thirst. The further north we travelled, the less chance we had of bumping into a

Japanese patrol, as all available troops would be needed in keeping the supply routes open or engaged in the fighting around Indaw.

Half a mile further on from the water, Lieutenant Musselwhite carried out the set bivouac procedure. We halted on the jungle path, and on the signal all turned to our left and pushed our way at right angles into the thick bush. After a few minutes on that bearing, we resumed our original direction for a few hundred yards. This was supposedly a sure way of covering our tracks. Whether or not this was the case, we always felt safer having carried out the procedure! Our leader selected a spot for his 'HQ' and we formed a rough circle facing outwards.

Fires were allowed for an hour, though there wasn't much tea left, but Sergeant Bouverie had a little and also some powdered milk which he shared with us. Bert, Buck and myself felt rather lost without the wireless communication to occupy our minds, but nevertheless we were glad to be able to rest. We had all lost weight, and our stomachs had shrunk since leaving Ledo all those weeks ago, so we had no great hunger. I opened a small tin of corned pork loaf, which weighed just three ounces, and that was quite enough. By this time, most men loathed the 'K' ration, and this tin had been acquired in exchange for a packet of five Camel cigarettes. Once the fires had been extinguished, we rolled up in our blankets with groundsheets over the top for warmth. Although the days were scorching and the ground dry and dusty, our blood had thinned, and in any case the temperature dropped drastically at night.

We made better progress the next day, though the two wounded men had to be helped along. One of the men had lost a great deal of blood and was as white as a sheet. Eventually we jettisoned the load that was on one of the mules, and literally strung the man to the saddle with parachute cord. We were all feeling the strain, and morale was at a low ebb. Only the will to survive kept us going. That evening, with little collective food left, we could not even find water after travelling all day through very dry and dusty teak forest in extreme heat.

However, just before dusk on the edge of the forest, we noticed some very scraggy cattle in a paddy field, and in one corner there was a murky muddy pond surrounded by cow pats. The whole thought was revolting, but we had no option. We filled our cooking tins with the green water and pooled the available sterilisation tablets. We then boiled the liquid and added tea. It tasted horrible, which it was, but there was no alternative and it kept us going. We gratefully started off at dawn, anxious to reach the stronghold. The small patrol ahead very soon entered the village of Alegyun on the Nami Chaung where there was plenty of water. Three friendly Burmese came along and said 'No Jap, you British,' but as we had no one to interpret, the conversation was limited.

After the water and this encounter, our spirits rose considerably, and we made rather better progress through Gwegyi, Hkoohs and Tahpala. That evening we hid away near the Nami Chaung and the large village of Konhka. We were back in the Manmaw reserved forest, not very far from Aberdeen, having travelled ten miles that day, in spite of the frequent halts to aid the sick and wounded.

Lieutenant Musselwhite was enjoying the situation and the opportunity to exercise his powers of leadership. He came round encouraging the sick and wounded, telling us all that the next day we would be back in the stronghold. Back in India, before the formation of the Chindit columns, his lighthearted approach and easy-going nature had been frowned upon and he had been down-posted. This lapse had never been forgotten by the Regiment. It was a prime example of the proverb 'Give a dog an ill name and hang him.'

Our energy returned the next morning, as we started well before dawn. We soon reached the village of Nyauggon which we had passed on the way in. At around midday, after progressively shorter marches and longer halts, we rested on the track just outside the village of Manhton. As we prepared to move, Brigade Headquarters, looking in much better shape than us, came past on the way to the stronghold. Behind the leading platoon, wearing a magnificent beard and sporting his monocle, Brigadier Fergusson halted the column and came over to have a word with Lieutenant Musselwhite. The latter lept to his feet and gave a magnificent salute.

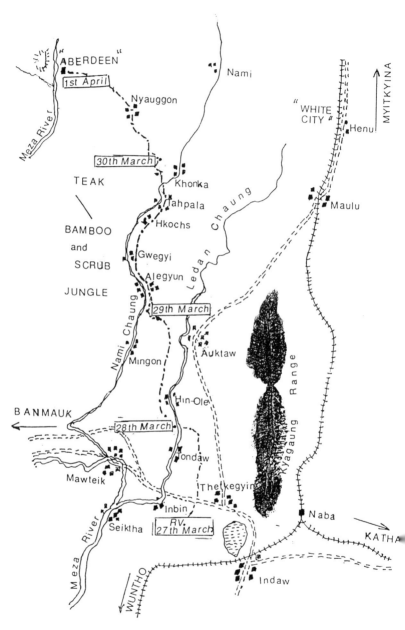

Escape route back to 'Aberdeen' with Lt. T. Musselwhite, after the Indaw Battle.

I did not hear the conversation, but according to the Brigadier in his later published account:

'Still nearer to Aberdeen, I encountered one platoon of 45 Column completely on its own, utterly ignorant of what had happened to everybody else, but completely happy in its absolute faith in its youthful commander, Tony Musselwhite. This young man, who had had a telling off at my hands more than once, had no inkling of what was going on, but was exhibiting complete unconcern to his men. We caught them up at a moment when they were halted at the side of the track, and as I reached the head of them, Musselwhite rose to his feet, a tall spare figure. "Good morning, Musselwhite," I said. "Good morning, Sir," said he, with a broad grin spreading over his face. "I will not deny, Sir, that I am exceedingly pleased to see you." "Well," I said, "I'll bet it's the first time you've been able to say that." He was killed a fortnight later.'

Surely the above-quoted conversation is a journalistic embellishment, and defies belief. Here we have Brigadier Fergusson, who has lost a major battle and all wireless communication with one of his columns for four days, making his first contact with one of its officers. One look at us by a trained soldier, let alone a brigadier, would have confirmed that we were not a platoon, but a collection of 'odds and sods' with a multiplicity of various weapons. His first words should have been 'What has happened to 45 Column, the CO, his officers and men, and how did you get back?' Actually, at that moment, Lieutenant Musselwhite knew much more than Brigadier Fergusson did about the debacle at Thetkegyin. In fact, probably much more than Brigadier Fergusson would ever get to know about the shocking breakdown in leadership. It is sad to read this now, but none of us knew what fate had in store.

Once Brigade Headquarters had passed, we followed them in to the stronghold at Aberdeen. The wounded and sick were helped down to the temporary hospital near the airstrip for eventual evacuation as soon as we arrived. We were then directed back to the hill overlooking the valley, which had been our start point on the 23rd March. So much had happened during the last few days, it was hard to believe that today was only Friday, the last day of the month.

Aberdeen was now a well established stronghold with permanent garrison troops. The airfield had been fashioned into a long flat runway, with landing lights on both sides and a flying control unit at one end. All was bustle and action as the small L1s and L5s took off to fly casualties back low over the treetops. The Dakotas operated mainly at night, due to the risk of attacks by the Japanese Zeros.

The surrounding hills had now been converted into separate smaller strongpoints. No. 1 strongpoint was near the end of the runway near the hospital and the Americans' light plane camp. No. 3 was on the opposite side of the runway and the River Meza and no. 2 was our camp further south, bounded by the Meza and the Kalat Chaung tributary. We were almost the first of either column to arrive back and once settled, our time was free to rest and sleep, free of all duties other than the collection of rations.

Brigadier Fergusson had sent a signal back to Rear Brigade asking them to fly in extra rations from India, and his request had been acted upon. For the next few days, we enjoyed the luxury of fresh eggs, green vegetables, dehydrated potatoes and tinned fruit, as well as the stand-by army rations of bully beef, biscuits, tea, sugar and powdered milk.

As more survivors from our two columns arrived back, the events of the last few days unfolded. Certainly the biggest shock and leading topic of conversation was the news that Major-General Orde Wingate was dead.' His plane had crashed into the hillside near Imphal over a week before, killing all on board. This was two days before 16th Brigade had made the assault on Indaw, so he could have had no influence on the actual direction of the battle. It is remarkable how many oficial accounts of the Indaw battle assume that General Wingate was in actual personal control. Even Shelford Bidwell in the *Chindit War* gets it wrong, 'The fiasco at Indaw remains the only example of Wingate in personal control of a large-scale operation in the field and reveals all his daring and all his weakness as a commander.' Major-General Orde Wingate had certainly planned the attack on Indaw. As for what he would have done had he lived, remains pure speculation and conjecture.

However, after the realisation that Wingate had perished had sunk in, the fate of our friends and comrades became uppermost in our minds. Wingate was the Special Force Commander, but he had always been a distant figure and death was much nearer to us here. Many men in the regiment had been killed or wounded and an even larger number was still missing. Of the two columns, ours had certainly suffered the fewer casualties. When Colonel Cumberlege had pulled out to make for the rendezvous, a number of our sections and platoons fought on bravely. However, getting no further instructions from the column commander they pulled out in independent parties to seek the now essential water. Fighting rearguard actions, the majority found the Ledan Chaung, and made their way back to Aberdeen, sustaining few further casualties. Though completely out of touch with Colonel Cumberlege and the senior column, no. 54 under the command of Major R.A.G. Varcoe fought on bravely.

Although the Japanese were well dug in, covering the lake and any adjacent water, they enjoyed commendable success, resisting sustained counter-attacks and killing many of the enemy. Then, just as they seemed to be gaining the initiative, disaster struck. A stray bullet hit one of the flame-throwers, igniting the fuel while it was still saddled to the mule. The mule, in its death throes ran amok setting alight an ammunittion dump. The fire rapidly escalated and within seconds the jungle was ablaze, with mortars and grenades exploding in the heat. So big was the conflagration that casualties were caused on both sides. During the subsequent confusion, a number of Japanese infiltrated the rear of the column, killing many of the mules tethered in a gully.

However, in spite of this setback, the column battled on grimly through the afternoon and night of the 26th March. By the afternoon of the following day, they were desperate for water. Any request for a supply drop was out of the question in this close encounter, so midway through the afternoon they fought a rearguard action in search of a stream.

There is no doubt that by now, the Japanese had summed up the situation and had set up check points to cover all possible sources of water around the Indaw area. Working westwards to the Ledan Chaung, just as we had two days earlier, 54 Column found the Japanese waiting for them. Some of the few mules that were left, smelling water, broke away from their handlers, giving away the position of the column. In addition, maddened by thirst, a few of the men threw caution to the wind and ran across the paddy towards the river with dire results.

54 Column had fought the Japanese with immense determination, and as we listened later, many individual acts of heroism came to light. Nevertheless, this had been a battle for water, and they had lost. Tired and haggard, the column reorganised, and shepherding their wounded, they began to return to Aberdeen. Their casualties overall were in the region of thirty per cent, and a few of my long standing friends had been killed or wounded. However, during the day we did receive some good news when Bill Warbutton, our four muleteers, without the mules which had been killed or captured and most of the HQ of our column arrived back at the stronghold.

Sadly, Major Adams, recently promoted from Captain, had been mortally wounded leading his company. As sport and recreational officer back in India, he had organised our football, rugby and cricket matches. In Ranchi he had organised several athletic meetings, running as a member of our cross country team. With both hips shattered, he bravely insisted on being left behind as casualties mounted. He was given a shot of morphia and left with his pistol and some grenades, after handing a note for his wife to his batman.

Within the next few days, several more stragglers arrived back at the stronghold, but the regiment had been reduced to little more than the strength of one column. Most of the brigade had met the same lack of success. Columns 51 and 69 of the Field Regiment Royal Artillery, as mentioned before, had never been in the fight after the long delay, due to the fruitless march to Lonkin. The two Queen's columns had had mixed fortunes, but they also had never joined the battle. Column 21 were caught by the Japanese whilst in camp just off the Banmauk-Indaw road, and very near to the spot chosen for our rendezvous before the battle. Their commanding officer, Lieutenant Colonel J.F. Metcalf was wounded in the ambush, and over half of their mules killed or captured. As a result of this, they could not move their wireless, heavy weapons or ammunition and were unable to proceed to Indaw as an effective unit. Column 22, which had been sent to block the Banmauk-Indaw road had had more success. They had ambushed a convoy and interrupted traffic, but this proved to be only a nuisance value to the Japanese, and when the Brigadier realised that additional help was needed in the battle for Indaw they were too far east to affect the main battle.

It could be said that a complete fiasco had been averted by the Leicester columns who were in a different military league. Led by Lieutenant-Colonel C.J. Wilkinson, a seasoned professional soldier, they nearly won the battle for Indaw on their own. Having fought as a regiment in the Middle East, they were a highly efficient and organised unit. Unlike the rest of the brigade, they had amalgamated the fighting elements of their two columns into one compact spearhead, consisting of machine guns and mortars for sustained fighting. Transport mules and support personnel had been safely tucked away and hidden in the jungle.

They came out of the hills from the east of Indaw, securing a water supply from a stream flowing through the small village of Inwa, where they dug in. Repeated stereotype attacks by the Japanese were repulsed with disciplined firepower, as wave after wave of attackers were mown down. Then at the crucial moment, no. 1 American Air Commando, summoned by Colonel Wilkinson using his RAF radio detachment, bombed the forward Japanese troops with pinpoint accuracy. He battled successfully for three days and two nights, killing over one hundred Japanese for the effective loss of just two officers and thirteen men killed, or wounded. The Leicester columns eventually made an orderly withdrawal but only because Brigadier Fergusson had called off the whole operation. Throughout the battle, Colonel Wilkinson nursed an arm,

233

broken in two places during the preliminary skirmish at Auktaw, so on arrival back at Aberdeen, he was flown back to India. He more than deserved his immediate award of the DSO and with another regiment as equally professional and dedicated in support, Indaw would have been secured.

There was no similar accolade for our leader, although Shelford Bidwell says that Colonel Cumberlege pulled out his no. 45 Column with commendable tenacity, and set out with two platoons to join the Leicesters. My own opinion at the time was that he pulled out with undue haste, failed to ensure that all platoons received the message, and made no effort to summon the powerful aid of the American no. 1 Air Commando with their B25s, which were equipped with 75mm cannons and depth charges.

Lieutenant Colonel C.R.T. Cumberlege and Major R.A.G. Varcoe were both evacuated to India due to sickness within a couple of days, and Major E. Hennings took charge of what was left of the combined 45 and 54 Columns. At this point it is opportune to mention just one of the many erroneous accounts which have appeared in print regarding our dismal failure at Indaw. Some of them contain much more fiction than fact and a great deal of conjecture. Perhaps the biggest howler is contained in *Back to Mandalay* by Lowell Thomas. He makes many factual errors in his version of events. For instance, he reduces the brigade to four hundred men and confuses the Leicester columns with those of the Reconnaissance Corps. The former had not been short of water, but we were. We had not called for air support from the American Air Commando. They had.

However, the biggest gaff of all is Thomas' story regarding the 16th Brigade. He says that, 'Tired and discouraged, they struggled back but Wingate took the setback in characteristic fashion, "We will retrieve the defeat and capture the airstrip at Indaw" said the man.' All very strong stuff. However, as General Orde Wingate had been killed in the aircrash on 24th March, two days before the battle commenced, then if we are to believe this story, the statement must have been transmitted from the Elysian battlefields!

After the fighting, there were of course many rumours, the most popular which said that we were to be flown back to

234

India right away. This probably owed its origin to both wishful thinking and the fact that two doctors with very white legs had been flown in to examine a section of the battered columns. They need not have asked questions, the evidence was plain to see. Even the fittest of us looked and were emaciated. We were suffering from general inertia. Living in the open, day after day and night after night, makeshift meals concocted most of the time from the monotonous 'K' ration, and carrying all our possessions and kit on our backs, had taken its toll.

If they had looked closer and asked questions, they would have been able to compile a list that included mental exhaustion, pallor, malaria, upset stomachs, jaundice, and a multitude of skin infections from jungle sores, boils, blisters, foot-rot, down to the more minor irritation of prickly heat.

12

With Calvert around 'White City'

We spent almost a week at Aberdeen, resting, sleeping and eating. Mail and newspapers from home were distributed, but it needed a great effort to put pen, or rather pencil as ball-point pens did not exist, to paper. It required even more effort to think of something original and permissible to write.

Before a week had passed, Major Hennings informed us that the Reconnaissance Regiment was to have a new commander, Lieutenant Colonel G. Astell, formally of the Burma Rifles, who had made his mark in the defence of the stronghold at Broadway. Major Hennings was to be his second in command, and we would now be two much smaller columns.

Although mules had been flown in, no attempt had been made to re-equip my section with a replacement no. 22 wireless set, batteries, charging engine or all other equipment that we needed to set up a radio station. After making several requests to speak to Major T. Moon, Brigade Signals Commander, or his deputy, Captain D. Kesting to no avail, we had to accept the situation.

Major Hennings told the columns that we had one more task to carry out, and that after that we would be flown back to India. We were to take over as garrison troops at the White City. Brigadier Calvert's men of the 77th Brigade had marched there in four days, to set up a stronghold after landing in Burma at Broadway. It was thought that although they had done plenty of fighting, they were comparatively fresh and that it would be a rest for us to take over these duties, while the equivalent number of the 77th Brigade did battle with the Japanese.

I approached Major Hennings again about our future duties, and he said that no doubt we would be detailed to help with shifts at the signal station in the stronghold. So on Easter Sunday, the 9th April, late in the afternoon, we once again marched out in single column towards White City.

A great deal had happened to us in the eighteen days since we had marched out of Aberdeen the first time, when few of our regiment had experienced fighting at close quarters and many had not heard a shot fired in anger. However, this time we knew what to expect. There was general nervousness and tension, coupled with the disappointment that we had more fighting to do before being flown out. On the other hand, the machine gun and mortar platoons had performed well, and gained confidence after their experience of close-quarter fighting with the Japanese. Also, the fact that we were destined to take over fixed lines of defence in established earthworks and dugouts was well received.

Of the next two days' march there is little to record. The first night we spent in the hills near Nyaunggon. After an early start the next morning, we soon reached the rendezvous where we were to meet up with a patrol from the White City. This was in an area of thickly wooded teak forest near the village of Nami. Here we waited and rested for what eventually became twenty-four hours. We were well hidden but near enough to the Nami Chaung to collect water for ourselves and the mules. We were about six miles from the stronghold and we could hear the almost continual noise of battle.

The following morning, Brigadier Calvert flew out of the stronghold in one of the American L5 spotter planes and landed at a nearby airstrip. There were several of these strips dotted around the stronghold, built by the troops who continually patrolled the area. We formed a closely packed semi-circle of nearly four hundred soldiers, and Brigadier Calvert stood on a rise in the ground and spoke to us. A stocky commanding figure, he had no problem in making himself heard.

His first few sentences gave little indication as to any change in our expected future role. He was proud that the Reconnaissance Regiment was now part of the 77th

237

Brigade. We had a first class leader in our new commander, Lieutenant Colonel G. Astell and we would remain with him under his direction, until the Japanese in this area had been defeated. Then after this successful action, we would be flown back to India. So far so good, but in the continual hushed silence, we heard about the rest of his plans. We would be part of a formidable force of over two thousand men who were to attack the Japanese surrounding the garrison. We would approach the Japanese from the outside, pinning them between us and the stronghold until they were destroyed or dispersed.

So that was that. We quickly realised that our promised garrison duties had vanished into thin air. We wondered who had made the change of plan. Brigadier Fergusson was certain that he had specified that what was left of the Reconnaissance Corps should be rested. He says in his book that 'it was suggested that I should lend the two depleted Recce columns . . . for a spell at White City . . . . He (Calvert) had not fully grasped that I had lent him the recce columns for static use only, in fact for a rest; but to have insisted on it now would have ruined his project.' Brigadier Calvert, on the other hand, makes no mention of garrison duties, he says, 'They were to fight their last action under my command.'

Actually, no one had suggested that the Reconnaissance Regiment should be rested as garrison troops. On the 3rd April, Major General Lentaigne, now commanding Special Force, held a conference at Aberdeen with all his brigade commanders. He discussed plans for reinforcing White City. Two days later he sent out an order that the Recce Corps and the 3rd West African Brigade should be sent to Calvert. It is quite possible the latter arrived first, and it was more convenient to slot them into the garrison.

Most accounts were written long after the event. For example, Brigadier Calvert recorded that our column were Devonshire men who had grown patriarchal red beards. In fact we were a cross-section of the UK population, and few of us sported red beards. Since his book was published, these words have been copied many times. Brigadier Calvert was averse to men with beards, and most of the troops in the stronghold were clean shaven. Basically, most of us would have preferred to shave daily, but had little option. We had lived in the open, carrying all our kit, arms and possessions and in that time we had marched over four hundred miles, since leaving the Ledo Road in Assam.

There was no job for my section in the coming battle. Although we were Royal Corps of Signals personnel, we would now have to operate as men-at-arms. In this situation, I felt that if we had to fight the Japanese, I would rather become part of the striking force amongst trained riflemen, than be left behind as a guard with the 'soft belly', the sick and the lame. So after a word with Major Hennings I was attached to one of the infantry rifle sections commanded by Lieutenant Winter. This was a scratch section, reformed after the losses at Thetkegyin. I was quite content to forget about my rank, as most of the section were better trained than myself in actual jungle fighting. In fact, most of the section did not realise I was an NCO. When a new clean bush shirt had been available at Aberdeen, there had been no chance to remove and sew on the old chevrons. Lieutenant Winter then gave us details of Brigadier Calvert's plan, as he knew it. We were to make our way through the village of Thayaung before continuing the advance to attack the suspected Japanese supply depot at Sepein.

On the next day, we began our advance at 1200 hours and soon reached Thayaung, which had already been captured by a column of the Lancashire Fusiliers. Apparently, it had been decided that this village was to be headquarters for the operation. During the day, most of the units involved moved into the immediate area ready for the next advance. It was here that we realised how many troops were involved. We were particularly pleased to see a column of the Gurkha Regiment, who had a great reputation as soldiers, and like the French Foreign Legion, were contracted to fight. By tradition, they were prepared to 'march, fight and die'.

During the night, there was the continual noise of battle from the stronghold, now only about three miles away. There had been talk about the Japanese six-inch mortar, and now we heard the heavy thump as the shells landed. Next morning we took part in the dawn attack on the village of Sepein. A column of the Lancashire Fusiliers were out on our right, and just ahead on the left were the Gurkhas. We kept our heads well down, as there was a great deal of cross-fire and we had no steel helmets.

The Gurkhas made good progress and overran several Japanese dugouts, killing all the occupants. Meanwhile, we were pinned down as we approached the village of Ponhon across the paddy. The only cover ahead was created by *bunds*, which kept back the water in the dry season and flooded the rice fields. It was madness trying to make progress wearing our haversacks, as they stuck up in the air and gave our every movement away. We had our first casualty in the section here, though it was only a flesh wound, and several haversack canvasses were torn by the snipers' bullets coming from the scrub ahead. This was my first experience of being caught in a blanket of enemy fire and feeling so helpless. During these very few minutes, I realised how well trained my comrades were and hoped that they would not see my fear.

Our predicament ended as quickly as it had begun, when the firing ahead suddenly ceased. The Lancashire Fusiliers had captured the village from the opposite side. The Japanese were retreating towards Sepein. We charged across the paddy, more in relief than in aggression and we were glad to reach the thin jungle on the edge of Ponhon. By now we were less than a mile from our objective. We crossed the road and then the metre gauge railway line,where it spanned the Nanthayan Chaung, without further opposition.

Suddenly ahead, in the direction of Sepein we heard the unmistakable scream of projectiles, followed by explosions which shook the ground. We fell flat and took up firing positions, expecting an attack. Then, as the barrage continued we realised it must be coming from our own troops. Shell after shell followed until the sky seemed to be alive, and over the scrub jungle ahead there appeared a massive cloud of yellow sandy dust and smoke.

It was a barrage from the 25 pounder Howitzers in the White City block, being directed by the Forward Artillery observation officer, who had left the stronghold to join the Gurkhas. The Howitzers had an effective range of something like seven miles, so Sepein was well within their range. At the time, we had no idea that this advance barrage was to take place, and it was a frightening experience due to the sheer noise.

We moved gingerly forward through the scrub jungle and took up defensive positions in the village without opposition, but nevertheless expecting a counter-attack from the Japanese. This never came, although there was the noise of machine gun, mortar and rifle fire from the village outskirts. Then word came back that the Japanese main supply base was not in Sepein after all, but a further mile to the south. It was heavily defended with foxholes and dugouts, and the Japanese had cut sections of the jungle away, to make fields of fire for the machine gunners.

They had almost certainly chosen these defence positions because of the lantana scrub which had grown out of hand in the village gardens. In our long march through the rain forest and almost impenetrable jungle from Ledo in Assam, we had not seen this plant. It grows into a large thick hedge, but leaves a gap between the ground and the first branches. The Japanese had dug in behind the lantana shrubs so that they would observe us coming at eye level, and they were making ideal use of this camouflage. I later found out that this shrub was a native of the West Indies. It had been introduced to Europe, and eventually imported by British officials and administrators in Burma to decorate their bungalow gardens. Since they left, it had completely overrun vast areas of jungle.

We tried to advance but ran into a solid wall of fire and began to sustain casualties. The problem was that they saw us clearly but we could only guess where they were. Any movement on our part provoked a fusillade. After an hour, during which we threw a pattern of grenades in the direction of the foxholes, covered by cross-fire from the Vickers machine gun section, we received the order to withdraw. We were not equipped for this type of warfare, and did not have the fire power to attack an enemy in well prepared positions. Furthermore, we had no entrenching tools to enable us to form even the most shallow of protecting hollows or trenches.

The first stage of our withdrawal was no more than a backward crawl across the paddy, covered by the machine gunners and the mortars. Once out of sight in the scrub

241

jungle, we made our way slowly back through Ponhon to the base at Thayaung, taking turns to carry our wounded, together with their arms and equipment. We remained there for two days, a supply drop was organised, and the wounded were taken to a hastily constructed strip in the lower valley and flown out by L1 and L5 planes.

Initially, we were naive enough to imagine that our task had been completed and we could now expect to be evacuated, but these hopes were soon to be dashed. First of all, we had been told that we were to be rested as garrison troops at the White City, then that we had just one more battle to fight, and now we were told that we had a further commitment.

This plan was once again supposedly the 'last battle', but we received the news with much scepticism. This time, we would advance on the Japanese who were attacking the White City, fall upon them from the rear, and then squeeze them against the stronghold until they were destroyed or scattered. We were told that the garrison troops would also attack from the fortress. By now, most of us were very cynical regarding our future and morale began to ebb.

To ensure that we were more mobile, we were to leave our packs, groundsheets and blankets behind, taking only our belts and webbing pouches to carry ammunition, grenades, water bottles and arms. This was a mixed blessing as far as I was concerned. Certainly the heavy pack had been an encumbrance and a target for the Japanese, but it was all I had. Since leaving my kitbag and other possessions back in India, this pack had contained my only link with sanity. The small piece of mosquito net to keep off the flying and creeping insects while I slept, the now tatty photographs of my wife, father, mother, brothers and sister and my map case and maps, as well as my diary.

As we stacked them up next morning, I wondered if we would ever see them again, or even get the correct one back. What would happen if we fought through to the White City? Surely it was unlikely that we would be permitted to return. However, this was no time to ponder. We left our hide-away in the hills to take up an attacking position three miles east of the railway, near Nahpi. Although I was burdened with six grenades, my trusty J9989 rifle, nearly one hundred rounds of ammunition and water bottle, the going was so much easier without the usual heavy haversack. We arrived there before nightfall, sharing a cache of 'K' ration dumped in advance. During the night, the Japanese again attacked the stronghold and we could hear the noise which had increased in volume over the last two nights.

In the morning, we edged steadily forward on a broad front due north towards the stronghold. There was a great deal of activity on both sides of our advance, but apart from a few snipers' bullets, and on one occasion, a clutch of mortar bombs which was too close for comfort, we encountered little opposition. At 5 p.m. we called a halt to our advance and set up our bivouacs in a dried up watercourse near the Maulu Chaung, between Nathkokyin and our previous hide-away at Thayaung. We were now very close indeed to the White City stronghold, no more than two miles away. As darkness fell, another attack began on the block, and we could hear the shouts and calls of the Japanese as well as the firing.

We crept about silently and did not light fires for our usual brew-up, to ensure that we remained undetected throughout the night. To say that we missed this nightly ritual would be an understatement. Lighting our small fires, balancing our various tins of water in the flames, had become one of our few pleasures after the long day's march. It was time to relax, gossip and look forward to the long rest ahead. Tonight was different. Without the basic comfort of a groundsheet to lie on or a blanket to ward off the chilly night air, we slept ready for action with our boots firmly laced.

We did not sleep for long. Moving forward at 0330 hours, we completely surprised a Japanese mortar platoon as dawn broke. If they had lookouts, no warning had been given because they were still asleep. We threw grenades into the centre of the patch, and shot most of those who had escaped the blasts and managed in a daze to get to their feet. Soon after, the battle against those who escaped began in earnest. Maybe we should have been told to fix bayonets before we advanced and quietly butchered them, though almost certainly some would have escaped. Three days before, I had acquired a bayonet and scabbard from one of the wounded men before he was flown out. Even so, I would have found this killing in cold blood most difficult. Had I been attacked by a Japanese wielding a bayonet it would have been different, I would have fought back because it would have been me or him. It is difficult to explain, but I felt no remorse at firing at these Japanese as they ran, maybe because we fired as a squad.

All along our front, progress was being made in spite of heavy mortar fire. Luckily it was rather inaccurate so a number of Japanese positions were overrun on both sides of our platoon. By mid-Morning we came to the main stream of the Maulu Chaung and found the Japanese well dug in. At one stage, the troops on our right crossed the stream and captured a 50mm mortar, complete with baseplate and tripod, and several Meizi · 38 rifles, having killed most of the Japs there. There was now a great deal of confusion. Machine guns from both sides raked at anything that moved, usually when our three-inch mortars, screaming overhead, landed behind them.

Although we were probably only half a mile from the White City block, the Japanese in between could not be shifted, and it was impossible to know whether the mortars landing around us were from friend or foe. One bomb landed in the bed of the chaung only twenty feet away, but luckily the deep soft sand took most of the blast. By now, we had lost our section sergeant, his arm torn to shreds, and casualties were mounting all around.

In spite of the fact that our machine gun section was covering the river, the Japanese did not vary their tactics one bit, but continually tried to cross over against the same line of fire, over their dead comrades. This suicidal action was the result of obeying orders to the letter in textbook style. Otherwise, they were well-trained, effcient fighters and hard to contain. They were probably the only contestants in World War II of whom it could truly be said 'They would fight to the last man and the last bullet.' At the time we could not understand this mentality. Actually the Japanese lower ranks were mainly conscripts, and in civilian life they led a frugal existence, living as smallholders or farmers.

Certainly the Japanese we fought against, especially those we saw close up at Thetkegyin were not the skinny, short, flat-footed, bow-legged characters who had been depicted in cartoons and propaganda leaflets. Those Japanese who came up the road from Indaw on the back of army lorries were six foot tall athletes, equivalent to our guardsmen. Apart from the Kung Fu fanatics, fitness was endemic in nearly all Japanese males. The majority of ordinary soldiers were quite used to carrying heavy loads as part of civilian life. Discipline was foremost in training, appearance and smart marching was not inportant, except in very formal parades.

NCOs and officers were mainly from a different social class, usually with higher educational achievements. Regular officers were often graduates of the military academy. That was why prisoners taken by the Japanese rank and file were often badly treated or killed, before a senior NCO or officer could intervene. The very big difference between us and the Japanese, was that they considered death more desirable than being taken prisoner. Invariably, prisoners taken by our troops were usually too weak or too badly injured to commit suicide. A Japanese soldier knew that his family would disown him, and that he would lose his army pension if he was taken prisoner. Because of his training and background, the Japanese was ready to fight to the bitter end, even if surrounded and out-numbered by troops in a ratio of fifty to one. He knew that if he died fighting, he and his family would be honoured; the latter receiving his army pension. Also, if the military situation afforded, his ashes would be buried in the national shrine of Yashkuni Jinga in Tokyo.

In spite of the Jap losses, our troops on the other side of the chaung appeared to be completely cut off. Although we had only been fighting a few hours, it seemed like an eternity. My mouth was dry and parched, but I dare not reach for my water bottle. Soon after midday we heard the sound of aircraft and I am sure that like me, most of our troops feared the worst. However, it was not the Japanese Zeros that had been strafing the White City stronghold, but Mustangs from the American no. 1 Air Commando, called up from India by Brigadier Calvert. It was not until the smoke of our mortars marked a target line of white vapour across the skyline some one hundred yards ahead, that we had an inkling of what was to happen.

There was an almighty roar as the Mustangs dived down, bang on target, dropping their 500lb bombs and 200lb anti-personnel fragmentation mines on the line of smoke. They followed this with a low level attack, using their 75mm cannon to good effect. We were petrified as the ground shook and seemed to come up to meet us; a blast of hot air seared overhead as debris rose on the horizon. Then there was absolute silence as a thick pall of smoke rose ahead, followed by the smell of cordite and burning flesh.

Almost at once, the order came to disengage and withdraw, as more fighting began and machine gun fire straddled the Chaung. We were all badly shaken and at that time we did not realise how near we had come to being captured. Soon we were in the shelter of the scrub jungle once again, and we passed a first aid post tucked away in a gully. The two medical officers and their orderlies were fighting a losing battle to patch up the wounded so that they could be moved. It was a ghastly sight. Some dead, some dying, lying on the hard ground amongst the trees. It was a great shock to realise that it was impossible to evacuate all these wounded men.

We had always blindly believed that if we were wounded, then we would be flown out by the light planes to a temporary casualty clearing station in Aberdeen or White City, before evacuation to India. The truth was, that here and on many other occasions, the system was overwhelmed by the number of casualties and the lack of stretcher bearers.

We moved back very slowly in single file, following the man in front and trusting that this was the way to safety. Suddenly, one of the men ahead collapsed, hitting the ground with a thud. He had lost consciousness, and as we hauled him to his feet, we realised that he had wounds in both legs. Although bandaged, he had lost a great deal of blood. We gave him water, taking turns to hold him up by the arms, one of us on each side. He was lucky. That day the medical team had to leave fifteen men behind, several mortally wounded, because casualties mounted while they were trying to help.

Having to leave men to die alone was a tragedy, but leaving them to be found alive by the Japanese, in full

246

knowledge of their probable fate was brutal. Any chance of survival after torture and eventual imprisonment was minimal, but it was hard to think of an alternative. Some brave men in full realisation of the situation, but mortally wounded, asked to be left with means to kill the enemy and then themselves.

The Chinese fighting in Northern Burma, shot troops who were too badly injured to continue the march when evacuation was impossible. Perhaps it was unfair to allege that they were callous and indifferent and had no respect for the sanctity of life. My view at the time would have been that, bearing in mind the Japanese mentality, it was kinder to kill a critically wounded man, than to leave him to be butchered by the enemy after torture, or be taken prisoner to suffer brutality and slave labour.

Time and time again, we waited for the stretcher bearers to close the gaps which formed in the long line, taking turns to help the walking wounded and carry their equipment. We felt nervous and exposed as we crossed the open paddy near Nathkokyin, but the Japanese had gone.

Later, when all the statistics of the battle were analysed, it was established that this was the end of the Japanese 24th Independent Mixed Brigade who had been attacking the White City. They had lost over 3,000 casualties, and their leader, Major General Hyashi was killed by the troops of the 6th Battalion Nigerian Regiment. He died leading his suicide troops, making one last attempt to capture the block with explosives fixed to their bodies, riding his white ceremonial horse.

However, there was little chance of the 77th Brigade taking advantage of this situation. The force overall had lost over 100 officers and men. At least double that number had been wounded. We could only lick our wounds.

Late in the afternoon, as the sun disappeared behind the western slopes of the Nami forest, we made our way wearily up the steeply sloping track to our sanctuary in the hills. A column of the Nigerian regiment which had been left behind to guard our packs had tins full of hot tea to help revive us, and they came down the incline to take over or help us with our stretchers. We had brought back over forty stretcher cases, and an additional seventy-plus wounded

247

men who needed urgent treatment. So many comrades were missing. It was quite impossible to know how they had fared, but several of my friends and two officers had been killed for certain.

Major Hennings, who had been the commanding officer of HQ Troop, when the 45th Reconnaissance Corps had been formed at Berkhamstead in early 1941, had been killed instantly. His watch and map case were brought back by his batman. Even more sadly, Lieutenant Tony Musselwhite, who had so recently led our scratch party safely back from Thetkegyin to the stronghold at Aberdeen had been left behind, mortally wounded. I pray he died before the Japanese patrols found him. Completely exhausted, both physically and mentally, I collected my haversack from the dump, curled up in my blanket and lapsed into oblivion.

I woke up the next morning feeling very tired and drained. There was an air of depression all around as we began to get organised again. We had all lost friends and comrades, and there were many tales of heroism and sacrifice. It has been said that the only way to get a Military Cross or a Military Medal, when all are heroes, is to get yourself killed in the right place at the right time, in front of the right people. I was rather a cynical view, but one which contained more than a grain of truth. Our spirits could not have been much lower, as we dragged on and up further into the hills to find a suitable site to build a landing strip.

Although my Royal Corps of Signals section was now together again, we had no equipment or mules, so our tour of duty was over, and we were left very much out of the picture. On the march from the Ledo Road, we had often cursed about the long hours, working at night to get the messages back to base, but now we missed the sense of involvement. All the signalling was now in the hands of the RAF detachment, which had joined us after the last battle. There was no sign of our friends Sergeants Bouverie and Hircock and we did not see them again.

Buck and I stripped to the waist and went to help level the stretch of paddy a few miles further on at a deserted village reference point 912213. I still had my map case and maps, a great source of interest and joy, as life was now one long monotonous trudge. The landing strip was soon completed and just before 1 p.m., two L5s circled the field.

The area was not really suitable for landing, but was the best that could be done. There was only one way in to land, and the strip was about fifty yards short of the recommended length and very uneven as usual. The first plane came down steeply and landed. All seemed well until he hit a bump towards the end of the runway and toppled over. The pilot was unhurt, but the second plane on the way down, was unsighted and as he landed, his wing tip caught the tail of the first plane and the fuselage crumbled. Thankfully, this pilot was also OK, and the strip was soon cleared. Eventually, nine of the seriously ill stretcher cases were taken off by back-up planes to Aberdeen, twenty miles away as the crow flies.

It was almost dusk before the last plane left, but without the two pilots of the crashed L5s, who had to join us as temporary members of the column. They did not look very happy about the situation. These American airmen took their lives in their hands, flying skilfully at tree-top level to avoid the Japanese fighter planes, and landing and taking off on makeshift runways. However, they had not reckoned on becoming infantrymen. We rested here for the next two days and six more men were lifted out, including the very relieved-looking Americans.

The hastily arranged supply drop was not very successful. Most of the parachutes floated well off target, and eventually we were issued with just three 'K' ration cartons, a day's supply. However, it was obvious to us that rations were stolen at this drop. Bert Fennell discovered a whole pile of outer 'K' rations cartons together with most of the contents, except that all the small packets of cigarettes had been taken. We were tempted and took a few tins and some fruit bars before I reported the find to the admin. officer. The tins were collected. If they were distributed, we heard no more, and we were not rewarded for our pains. We had no qualms about stealing the few items as somehow the situation had changed,even though it was a silly thing to do.

On Sunday, 23rd April, we began to make our way back to Aberdeen, travelling as one column, led by Lieutenant Colonel G. Astell. There was no official information given out, but a strong rumour that we were to be flown out at last.

Most of us, who had heard it all before, took the hearsay with a pinch of salt. To get to the Aberdeen stronghold, we had to recross the area where we had fought our recent battle, negotiate the huge areas of paddy and cross the supply road and railway between Katha and Mawlu. This seemed a grim prospect.

Our worst fears were soon realised. As we left the shelter of the jungle, our forward section bumped into a Japanese patrol. The order for dispersal was given, and the column quickly formed up on the edge of the forest and waited, hidden in the thick scrub. The fighting was soon over, as the Japanese were quickly overpowered or put to flight. They were probably as battle weary as us. However, we had sustained further casualties with four men wounded, but luckily all were able to walk after treatment. Our RAF detachment contacted the 77th Brigade in the White City fortress, and we were instructed to make a short march and link up with the 77th Brigade troops operating outside the stronghold. We were able to link up with them, and spent the night near the Nathkokyin Chaung.

We still retained our discipline, but quite frankly this recent minor skirmish had been the last straw. We had been battle scarred, but now we were battle 'scared'. This situation must have been patently clear to our commander Lieutenant-Colonel G. Astell and Special Force Command. Late that night, the order came that we were to about turn and take the safer route to Broadway, as well as the official news that we were to stand down and be flown back to India.

13

March to Deliverance

The news was a wonderful stimulus; our spirits rose considerably and the following morning we were on our way soon after 5 a.m. with renewed energy. This was definitely the first morning since leaving the Ledo Road that my initial waking thoughts had held enthusiasm for the day ahead. At least we had an objective with the prospect of an end to our tribulations.

Our route took us up the narrowing valley, towards the source of the Nathkckyin Chaung, a long gradual climb to the Gangaw range of hills. Progress was painfully slow. Apart from those who were suffering from the overall ordeal, we had more than forty walking wounded and five more seriously injured men, propped up on mules or ponies. Furthermore, we had to take turns in carrying the sten guns, rifles and equipment of the injured.

Although we were now heading away from the Japanese lines of communication, and able to see light at the end of the tunnel, we marched under a cloud of apprehension. We were on the last lap to safety, feeling jittery and frightened of our own shadows. Early on that morning, a man ahead dropped his sten gun. Just the clatter as it hit the path made us stop in our tracks. Later, during the three hour rest in the heat of the day, we heard rifle shots, intermittent at first, but then increasing to a continuous fusillage.

We formed ourselves into a laager position, with the infantry and assault troops round the perimeter. The situation was tense and we 'stood to' ready for action. Meanwhile a patrol was sent forward to investigate, and after waiting for what seemed an interminable period, they

'White City' battle area, and line of march with wounded to 'Broadway' 22 nd April to 1st May, 1944.

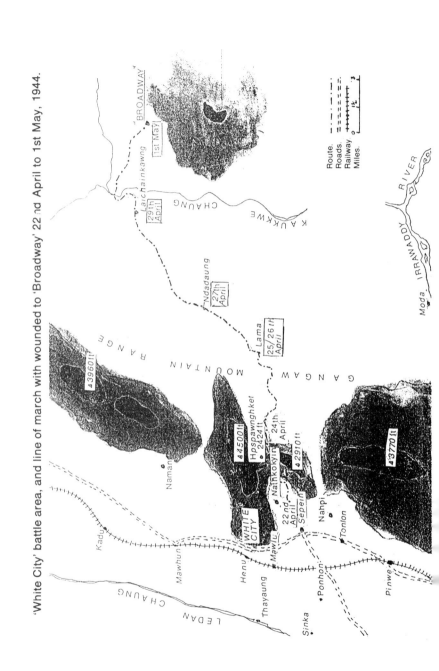

returned looking very cheerful. They reported nothing more than a forest fire, no doubt caused by the heat and dry vegetation at this time of year. The menacing rifle fire was caused by the flames as they spread through a bamboo thicket. The dry canes exploded with an uncanny resemblance to the sound of gunfire. We knew that dry bamboo detonated if burnt, and we had been trained not to use this dry timber to light fires. In fact, any section causing such a report was ordered to extinguish its blaze and go without hot food and char at that halt.

If we needed an excuse for our over-reaction, it was obvious that all nerves were on edge, and the clatter ahead had been most realistic. After another slow and strenuous climb, we laagered that evening near the village of Hpspawnghket way up in the Gangaw range at the foot of a high peak of 2,424 feet. We had tea, sugar, powdered milk and some rice but little else. Exhausted and hungry, we slept early, curled up in our blankets against the cold night air. Here in the hills there were great fluctuations in temperature.

We made another early start the next morning, soon after 5 a.m. Everyone was now eager to reach the end of his journey. Today we made better progress. The jungle paths followed the contours between the high hills, and most of the going was flat. We continued in a north easterly direction, passing through several Kachin villages, seemingly untouched by the war around them. The names of these villages in the order that we passed through them that day were Manawng, Hpawat and Nahkaw. Even to this day, it is unlikely that the hand of progress has reached this isolated and exotic area of far Northern Myanmar. We had a short midday halt and reached the village of Lama by the side of a fast moving stream. On the other side there was another village marked as Gamaw on the map.

We watered here for the night and hid away in the jungle. We were now desperate for food, and several of our casualties needed urgent hospital treatment. Our medical officer with his limited resources, was now overwhelmed. There were several cases of gangrene amongst the wounded, and men with chronic malaria. Messages were sent in an effort to organise a supply drop for the following day, and arrange for light planes to fly in and evacuate the seriously-ill men. In the morning a landing strip was hastily fashioned on the ribbon of paddy between the two villages, and we anxiously awaited the outcome of our appeal for help. Everyone, officers included, had now become ultra-cautious. We realised that the end of our struggle was near, and an irrational fear that the Japanese might be waiting to pounce had infiltrated our reasoning.

Just before midday, we were flabbergasted when a helicopter circled the clearing and landed. I certainly had never seen one before and it was quite likely that very few of our company had either, though I had a Spanish stamp in my boyhood collection of a 1935 Autogyro over Seville. I did not realise at the time that the helicopter was a further development of this machine.

The helicopter took off with the two most serious stretcher cases and returned late in the afternoon for a further two. In addition, eight of the very sick or seriously wounded were flown out by L5s. This R4 Sikorsky helicopter was the first successful and practical machine, and it evacuated a total of eighteen men during the Special Force operation. Actually, the pilot, Lieutenant Harman of No. 1 American Air Commando was the first pilot to fly a helicopter in combat conditions, operating it from the Aberdeen stronghold.

This helicopter had been developed in America by Igor Sikorsky, a naturalised Russian engineer who had constructed the first prototype in 1939. His company eventually became one of the outstanding designers and manufacturers of vertical take-off aircraft. Like the L1 and L5s, these planes were flown or shipped in parts from the USA and assembled in India. As an experiment, four R4s were sent out in two halves, for Special Force Air Commando, but due to mishaps and enemy action, only two were pieced together. The first of these hit a telephone wire and crashed killing the two occupants, leaving just this one which amazed us that day. Many more of these helicopters were later sent to Europe to join the RAF and the Royal Navy, before the end of hostilities.

However, there was no supply drop, apparently due to adverse weather conditions in Assam. Much later, I learned that it had been more likely due to the battle in Manipur State, where the town of Imphal had been completely cut off so that all supplies and ammunition had to be dropped by parachute. This was a bitter blow and we spent a hungry and miserable night, only alleviated by the promise that a drop had been arranged for the following evening.

On the next day, the 27th April, we struggled on to Ndadaung at reference point 114400. The tension had become most evident, as we trod wearily in column file. Some men fell out, and we all had to wait and help them as they struggled to keep up with the column. Those few of us who were fit were desperately tired, rumour was rife, and we were trigger-happy. However, that night at Ndadaung we had a first-class supply drop, giving us adequate rations for four days. Our hunger disappeared and with it the depression and the awful feeling of emptiness, in more than one sense of the word.

The following day, feeling in better spirits, we marched with much more purpose. Our many wounded and sick were now helped by the fact that the route was mainly downhill, making the journey so much easier. Late that afternoon, we sighted the valley of the Kaukkwe Chaung through the jungle edge, and hid away for the night in a deep, dry *nullah* near the village of Laichainkawng. We lit fires for one hour, brewed up, and even enjoyed the 'K' ration we had learned to hate. We were also cheered by the fact that Broadway was almost in our sights.

The next morning, we left the hills and passed through the wide flat marshy country bordering the Kaukkwe Chaung. It was very different from the usual river surrounds. The map showed no villages, just lagoons, bamboo thickets and stunted trees. Time and time again, the track threaded its way through marsh and large tracts of water. Twice during the day, we had to ford small streams. The third time, we had to cross the Kaukkwe and the water was up to our waists, but that was no problem as we had done all this before. The sun was hot and so we would soon dry out. All the time, at the back of our minds was the thought that we were on the way to safety and this was a stimulus to our efforts. Although we had only a short distance to go to reach the stronghold, it had been decided that we would postpone our arrival until the day after.

We pulled off to slightly higher ground surrounded by bamboo thickets to bivouac, for what we hoped would be the last time in Burma. This area was an unspoiled nature reserve, a watering place for birds and animals, with no village within miles. Of course, the whole area we had travelled was unspoiled. Most of the names I have recorded were nothing more than a few huts on the trail. Even the larger villages only had a few streets with wooden houses, a shop or two and in the centre,the sacred pagoda.

We were more than ready to move the next morning, and as we started we were joined by a patrol which had been sent out to accompany us for the last few miles. When we arrived at Broadway, we were amazed at the vast open space. Apart from the runway, nothing could be seen, as everything had been hidden away. Somewhere, there were hundreds of troops, but the enemy would not have found them.

By now the Japanese had actually given up their attack on the stronghold. They had more than enough on their hands, trying to reopen the railway blocked by the 77th Brigade at Maulu, as well as sending emergency reinforcements to join in the battle for Imphal. Of course, we did not know this at the time so we were astonished and elated by the air of composure, as well as nonchalance shown by the garrison. Why indeed had we spent the last few days in near panic? They told us that there were no Japs around for twenty miles.

We were indeed very impressed by the long 5,000 foot airstrip, which was now established with runway lights and Tannoy control, and by the way we were directed to our departure area to await our aircraft. My mind is rather hazy regarding the last few hours, but in spite of all the assurances, we were still on edge. I was mindful of the proverb: 'There's many a slip 'twixt cup and lip.'

When the two columns of the 45th Reconnaissance Regiment had set out from Tagap Ga on the Ledo Road at dawn on the 12th February, we had a complement of over 900 men, fit and fully trained. Now, only seventy-eight days later, just over 400 men and thirteen officers struggled painfully into the stronghold. In actual fact, some of these had not been in the original party. There had been replacements, stragglers we had brought with us from the last battle, including a detachment with two RAF officers. None of us was fully fit, and many were in a pitiful condition.

Soon after dusk, the runway lights were switched on and an hour later, the first of the C47 Dakota aircraft arrived. We were organised into parties of thirty ready for departure, and were quite happy to doze and await the summons to move. Those mules who had survived the long journey were not so lucky. They remained behind, to be taken over by one of the West African brigades. Surely they deserved a break as much as we did. When they had first arrived, they had been resented, especially by those detailed to handle them. Later, those men who fed them, watered, groomed, saddled and led them over the Patkai hills, not only respected them, but held them in affection. It has been said that some muleteers wept more for a mule which had been killed than at the death of a comrade.

Soon after 2200 hours, we boarded our plane and all I remember is curling up in my blanket on the deck. There were no seats in these transport planes. The plane taxied a long time before the engines roared into life, and we bumped heavily along the landing strip. Within a couple of hours we had landed back at Broadway. The official reason for returning was the bad weather over the mountains, though at the time, I remember the Canadian pilot telling us he was short of gas. A story circulated later, saying that several of our party thought they were back in India and jumped out shouting 'Charwallah', with brew tins at the ready. I cannot recall this happening at the time. It is doubtful if any had the energy. Maybe it happened on another plane, or maybe it is a story that has improved with the telling. Eventually at around 0200 hours we were airborne again and this time there were no hitches.

Considering the hasty decisions that had to be made when these airstrips were established, especially the siting and construction, these runways and the standard of flying was outstanding. Broadway was well positioned with flat terrain around, but Aberdeen was a pilot's nightmare. The surface and length were adequate, but the hills at the northern end were much too close for comfort, and all

257

planes had to take off and land at the southern end. Only one plane crashed during the whole of the Special Force Chindit Operation, and that was at Aberdeen, just after take off. Apart from this one crash, there were no other losses of planes at these airfields, either by accident or enemy action.

The plane that crashed had taken off at the identical time on the very same night that our C47 lifted us out of Broadway. On board, there had been a party of thirty men of the Leicester Regiment who had fought so bravely and courageously at Indaw. Failing to gain height, it had hit the jungle fringe at the end of the strip and sadly the passengers and crew were all killed.

There had been casualties caused by the Japanese bombing raids of course, and one of these was Trooper Bill Key, originally a despatch rider in Ray Scully's platoon. When Bill had been left behind before our first battle, to recover from malaria and help on the airfield, we thought he had been lucky. He was killed during the first air attack two days later. Such are the fortunes of war.

Our flight was uneventful, and we landed at Comilla just after dawn. I remember the blur of green jungle as we approached the strip and taxied to a halt. It was early morning, Tuesday, 2nd May. We were tired and weary but the relief was overwhelming. The war was not yet over and we had won no victories, but we felt immensely fortunate to have survived our ordeal. The heavy pall of uncertainty had been lifted. We were now back to comparative civilisation and safety.

The reception camp was quite near the edge of the airport, and our first realisation was how smart and clean the troops looked, compared with our scruffy tattered appearance. Large canvas marquees with charpoys, clean sheets and blankets awaited us. We were led to showers in a real brick building, and afterwards it was absolute bliss to change into new clean jungle-green kit.

I had hoped to have my photograph taken with this luxuriant growth of beard, but we were orderd to shave off our beards straight away. Besides, my camera was still in my kitbag back at base. While we were existing on 'K' ration rice, and the occasional extras, we looked forward to the

258

enjoyment of having regular cooked food again, but the meals on the first day were a disaster. Every effort had been made to feed us well, but our stomachs had shrunk during the expedition and we were not yet ready for large meals. Those who were gluttonous made themselves very ill indeed.

We were examined by the medical team and given blood tests. Those whose results showed imminent signs of malaria were transferred to the military hospital straight away, to join the wounded men already there. We were ordered to continue to take our mepacrine anti-malarial tablets until further notice. The first night sleeping between cool sheets, instead of on the ground wearing our clothes, was absolute heaven and we relished every moment. More men from the Brigade columns continued to arrive, and the next day we made ready to fly north to Sylhet. Comilla had limited space and facilities, whereas Sylhet was the main Chindit base. The Special Force Headquarters, including our Rear Brigade were there, and since the retreat from Imphal the Special Force Signals network complex were also there.

This time, we travelled in comparatively luxurious style in a C47 Dakota, fitted with real passenger seats. When we were lifted out of Broadway to safety, the fear of flying was not an issue. Leaving Burma behind had been the sole consideration. Now we were back safely in India, several of my companions were nervous of everything, including flying. It is amazing how situations change priorities. Once the plane touched down on the runway at Sylhet, we were back to the typical army garrison routine.

We alighted and marched in threes through the camp area to our allotted bamboo huts. It was marvellous to be able to meet up with those of the Signal personnel who remained in India to operate the base radio sets and maintain communication with our two columns. It was especially pleasing to greet Wilf Rogers, Eric Nightingale, Denis Elkins, George Bell and Sergeant Dennis Stringer.

That afternoon we fell in and again marched in regimental fashion to collect our kitbags and other personal belongings, which had been stored while we were in Burma. I was particularly pleased to get hold of my camera again.

Some of our column had been flown directly back to Sylhet and they were lucky that they still had not been ordered to shave off their beards. They were able to have their photographs taken, complete with the three months' growth.

Later during the day, we were issued with steel helmets and respirators for training as proper soldiers again! Parades were soon the norm, we marched to meals, endured kit inspections, and guard mountings were reintroduced with all the old procedures and 'bull'.

Just as I began to wonder if jungle life would be preferable, the malarial parasites in my body surfaced and took over. To say that I felt ill would be a downright understatement. The paroxysms of shivering, fever and sweating left me helpless, and for a time I had no more interest in life. How my companions had managed to keep going when struck down in Burma defies belief. Malaria had been expected to materialise in most of us, so the military hospitals were well prepared. After treatment and many doses of quinine, I was well enough to return to duty in just under three weeks. However, several years were to pass, well after the war had ended, before the malaria attacks finally ended.

During the first few weeks in Sylhet, the main bone of contention was that the blue and gold Chindit emblem had already been issued to rear echelon troops who had never been into Burma. Those of us who felt that we were really Chindits had to wait, in some cases many weeks, before further consignments arrived. Seeing these 'base wallahs' wearing such insignias on their smart army uniforms made many men see red. Later, in leave areas this caused jealousy and resentment quite out of proportion, and Chindit fought Chindit.

Army orders continued to contradict and confuse. On 7th May we were informed that we could write letters home, saying we had arrived back safely in India from Burma and describe our adventures, providing we did not mention details, such as place names, weapons and casualties. Ten days later, this was rescinded stating that no mention should be made of our experience and that 100 per cent secrecy must be observed. The war against Japan was certainly not over yet and soon the Chindit ranks would be reinforced to train for future operations.

However, this must be the end of my story. Those who were lucky enough to see out the Chindit War and the battles that followed, or to endure the constraint of capture and the horrors of Japanese prison camps coupled with slave labour, are growing older and memories are fading. We Chindits were but a small force compared to the vast army of troops who fought against the Japanese in the Far East. However, we were all part of the 'Forgotten Army'. Soon there will be none of us left to remember our comrades, all so young, who were left behind. Nevertheless, there will be permanent tributes like the inscription carved in the hillside at Kohima, where one of our Chindit Brigades fought so bravely alongside the 2nd British Division. We will never forget the words:

When you go home,
Tell them of us and say
For your tomorrow,
We gave our today.

Let us trust that even the dust of time will not obscure these and all the other words of memory written clearly in the pages of history.

14

Final Judgement

So what assessment can be made of General Wingate, his theories, the Chindit battles and the overall value of the operation? As a junior NCO attached to one of the columns of the 16th Brigade, I can only express my own considered opinion.

There is no question of making an all-embracing criticism of General Wingate as a commander. Numerous historians have done this. There is however no doubt that Wingate was a maverick. His autocratic and abrasive style aroused animus in many of his day to day contacts. He had a history of depressions and a deep seated fear that everyone, everywhere, was doing their best to frustrate him. Nevertheless, there is no doubt that General Wingate's concept of Long Range Penetration was a vision well ahead of its time. The idea of inserting troops behind enemy lines, directing operations from base, and making supplies and close bombing support available by air was brilliant.

Also, there is no doubt that the Commander-in-Chief in Delhi, General Auchinleck, was very much against the details of the plan formulated at the Quadrant Conference. He considered the breaking up of the 70th British Division a tragic mistake. However, when his objections were overruled, he lost no time in implementing the orders. On the other hand, his staff officers at GHQ mainly showed bewilderment, bitter resentment, hindrance, hostility and bloody mindedness towards the Wingate operation from the outset. General Wingate's ideas had upset their routine and deep set traditions where rank and length of service hold predominance in campaign planning. Many of these staff officers had seen no fighting whatsoever, and still clung to the blackboard lessons blueprinted from the First World War.

The new breed of guerrilla soldiers, brutally energetic like Wingate, and Calvert who had preached modern jungle fighting in the Bush Warfare School, had taken over upsetting the orderly day to day routine of GHQ Delhi. In fact, it was said that Special Force, the 3rd Indian Infantry Division, had more enemies in Delhi when it was formed, than it subsequently met in Burma. In fairness to the military establishment in India, Special Force tied up one sixth of the army in India, in a limited role as lightly armed guerrillas. The 70th Division, battle hardened, with a nucleus of regular established units, some mechanised, was broken up. Certainly many historians consider that it would have been very worthwhile to have retained the 70th Division as an entity under its more than able commander, Major General W.G. Symes, and considered only the 77th and 111th Brigades for the Chindit operation. As it was, trained mechanics, drivers and gunners were either re-equipped as infantrymen or given the menial task of muleteering. Experienced officers, if over forty years of age, were replaced and insome cases unit morale suffered and their *esprit de corps* was lost.

Until the American Air Commando came on the scene with their fleet of transport Dakotas and gliders, the plan was that the whole of Special Force should march into Burma. The availability of this air transport to supplement the British Air Force Command led to a fresh line of thought. Eventually, the 16th Infantry Brigade were the only troops out of over 15,000 of Special Force who marched from Assam to Northern Burma. So when Brigadier Bernard Fergusson was ordered to march our brigade over the Chindwin, the odds were heavily stacked against him. This march contributed in no small way to our failure in the attack on Indaw. When we eventually arrived in the battle area, after an accumulation of delays and mishaps, we were completely exhausted by the long life-sapping march.

One reason for the march was that of surprise. In the event, the only surprise to the Japanese was the airborne invasion of the rest of the troops which began on 5th March, while we were still crossing the River Chindwin. What is more, the 77th and 111th Brigades quickly became organised fighting units within days of landing, after very short marches. It could be strongly argued that sufficient planes and gliders were not available to transport an additional brigade.

This certainly looked like a valid reason at first glance. However, let us consider the timing of our start and other possible options. We began our march from the Ledo Road at the beginning of February and did not arrive at the site of the eventual stronghold Aberdeen until 23rd March. Even by this time, the brigade only had six columns while nos. 51 and 69 were still trying to catch up after the diversion to Lonkin.

During this period it was necessary to drop supplies of food and equipment, provide boats to cross the Chindwin and land diversionary troops down river to mask the location of our crossing. The overall wastage of air time, machines and supplies must have been very substantial during those seven weeks. It should not be forgotten that even the most efficient air drop spread the load over as much as a mile of jungle, and these drops were few and far between. Overall, little more than 50 per cent of supplies were recovered. Furthermore, there was the wastage of all the abortive flights when columns could not be located. Considering the operation as a whole, a number of planes was written off during the initial landings at Broadway and Chowringee. Unfortunately, General Wingate was averse to the use of available paratroops. The reason he gave was that they could not reach his exacting training standards in the time available.

A 'pathfinder' party, dropped in advance of the main body of troops could have reconnoitered the whole area reported back and surely reduced the initial carnage Quietly and purposefully, they could have checked the landing grounds and organised the filling up of bunds and ruts, if necessary with the use of local labour. Similarly Aberdeen could have been established weeks earlier with the added use of RAF air reconnaissance.

If the alternative option had been taken to fly the brigade into Burma, surely it would have been more successful and profitable all round. It should be remembered that the only reason that the 14th Brigade fly-in was delayed, was the fact that Aberdeen was not ready. They actually began to arrive as soon as the strip had been levelled by the bulldozers of the American engineers on the 23rd March. On that date most of the 16th Brigade had not left the stronghold,and 45 Column did not leave for the battle of Indaw until two days later. If Aberdeen had been ready even two weeks earlier, then both 14th and 16th Brigades could have made a combined direct assault. Indaw was virtually undefended until a few days before our eventual attack. In the event, the 14th Brigade, who were fresh and well trained never did join the battle.

This is all conjecture, but had we captured Indaw and reinforced it with defenders, the Japanese would have needed to divert even more troops to restore the blocked supply lines. Their attack on India via Manipur could well have been seriously disrupted. Overall, my considered opinion is that the march by the 16th Infantry Brigade was a contrived publicity stunt, and an absurd act of showman-ship by General Wingate. Admittedly, he proved that the Patkai hills and the tropical jungle could be mastered, but the wastage in supplies, equipment and expended energy far outweighed the effort.

Our eventual attack on Indaw on the 26th March was a complete fiasco apart from the Leicester's excellence. Our attack was not in accordance with Chindit principles, which were to act primarily as guerrillas, emerging from the jungle to ambush enemy convoys or to blow up railway and ammunition dumps, before slipping away and hiding in the ubiquitous jungle. Here we had to attack prepared positions without adequate fire power, and with the encumbrance of full packs and equipment. Also, it was surely a mistake to attack from several directions under separate commands. Out of the eight columns, two were still way behind, and a further two, the 21 and 22 Columns were sent on diversionary tactics, which had no effect on the immediate battle. So for the actual assault we were reduced to four columns, the 45 and 54 Columns of the Reconnaissance Corps, and Columns 17 and 71 of the Leicesters. Further-more, there was the loss of radio contact at a vital time.

Although it was a complicated network, our wireless communication had been reasonably efficient. However, when the Japanese reached Manipur and began the attack on Imphal and Kohima, a serious problem was created. On 24th March, Rear Brigade Signals closed down and moved back to Sylhet. For a whole week the powerful transmitters were silent. Admittedly, efforts were made with the no. 22 sets, to contact the brigade, but at these vast distances the combination of static and interference nullified our efforts to maintain communication. There is no doubt at all that this almost complete blackout of signals was a major factor in the failure of Brigadier Fergusson's attack on Indaw. Without wireless, Fergusson was like a blind man. He had no communication with his columns via Rear Brigade Signals, and similarly he could not receive or give intelligence reports and information.

This fact has been glossed over by many historians and at the time, by the military themselves. For instance, in *Burma. The Longest War* the author Louis Allen quotes a breakdown in communication of only twenty-four hours. General Wingate's Chief-of-Staff, Brigadier Derek Tulloch makes an even more serious error in recording the event in his book *Wingate in Peace and War.* He blames Fergusson for the breakdown: 'Fergusson's wireless communication broke down and therefore he was unable to inform Special Force of his plight.' Without my labouring the point too much, what he should have said was: 'Special Force Rear Brigade signals ran for cover and so Brigadier Fergusson was unable to communicate with them!'

It is very likely that this lack of communication caused the mix up over the use of the 14th Brigade. Brigadier Fergusson was under the impression, probably false, that he would have their help in capturing Indaw, but no signal of the changed plan arrived. At the risk of repetition, the importance of the radio network must be emphasised. It was the lifeblood of our type of warfare. Rear Brigade HQ should have been located alongside the air supply base from the beginning of the operation.

There was another problem. Little information was passed between brigades about their future intentions, and therefore individual columns of different brigades often

266

crossed each other's routes. It so happened for example, that after a split landing at Broadway and Chowringee, the 111th Brigade were on the way to link up west of Indaw. On the way, Columns 26 and 90 of the 1st Battalion of Cameronians, passed through Nyauggon two days before our brigade. They laid a 'red herring' by telling the villagers that they were on the way to attack Indaw. The likely possibility is that this information was passed on to the Japanese, giving them plenty of time to prepare for us. This excessive security about not telling individial commanders what was happening was a bad plan which boomeranged and defeated its own objective.

Finally, there remains the question of what the Chindits achieved. Certainly they achieved no more than other allied units who also fought hard, received and inflicted casualties and made mistakes. Special Force was really too large as a guerrilla force and not equipped with the heavier weapons to make it an airborne strike force. Lieutenant General Sir Reginald Savoury said much later, 'In my opinion any reasonably trained, well led infantry regiment could have done all that Wingate's forces did.' General Sir William Slim's retrospective assessment was that 'The cult of special forces is as sensible as to form a royal corps of tree climbers, and say that no soldier who does not wear its green hat with a bunch of leaves stuck in it, should be expected to climb a tree.'

However, both these remarks miss the point. Most of the Chindit forces were trained and well led, and did not pretend that they were more accomplished than other units in the field. It was the idea not the troops that was different. New concepts always evoke criticism, regarding the orthodoxy of the moment as the only right method of battle. General Orde Wingate transformed the art of war by the use of air power and wireless in a novel way. He also raised morale, both in India and the UK and he showed that the Japanese could be outclassed in jungle fighting. The significant benefits for the allies was that the second Chindit operation was hailed as a great victory and the fable of Japanese invincibility was destroyed for ever. Now the troops in India could face the Japanese and the future with a new-found confidence.

APPENDIX 1

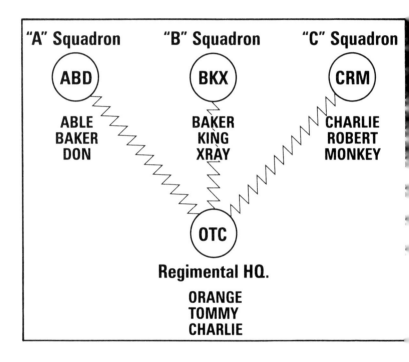

"A" Squadron   "B" Squadron   "C" Squadron

ABD   **BKX**   **CRM**

ABLE   BAKER   CHARLIE
BAKER   KING   ROBERT
DON   XRAY   MONKEY

OTC

Regimental HQ.

ORANGE
TOMMY
CHARLIE

There was no special significance in the call sign letters
chosen, so they could be changed at any time. In fact the
phonetic alphabet that we used at this time was gradually
changed over the wartime years, probably to dovetail into
the procedures used by the other services, especially the
Americans. For example, around this time, Fox was
changed to Freddie, Dog to Don, How to Harry. Also, the
Americans used Roger instead of Robert and for William
they used Wilco which meant 'message understood and will

be actioned.' Roger meant 'message received and understood.'

Standard phonetic procedure at this time was as follows:

A. Ac.	J. Johnnie.	S. Sugar.
B. Beer.	K. King.	T. Toc.
C. Charlie.	L. London.	U. Uncle.
D. Don.	M. Monkey.	V. Vic.
E. Edward.	N. Nuts.	W. William.
F. Freddie.	O. Orange.	X. X-ray.
G. George.	P. Pip.	Y. Yorker.
H. Harry.	Q. Queen.	Z. Zebra.
I. Ink.	R. Robert.	

Below is the modern version of the phonetic alphabet used in all international communications by air, land, sea forces and the police. These words will be very familiar to TV and radio listeners:

A. Alpha.	J. Juliette.	S. Sierra.
B. Bravo.	K. Kilo.	T. Tango.
C. Charlie.	L. Lima.	U. Uniform.
D. Delta.	M. Mike.	V. Victor.
E. Echo.	N. November.	W. Whisky.
F. Foxtrot.	O. Oscar.	X. X-ray.
G. Golf.	P. Papa.	Y. Yankee.
H. Hotel.	Q. Quebec.	Z. Zulu.
I. India.	R. Romeo.	

So that it will be seen that only Charlie and X-ray have survived over the years.

We also reported the strength of radio signals being received. For this we used the international scale, which had five degrees of signal strength, whereas we had previously used a code of signal strength 1 – 9. These were:

1. Hardly perceptible.
2. Weak.
3. Fairly good.
4. Good.
5. Very good.

So, for example, a station which had been called and asked for signal strength, could answer back: 'Hello OTC, hearing you strength 4. Over.'

Here is an example of a message to be transmitted to all stations while we were on the exercise on the way back to

Ranchi. There was no security problem, so this message could go in 'clear'. Had the wording have been liable to interception or of used to an enemy, it would have been transmitted in cypher. The originator of the message would write his despatch in the central portion of the form. Only the signal operator was allowed to record in the space allocated above and below. Once handed in, the operator would note the time (THI) 0905, fill in the call signs, the number of groups in the message (23) and transmit at the earliest opportunity. On this particular exercise, stations would not open up until the next stop (0950). In this instance, had the message been vital, a motorcycle despatch rider would have been used.

Army Form C.2130. (Pads of 100.)		MESSAGE FORM				Serial No.
CALL AND INSTRUC-TIONS	IN			No. of Groups. GR. 23	Office Date Stamp	
	OUT	*ABD BKX CRM v OTC*				
TO		(ABOVE THIS LINE IS FOR SIGNALS USE ONLY) *ALL SQUADRONS*				
FROM	*REGT HQ*		Originator's Number *A/116*	Date *24*	In Reply to Number	

LAAGER	*TONIGHT*	*AND*	*25*	*CAWNPORE*	*CANTONMEN*
E.T.A.	*1500 HRS*	*⊙*	*OFFICERS*	*REPORT*	*LANCS*
FUSILIERS	*MESS*	*1900 HRS*	*24*	*AND*	*1200 HRS*
25	*⊙*	*GUESTS*	*OC*	*BARRACKS*	

THIS MESSAGE MAY BE SENT AS WRITTEN BY ANY MEANS [EXCEPT] [*] [INCH.] WIRELESS	THIS MESSAGE MUST BE SENT IN CIPHER IF LIABLE TO INTERCEPTION OR TO FALL INTO ENEMY HANDS	ORIGINATOR'S INSTRUCTIONS DEGREE OF PRIORITY *IMMEDIATE*		TIME OF ORIGIN *0850*
SIGNED *Parsons AW Capt*	SIGNED (BELOW THIS LINE IS FOR SIGNALS USE ONLY.)			T.H.I. *0905*

SYSTEM IN	TIME IN	READER	SENDER	SYSTEM OUT	TIME OUT	READER	SENDER	SYSTEM OUT	TIME OUT	READER	SENDER	T.O.R.
				R/T	*0955*	*ABD* ✓ *BKX* ✓ *CRM* ✓	*W King* *OTC*					

Originator may delete "except" and insert "including"   690816 Wt 36391/3368 275m Pads 11/41 wr 51-1836

Note that O was written in the message for 'stop', and would be so pronounced. Only the date, excluding the month, was recorded in the date space. The degree of priority such as 'important' could be inserted by any officer. 'Immediate' could be originated by the Regimental Commander, or Senior Staff Officer, but higher priorities were often used and the system abused. So, here the message was sent out at 0955 hours by the operator on the set at regimental HQ (OTC), who would have received acknowledgement from each of the squadron radio set operators.

The message was self explanatory and the senior officer with each of A, B and C Squadrons would have passed the good news to all officers. On arrival at Cawnpore on Christmas Eve, they were in fact invited to meals and a booze-up in the Lancashire Fusiliers' mess. In actual fact this laager had been arranged by the Army Command Administration, long before we had left Bombay.

APPENDIX 2

In Wingate's defence, if defence is needed, the book *Wingate in Peace and War*, written by Major General Derek Tulloch and published by Macdonald, should be read. Tulloch was Wingate's Chief Staff Officer during the 1943-44 Burma Operation, and in my opinion gives an excellent account of the difficulties Wingate encountered. Another outstanding and unbiased volume is *The Chindit War* by Shelford Bidwell, which records the whole of the 1944 campaign.

I have deviated from my personal story in order to compare the recordings of the military scribes with my own experience at that time, backed by the day to day entries in my diary. There are two measured convictions recorded by Major General Tulloch which tend to confirm my own belief. On page 135 of his book, he states: 'The senior army and navy authorities in India were convinced that the plans for offensive action in Burma in 1944 were political manoeuvres, and there was no intention of their being carried out.' Also on page 142: 'There is little doubt in my mind that General Symes, indeed, had been "briefed" to hold himself in readiness for a revision of his brigades back to a normal division.'

APPENDIX 3

The time in Bangalore soon passed and the regimental advance party left on Saturday, 25th September, followed by the road party with our vehicles on the 30th September. Sergeant Stringer left with the former detachment, so for the remainder of our stay I was acting Troop Sergeant. It was obvious to all, during the last few weeks in camp with reduced numbers, that interest in future training had been lost. In Christopher Sykes's comprehensive biography of Orde Wingate, there is an interesting passage which confirms my own observation: 'On arrival at Bangalore, Wingate found that very little had been done to implement the break up, but he had the wisdom not to make one of his furious scenes. He met most of the officers, made a good impression, insisted that the move to Gwalior should be made immediately, and this was done. The Division went north in the first week of October.'